Quality of Life in Cities

In the last few decades, urban quality of life has received increasing interest from policy makers who aim to make cities better places to live. In addition to the aim of improving quality of life, sustainable and equitable development is also often included in the policy agendas of decision makers.

This book aims to link quality of life to related issues such as sustainability, equity, and subjective well-being. While less than one-third of the world's population lived in cities in 1950, about two thirds of humanity is expected to live in urban areas by 2030. This dramatic increase in the number of people living in urban areas serves as the backdrop for this book's analysis of cities.

This book will be useful to students and researchers in economics, architecture and urban planning, sociology and political sciences, as well as policy makers.

Alessandra Michelangeli is Associate Professor of Economics, Department of Economics, Management and Statistics (DEMS), University of Milan-Bicocca, Italy.

Routledge advances in regional economics, science and policy

1 **Territorial Patterns of Innovation**
An inquiry on the knowledge economy in European regions
Edited by Roberta Capello and Camilla Lenzi

2 **The Political Economy of City Branding**
Ari-Veikko Anttiroiko

3 **Structural Change, Competitiveness and Industrial Policy**
Painful lessons from the European periphery
Edited By Aurora A.C. Teixeira, Ester Silva and Ricardo Mamede

4 **Airports, Cities and Regions**
Edited by Sven Conventz and Alain Thierstein

5 **Rural and Regional Futures**
Edited by Anthony Hogan and Michelle Young

6 **Untamed Urbanisms**
Edited by Adriana Allen, Andrea Lampis and Mark Swilling

7 **Explorations in Urban and Regional Dynamics**
A case study in complexity science
Joel Dearden and Alan Wilson

8 **Quality of Life in Cities**
Equity, sustainable development and happiness from a policy perspective
Edited by Alessandra Michelangeli

Quality of Life in Cities

Equity, sustainable development and happiness from a policy perspective

**Edited by
Alessandra Michelangeli**

LONDON AND NEW YORK

First published 2015
by Routledge
2 Park Square, Milton Park, Abingdon, Oxon OX14 4RN

and by Routledge
711 Third Avenue, New York, NY 10017

Routledge is an imprint of the Taylor & Francis Group, an informa business

© 2015 selection and editorial material, Alessandra Michelangeli;
individual chapters, the contributors.

The right of the editor to be identified as the author of the editorial material,
and of the authors for their individual chapters, has been asserted in
accordance with sections 77 and 78 of the Copyright, Designs and
Patents Act 1988.

All rights reserved. No part of this book may be reprinted or reproduced or
utilised in any form or by any electronic, mechanical, or other means, now
known or hereafter invented, including photocopying and recording, or in
any information storage or retrieval system, without permission in writing
from the publishers.

Trademark notice: Product or corporate names may be trademarks or
registered trademarks, and are used only for identification and explanation
without intent to infringe.

British Library Cataloguing in Publication Data
A catalogue record for this book is available from the British Library

Library of Congress Cataloging in Publication Data
Quality of life in cities : equity, sustainable development and happiness from
a policy perspective / edited by Alessandra Michelangeli.
   pages cm.
   (Routledge advances in regional economics, science and policy)
   Includes bibliographical references and index.
   1. City and town life. 2. Quality of life. 3. Sustainable urban development.
   I. Michelangeli, Alessandra.
HT119.Q346 2015
307.76–dc23   2014041068

ISBN: 978-1-138-79041-4 (hbk)
ISBN: 978-1-315-76421-4 (ebk)

Typeset in Times New Roman
by Sunrise Setting Ltd, Paignton, UK

To Adele, Allegra and Luca Eugenio

Contents

List of figures	x
List of tables	xi
List of contributors	xii
Preface	xv
Acknowledgments	xvii

1 Urbanization: an overview   1

ANDRÉ DE PALMA AND ALEXANDRE GUIMARD

1.1 *Foreword 1*

1.2 *History of urbanization and first modeling stages 7*

1.3 *Regularities about the internal structure of cities 19*

1.4 *The distribution of cities 25*

1.5 *Forecasts 28*

1.6 *Concluding comments 34*

Notes 35

Bibliography 36

2 The hedonic value of urban quality of life   44

FRANCESCO ANDREOLI AND ALESSANDRA MICHELANGELI

2.1 *Introduction 44*

2.2 *The value of (dis)amenities in a partial equilibrium model 46*

2.3 *The hedonic spatial equilibrium model 49*

2.4 *The value-adjusted quality of life index 51*

2.5 *Which amenities for the hedonic quality of life index? 53*

2.6 *Quality of life and city size: the role of the cost of living 61* viii *Contents*

 2.7 *Concluding remarks: challenging problems and*
   promising developments in the quality of
   life literature 62
  Notes 63
  Bibliography 63

3 Measuring urban quality of life: a life satisfaction approach 66

LUCA STANCA

 3.1 *Introduction 66*
 3.2 *The economics and happiness revolution 68*
 3.3 *Life satisfaction, environmental valuation*
   and quality of life 70
 3.4 *Data and methods 72*
 3.5 *The life satisfaction value of amenities 79*
 3.6 *Quality of life in Italian cities 79*
 3.7 *Conclusions 85*
  Bibliography 86

4 Cities, equity and quality of life 91

MARCO GIOVANNI BRAMBILLA, ALESSANDRA MICHELANGELI
AND EUGENIO PELUSO

 4.1 *Introduction 91*
 4.2 *Why is excessive inequality bad for cities? 92*
 4.3 *Inequality and space 94*
 4.4 *Equitable cities: measurement issues 99*
 4.5 *Equity as equality of opportunities 101*
 4.6 *Territorial justice 102*
 4.7 *Positive models 104*
 4.8 *Preferences, quality of life, and values 105*
 4.9 *Conclusions 105*
  Notes 106
  Bibliography 106

5 Urban sustainability and individual/household well-being 110

CONSTANTINOS ANTONIOU AND NATHALIE PICARD

 5.1 *Introduction 110*
 5.2 *Urban sustainability and quality of life 111*
 5.3 *Urban sustainability indicators 115*
 5.4 *Microsimulation models for the analysis of*
   urban sustainability 118

Contents ix

5.5 *Individual vs. household well-being and*
     individual vs. household decisions 119
5.6 *Conclusions* 138
     Notes 139
     Bibliography 139

6 Agglomeration economies and urban location benefits: the debate around the existence of an optimal city size

143

ROBERTO CAMAGNI AND ROBERTA CAPELLO

6.1 *Introduction* 143
6.2 *Criticisms of the optimal city size* 144
6.3 *Agglomeration economies and territorial capital* 146
6.4 *Empirical evidence from European cities* 154
6.5 *Conclusions and policy implications* 161
     Notes 162
     Bibliography 162

Index 167

Figures

1.1	Accessibility to a local market	12
1.2	Bid rents function of distance from the city hall	16
1.3	The distribution of residents in NYC and Atlanta	21
1.4	The length of metro networks vs. population density	23
1.5	The length of metro networks vs. GDP of cities	24
1.6	The rank-size rule for the 135 largest US metropolitan areas in 1991	27
2.1	Comparison between the value-adjusted quality of life index and the Roback (1982) index	54
3.1	Life satisfaction across cities, by year	74
3.2	Quality of life index, overall	81
3.3	Quality of life, individual domains	84
4.1	Income endowments of eight individuals living in two areas (panel *(a)*) or in four areas (panel *(b)*)	97
4.2	Case of individuals located such that their incomes do not overlap between areas	97
5.1	Popularity (expressed through Google ngrams) of three relevant terms: (1) indicators, (2) quality of life, and (3) sustainability	111
5.2	Accessibility measures, by education level	130
5.3	Extended nested model explaining credit constraints, tenure status, dwelling type and location	134
5.4	Probability of liquidity constraint, by income group	135
5.5	Proportion of constrained households per commune	136
5.6	Per cent change in demand when credit constraints are alleviated	137
6.1	Efficient city-size for different urban functions	151
6.2	Urban average location advantages and costs for different urban sizes, higher urban functions, and degree of networking	158

Tables

3.1	Individual characteristics, descriptive statistics	73
3.2	Life satisfaction, city ranking	75
3.3	Well-being and individual characteristics	77
3.4	Well-being and local amenities, net effects	78
3.5	Well-being and local amenities, gross effects	80
3.6	Quality of life (overall), city ranking	82
3.7	QoL indices, pairwise correlations	85
4.1	Interpreting the Gini coefficient	94
6.1	Indicators of city effect and urban overload indicators	155

Contributors

Francesco Andreoli is a researcher in Economics at CEPS/INSTEAD, Luxembourg. His research focuses on welfare evaluation and public policy analysis, with a particular devotion to the equality of opportunity perspective.

Constantinos Antoniou is Professor of Engineering at National Technical University of Athens (NTUA), Greece. His research focuses on modeling and simulation of transportation systems, Intelligent Transport Systems (ITS), calibration and optimization applications, road safety and sustainable transport systems.

Marco Giovanni Brambilla is a civil engineer with a specialization in Transport from Politecnico of Milan, Italy, and a PhD in Economics from Catholic University of Milan, Italy. He works as a consultant in the private sector and he has been involved in a number of projects funded by different Directorates-General of the European Commission. His professional interests and activities are concentrated on ex-post evaluations of transport policies, ex-ante appraisals of transport infrastructures investments, and capacity building on project appraisal of governments' employees.

Roberto Camagni is Professor of Economics at Politecnico of Milan, Italy. He is also head of the Department for Urban Affairs at the Presidency of the Council of Ministers, Rome, under the Prodi Government (1997–98); Vice President of the Group on Urban Affairs of the Territorial Development Service of the OECD (since May 1998); President of the GREMI, an international association for the study of innovative environments or "milieus," located in Paris, Sorbonne University (since 1987); President of ERSA, the European Regional Science Association (1989–99); President of AISRE, the Italian Section of the Regional Science Association (1989–92); Councillor (1992–95), and member of the Council of the ASRDLF, the French Regional Science Association (since 1993). Roberto has worked for the EU, the OECD, DATAR, Plan Urbain, the Italian Ministers of Public Works and Industry and many Italian and European Regional Governments in the fields of innovation diffusion and regional and urban development planning. He is the author of many publications on urban and regional development, and regional and urban policy. He was also awarded the 2010 European Regional Science Association European Investment Bank prize for his scientific contributions to Spatial Economics.

Roberta Capello is Professor in Regional and Urban Economics at the Politecnico of Milan, Italy, and past President of the Regional Science Association International (RSAI). She is Editor-in-Chief of *Papers in Regional Science* (Wiley-Blackwell, London) and of the *Italian Journal of Regional Science* (Franco Angeli, Milan). She is a past co-editor of *Letters in Spatial and Resource Science* (Springer Verlag, Berlin) and author of many scientific papers and a textbook in Regional Economics, published in Italian and English.

André De Palma has a PhD in both Physics and Economics. He has held faculty positions at Queen's University, Canada, Northwestern University in Illinois, USA and the University of Geneva, Switzerland. He is a specialist in industrial organization, transportation economics, and decision making under risk and uncertainty. He has published seven books and 228 articles in international journals. According to RePEc (2013) he is ranked first worldwide in Transportation Economics (score: 1.62). He belongs to the top 1 percent of economists wordwide in RePEc's overall ranking (at number 360).

He has also consulted for major financial organizations in the US, Spain, Switzerland, France, and Belgium.

Alexandre Guimard is a PhD student and research assistant at Ecole Normale Supérieure de Cachan, France. His primary research interest is urban geography.

Alessandra Michelangeli is Professor of Economics at the University of Milan-Bicocca, Italy. Her research focuses on urban quality of life, multidimensional well-being, inequality and measurement of wealth. She has extensive experience in microeconometrics. She is the author of many scientific papers and of a book on the quality of life in Italian cities published by Bocconi University Press.

Eugenio Peluso is Professor of Economics at the University of Verona, Italy, and research associate at Statistics Norway. His research focuses on inequality measurement, equality of opportunity, political economy, and voting theory.

Nathalie Picard is Professor of Economics at Cergy-Pontoise University, France. Her academic specialities are microeconometrics and public policy evaluation. Her current research interests include urban sustainability and spatial economics.

Luca Stanca is Professor of Economics at the University of Milan-Bicocca, Italy. His research focuses on applied econometrics, behavioral economics, and experimental economics. He is the Director of the Center for Interdisciplinary xiv *Contributors*

Studies in Economics, Psychology and Social Sciences (CISEPS) and of the Experimental Economics Laboratory (EELab) at the University of Milan-Bicocca, Italy. He has been Research Associate at the Center for Economic Performance (London School of Economics), and is currently Research Associate at the Laboratory for Comparative Social Research, High School of Economics, Moscow, Russia. He is co-editor of *International Review of Economics*, and associate editor of the *Journal of Socio-Economics*.

Preface

In the last few decades, the topic of urban quality of life has been receiving increased interest from a wide array of policy makers—both at local and national level—aiming to identify factors on which action must be taken to make cities better places to live in. Beside the aim of improving quality of life, sustainable and equitable development are often included in the policy agendas of decision makers. Perhaps the best-known example is the Commission on the Measurement of Economic Performance and Social Progress created at the beginning of 2008 on the French government's initiative. The main purpose of the Commission was to develop measurement tools of well-being, as well as measures of economic, environmental, and social sustainability. Another example is Urban Audit, the European Commission sponsored project, created in 2003, whose ultimate goal is to assist cities to improve the quality of urban life, identify best practices, support the exchange of experiences among European cities, and provide reliable and comparative information on the dynamics of urban life both within the cities and between them. This book aims to link the analysis of urban quality of life with other strictly related issues such as subjective well-being, sustainability, equity, and urban efficiency.

These topics are widely taught in a large variety of Economics, Sociology, and Political Science courses, both at undergraduate and postgraduate levels, and this book would appeal mainly to: researchers/academics in economics, sociology, urban planning, and political sciences; theoretical, applied, and policy-oriented scholars; MSc and PhD students in these and related topics; readers and policy makers at the EU, both at country and urban levels; and other readers interested in fashionable issues such as quality of life, sustainability, happiness, social equity, and urban policies.

The book is composed of six chapters, each addressing one of the above topics. Each chapter can be read as a stand-alone text, without the necessity of consulting other chapters for information. However, the entire book is an integrated text with respect to giving an in-depth analysis of well-being—at the city level—from different perspectives. Chapter 1 explores the history of cities, the spatial distribution of cities around the world, their internal structure and optimal size. The aim of the chapter is to convince the reader about the importance of studying citizens' xvi *Preface*

well-being in a world where the proportion of population living in urban areas is dramatically rising. Well-being should be understood not only as urban quality of life, but also in subjective terms and in a dynamic perspective that takes into account current and future resources. Chapter 2 presents the hedonic approach, perhaps the most common framework used by urban economists to measure urban quality of life. The chapter presents a wide range of extensions of the standard approach, both on methodological and empirical grounds. In particular, the chapter is innovative in extending the traditional methodology by proposing a new measure of quality of life, where infra-marginal units of amenities are assessed through the willingness to pay for non-marginal quantities of amenities. Some specific issues, such as the relationship between city size, cost of living, wealth, and quality of life are also addressed.

Chapter 3 examines, both theoretically and empirically, the relationship between quality of life and subjective well-being. After surveying the recent literature on this complex relationship, the chapter presents an empirical analysis of quality of life and subjective well-being in Italian cities. More specifically, two specific issues are investigated. First, is quality of life related to well-being? Second, what domains of quality of life (i.e. types of local amenities) are more relevant for individual well-being?

Chapter 4 focuses on equity concerns at the urban level. The first part of the chapter explores the idea of the "just city," which is enshrined in both planning and economic literature. The second part of the chapter attempts to bridge the gap between the urban economics and inequality measurement literature. Starting from the premise that these two fields of economics share a multidimensional view of quality of life, a recent methodology is presented to assess urban quality of life when equity concerns arise.

Chapter 5 proposes a framework that links urban sustainability with individual well-being and quality of life. While there are many definitions of sustainability, this chapter looks at sustainability as the sum of several components, one of which is the quality of life.

Chapter 6 presents a critical view of theoretical works on city size and its relationship with urban quality of life and efficiency. Consistent with recent advances in this strand of literature, the chapter shows that, for a given city size, functional characteristics of cities and their spatial organization within the urban system play an important role in determining urban efficiency and enhancing quality of life.

Acknowledgments

I am grateful to my editor at Routledge, Rob Langham, for his encouragement and help in the preparation of this book. Gratitude is also due to the three anonymous reviewers commissioned by Routledge who provided valuable suggestions and feedback.

I thank all chapter authors, who are leaders in their respective fields and who agreed to contribute to this book with their knowledge and experience from their own research.

André De Palma and Alexandre Guimard, authors of Chapter 1, would like to thank Peter Newman, Xavier Gabaix, Edward Glaeser, and Alain Bertaud for their permission to reuse their figures, and for their suggestions.

Luca Stanca, author of Chapter 3, is grateful to the statistical office of the Lombardy region for granting access to the micro-level data.

1 Urbanization

An overview

André de Palma and Alexandre Guimard

1.1 Foreword

Historically, the concentration of people has always shifted. Individuals concentrated at some specific places for short periods of time and moved their habitats from one place to another. Several reasons may lead to "ephemeral cities": events and effects of seasonality, or nomadism. First, the "ephemeral city" can be a place where a group of people meet from time to time. For example, individuals can periodically meet at some particular places (markets) to exchange goods, but this does not necessarily lead to the emergence of cities. The reason for temporary concentrations could also be religious. As an example, people met in Mayan sites (with no permanent residents) for ceremonial settings (Kostof, 1993). According to Mumford (1961), when people were still nomads, sepultures were a point of concentration. Second, communities moved their habitat over time for reasons related to climate, natural resources (soil erosion, water resources, etc.) and livelihood. Before the Neolithic Age, for example, individuals hunted and fished to feed themselves and frequently moved their habitat.

As a matter of fact, the concentration of a large population size is not the prerogative of man. Indeed, a number of animals are referred to as social because they live in a community. These communities may include thousands of insects, as in ant colonies, or even several millions of insects, as in communities of termites. These systems are extremely well regulated. For example, workers in the nests of termites manage to keep the temperature of the nest close to the ideal temperature (Deneubourg and Franks, 1995). These regulations are very different from those implemented in many other animal societies. These phenomena of self-organization involve large-scale systems, which could provide fruitful sources of inspiration for researchers in social sciences.

At around 6000 BC, only a few thousands of people lived in cities, which is not many compared to the millions of people who are currently living in metropolitan cities such as Tokyo, Delhi, Mexico or New York City (NYC). The way cities emerge and grow depends on the historical context. We can roughly distinguish two types of cities, the pre-industrial cities and the post-industrial ones (Sjoberg, 1960): "Preindustrial cities depend for the production of goods and services upon animate (human or animal) sources of energy – applied either directly or indirectly

2 *André de Palma and Alexandre Guimard*

through such mechanical devices as hammers, pulleys, and wheels." By contrast, post-industrial cities depend on "inanimate sources of power [...] used to multiply human effort" and allowed by the invention of steam machinery. After the Industrial Revolution, production processes and modes of transportation stayed roughly the same over time. The city was dense (Newman and Kenworthy, 1996), with mixed land use, and "city dwellings often serve as workshops" (Sjoberg, 1960). After the Industrial Revolution, plants and new modes of transportation changed cities. The city became more spatially specialized and spread out. Urban sprawl increased even more after World War II and found its apogee with the automobile city during the 1970s, due to the democratization of the private car.

Cities are defined quite differently across countries and over time, and this makes comparisons very difficult: "Because of national differences in the characteristics which distinguish urban from rural areas, the distinction between urban and rural population is not amenable to a single definition applicable to all countries" (Chen *et al.*, 2013). In China, for example, urban administrative areas, "often include large stretches of farmland and sizeable rural population, thus inflating the urban population figures" (Chan *et al.*, 2008). The *hukou* system, which "acted as an internal passport arrangement regulating mobility and granting people citizenship in the locality," makes the task of counting urban population in China even more difficult since a lot of migrants are not treated as permanent migrants in census data. However, it is necessary to have a common definition of what is a city in order to compare them around the world.

According to Mumford (1938), the city is "a point of maximum concentration for the power and culture of a community." Marshall (2007) recalls the definition of urban areas by the US Census Bureau:

> The US Census delineates "urban areas" as areas based on the population density of a census block or block group being greater than 1000 people per square mile and the population density of surrounding census blocks being greater than 500 people per square mile. Urban areas (UAs) must have a population size of 50 000 or greater. UAs are delineated at the start of each decade.
> (US Census, 2004)

In France, the continuity of settlements and the concentration of individuals are the key statistics of cities. The definition of cities changed with the introduction of new concepts over time, such as urban areas. In France, according to INSEE, "an urban unit is a municipality or a set of municipalities presenting a zone of built up continuous (no cut of more than 200 meters between two constructions) ... and with at least 2,000 inhabitants." Since 1997, INSEE introduced the new concept of urban areas by allowing remote settlements to be part of a larger urban core. However, the core must have a large labour market (10,000 employees for large urban areas). Thus, many remote settlements are excluded because they are not included in an urban core that is big enough in terms of total employees. This biases the analysis of cities over time and may lead researchers to think that rural areas resist the urbanization process, whereas actually, according to Lévy (2013), urbanization in France has been achieved. The proportion of urban areas is at its maximum level since even the more remote "rural" areas are connected to urban cores (peri-urbanization).

Worldwide, just a few years ago (by 2007), there were as many people living in cities as in rural areas. Urbanization is increasing in such a manner that, in 2050, 70 percent of the total population will live in cities. In less developed countries, the growth of cities is substantial. In developing countries, between 2010 and 2015, 183,000 individuals will move to cities each day, leading to 91 percent of urban growth worldwide (UN Habitat, 2013). According to the United Nations (2012), in less developed countries, urban populations will grow from 2.7 billion in 2011 to 5.1 billion in 2050. As a result, control of urbanization is often difficult to achieve.

This large gain is due to population growth and to rural exodus. From the date of writing to 2050, the total population worldwide will increase by 30 percent and the urban population by about 70 percent, implying a large increase in the urban proportion. Total population figures worldwide will grow from 7.130 million residents in 2013, to 9.306 million residents in 2050 (INED).[1] The urban population will grow from 3.6 billion in 2009 to 6.4 billion in 2050 (UN, 2012). Between 2011 and 2030, both in the developed and the less developed countries, the urban population will increase more than the total population (0.52 percent vs. 0.23 percent and 2.02 percent vs. 1.07 percent respectively), but this trend will be evident in less developed countries. In developed countries, the increase of the urban proportion will be moderate: it will increase by 100 million residents between 2011 and 2050, whereas the total population will increase by only 70 million. In China, from 2035, the total population will decrease (by -0.14 percent between 2035 and 2040) while the urban proportion will keep growing (from 47 percent in 2010 to 61.9 percent in 2030) because the rural exodus will remain in place.

Fast urban growth will mainly occur in medium and large cities. Mega-cities, defined as cities exceeding ten million inhabitants, are responsible for only 9.9 percent of total urban growth in 2011 and will increase by only 13.6 percent in 2025. Between 2000 and 2010, the number of cities above ten million inhabitants increased by 35 percent; it grew from 17 mega-cities in 2000 to 23 in 2010.

Urban growth is not homogeneous among regions. For example, the population of Cleveland decreased by 27.4 percent in only 12 years. The number of inhabitants decreased from 501,662 in 1999 to 393,806 in 2011 because of the industrial crisis. Urban growth is thus a function of historical time periods, but may differ across countries and cities. Cities do not grow in the same way, and there exist distinct urban growth patterns between cities around the world. Some cities grow faster than others and some are spreading out more than others. Large investments in road infrastructures and a high car detention can explain these disparities.

Despite the uniqueness of each situation, several regularities have been documented concerning urban development. A scaling law informs by how much in percentage terms cities' characteristics increase or decrease, with mostly a 1 percent increase of city size being noted. There exists a scaling law between energy consumption and city size, a scaling law between levels of crime and city

4   *André de Palma and Alexandre Guimard*

size, a scaling law between revenues and city size, and a scaling law between the city size and urban sprawl. The literature indicates by how much, on average, urban sprawl increases in percentage terms for a one percent increase of city size (Fuller and Gaston, 2009). At a lower-scale level we also find some regularities, such as the constant share of travel expenditures in total revenues (Schafer, 2000). In addition, it is not surprising to find regularities at the scale level of cities, in particular to find a rank-size rule, i.e. a law that relates the population size of a city to its rank in the country's or world's ranking of cities by population.

The Zipf's law (rank-size rule) postulates that city growth rate is independent (of city size) and identically distributed, such that cities are Pareto distributed. A related issue is obviously to explain the growth rate of cities, that is, why and by how much cities are growing. The concentration phenomenon of individuals and businesses is the outcome of two opposite forces: agglomeration forces and dispersion forces.

First, low transportation costs associated with high economies of scale encourage firms to be concentrated. A wider market access at the city core encourages firms' concentration. Second, at the city core, firms benefit from agglomeration economies through the effects of sharing and/or matching and/or learning due to more input suppliers and a larger labor market. For mature cities, knowledge spillovers are crucial. As explained in Glaeser *et al.* (1991), knowledge spillovers are promoted by diversification (Jacobs, 1969) or specialization of industries,[2] and by either competition or monopoly. By contrast, competition, high rents and high wages encourage firms to locate farther away.

For households, agglomerations forces are related to high wages, the variety of the labor market, social amenities, the variety of goods and high transportation costs. The living conditions within cities are on average better than in rural areas and may explain why people are leaving rural areas for cities. As an example, in China, in 2002, on average, urban residents were more than twice as rich as rural residents (Sicular *et al.*, 2007). Per capita income increased by 152 percent in cities around the world between 1960 and 2010. Cities provide inhabitants better access to sanitation and water. Migrants who move to cities make their choice on the differential between the living conditions of rural and urban areas. Many refugees move to cities as well. In contrast to migrants, refugees "are forced or compelled to relocate by external forces" (Bates, 2002). Those people have to reach cities in order to survive. Indeed, global warming increases the number of environmental refugees who tend to live in urban slums. Cities also host a large number of war refugees. Dadaab in Kenya is the largest refugee camp in the world, where 500,000 refugees are now living. Originally built by the United Nations to be ephemeral, the refugee camp is now more than 20 years old. By contrast to agglomeration forces, which cause people to concentrate in one locality, high rents, negative externalities such as noise, air pollution and the level of crime at the urban core, as well as preferences for natural amenities, encourage households to locate in smaller cities or in suburbs of large metropolitan areas.

With new and faster modes of travel, households have incentives to relocate farther away from city centers. When urban developments are neglected, developers expand the city in the surroundings that foster urban sprawl. Market failures lead some researchers to think that urban sprawl is naturally not optimal (Brueckner, 2000). First, commuters do not face the social cost of travel—the private cost does not take into account the negative externalities imposed on others. Second, land price is underestimated because it does not fully internalize the amenity value of the open space.[3] Third, the cost of an additional development in infrastructure is equal to the average cost of infrastructures and not to the marginal cost. As a result, the infrastructure cost of an additional development is under-priced.

The location of firms is partially explained by agglomeration economies. Some agglomeration economies are based on externalities, i.e. on positive effects from others (suppliers, firms or workers) that are not internalized. In the presence of externalities, the market price does not reflect the social value. For the case of urban development, the price of being located at some places differs from the social value. Thus, the concentration of firms is naturally not optimal. For Hotelling (1929), cities were excessively large because of unpriced negative externalities. But "urban externalities are not necessarily negative, and increasing returns might be a strong force in favor of geographical concentration" (Fujita and Thisse, 1997). Hence, cities may also be too small. One thus has to anticipate the natural growth path of cities to develop tailored policies related to urban development.

By using the regularities relative to urban growth and individual behaviors, one can forecast the size and the internal structure of cities. Policymakers must either promote or restrict some specific urban developments in order to reach the optimal city size. Furthermore, important challenges are related to the internal structure of cities. The challenges that policymakers have to face include traffic congestion, air pollution, natural disasters and social inequalities. For instance, there will be a large increase in the development of seaside cities in Asia, where natural disasters will be more frequent during this century. Developed countries are not exempted from natural disasters, which are indicated by forecasts about the San Andreas Fault. According to the US Geological Survey of 2008, "... in the next 30 years ... the overall probability of a magnitude 6.7 or greater earthquake in the Greater Bay Area is 63%." Moreover, larger cities are more exposed to terrorism risk because of the "target effect," i.e. very dense areas allow terrorists to target many people (Glaeser and Shapiro, 2002), and this explains why the density-weighted population can be a first simple proxy to evaluate risk exposure (Willis, 2007). The policymaker has limited resources to address all these challenges, and needs analytical tools to decide how to allocate these optimally (see Chapter 20, by Yoshitsugu Kanemoto, in de Palma *et al.*, 2011).

Moreover, there is a need to define the objective function, that is, there is a need to define the ideal city. Theories of ideal cities have been proposed by many researchers, architects and geographers, who have encountered many difficulties in developing those theories. For example, Brasilia—built between 1956 and 1960 by Lucio Costa and Oscar Niemeyer—was an application of theoretical ideas developed by Le Corbusier, and it was clearly a failure in terms of transportation. The city is car-dependent because of its specific urban shape. Even if buildings include

6 André de Palma and Alexandre Guimard

mixed services, the city itself is not a system of compact neighborhoods with mixed land use. It is divided into sectors and driving is necessary to travel among the different places. This is completely in contrast with the current vision of the ideal city as a system of compact districts, with mixed land use, green spaces and a rich social life. Currently, the community prefers to define what is a sustainable city (Proost and van der Loo, 2013), and many definitions of sustainability have been proposed. In the sense of Brundlandt in 1987: "Sustainable development is development that meets the needs of the present without compromising the ability of future generations to meet their own needs." In order to carry out sustainable policies that do not depend on the scale level, economists usually consider that the policymaker must integrate several components in order to make better decisions. The policymaker must have an intergenerational preference representation and preferences for social equity, and he must internalize the negative externalities created by the city. As an example, the welfare function, useful to evaluate the efficiency of each policy relative to others, should include the policy impacts on households, intercity migration and the negative externalities of air pollution borne by other cities (e.g. the rise in sea level, the costs of environmental refugees, and so on).

One may wonder to what extent policymakers have incentives to develop sustainable cities. Usually, policymakers' interests are focused on satisfying voters and attracting productive firms, individuals and foreign investments. More competition between cities will not necessarily lead to more sustainability. Yet urgent issues have to be addressed. Policymakers must set up tailored sustainable policies. We can identify three major areas of expertise for policymakers: transportation policies, land-use policies and social policies. They intend to address the major and growing issues of cities, which mainly include congestion, air pollution, urban sprawl, income inequality and social exclusion.

A transportation policy (including cordon pricing, zoning, a linear road pricing scheme, transit and road investments) is useful for dealing with congestion, exclusion, air pollution (at the city-scale level and at the global-scale level) and urban sprawl in the long run. Indeed, in the long run, transportation policies that change accessibility thus influence the location of households as well as businesses. Hence, a transportation policy not only deals with travel flows; it can, for example, foster the effects of land-use policies that are dealing with excessive urban sprawl.

Land-use policies such as urban boundaries, development taxes, impact fees, green cordons and targeted subsidies to renew buildings are particularly dedicated to dealing with excessive urban sprawl, addressing the problem of the decreasing share of open spaces and the decline of biodiversity, and protecting historic buildings. Land-use policies are not disconnected from other targets. For instance, they have inevitable consequences on transport demand. Specific renewal programs may want to deal with too much partitioning of social classes. However, a city manager is not exempted from the necessity to carry out specific social policies.

Social policies are particularly necessary to cut the increase of income inequality and provide public goods and services ranging from education to health and economic assistance.

Hence, policies are interconnected. Each expert must take into account the impact of other policies on his own field. The implication is that policymakers must work together to develop an efficient global policy enacted by the policy tools that are available. Because resources are limited, all goals cannot be achieved at the same time. Policymakers must make a trade-off between targets and invest more in one given policy than in others, depending on how much each goal is weighted when defining the welfare function (Hediger, 2000).

Hence, the sustainability of a city is not only dependent on the current and/or coming successful picture of the city as seen through the prism of per capita revenues and urban growth. The sustainability of a city will depend on its capacity to be sustainable, not only economically, but also socially and environmentally.

The goal of this chapter is to describe and explain the development patterns of cities. Behind the uniqueness and the contextuality of urban pictures, we find some strong regularities in urban development and individual behaviors. This allows us to imagine the future outlines of major cities across the world and the main challenges for our current century. We deduce the need for public policies and cooperation at the global-scale level to address the world sustainability.

The chapter is organized as follows: in Section 1.2, first, we briefly describe urbanization over time and space, from the very first cities in history to current Megalopolises such as Tokyo, Delhi and Shanghai. Second, we recall standard models dealing with urban development to see to what extent they can explain the observed urbanization phenomenon.

In Section 1.3, we will shed light on the regularities concerning the internal structure of cities. The size of a city appears to have a major impact on a number of its characteristics. Some regularities (the scaling law of cities) concerned with the internal structure of cities promote either agglomeration or dispersion.

In Section 1.4, we will discuss the regularities between cities. First, we will explain the distribution of cities in terms of their size (the Pareto distribution of cities due to the Zipf's law). Second, we will describe and explain the strong regularities found in the location of cities across the world.

In Section 1.5, we will shed light on the main forecasts in developed, emerging and developing countries. The demographic forecasts for the end of the current century, combined with the regularities of cities, allow us to surmise the major changes and challenges to be faced by cities around the world.

We conclude with the need to coordinate policymakers around the world to address the externalities created by cities, such as air pollution and the necessity of redistributive systems.

1.2 History of urbanization and first modeling stages

Performing a cross-sectional analysis, one can observe that all cities are different in terms of size, urban shape, the density distribution within the urban core, congestion and other internal characteristics. With a longitudinal analysis, we can also notice some regularities in the urban development of cities. Over time, radius of the city grew from 2.5 kilometers to 20 kilometers, when the walking city changed

8 *André de Palma and Alexandre Guimard*

to the automobile city (Newman and Kenworthy, 1996). However, time spent on transportation remained roughly constant over time, at approximately one hour per day. The increase in travel speed allowed people to extend the distances they travelled. According to Marchetti (1994), humans have cave instincts; therefore, the time exposure outside the cave is limited to one hour. There are also other theories that explain the statistical regularity of spending one hour on transportation.

To understand the size, spatial distribution, and shape of cities, it is necessary to analyze the history of cities and their urban development. Based on observations, researchers have built models that provide useful insights to explain the process of city development.

1.2.1 History of cities

1.2.1.1 Early stages of urbanization

At the early age of human societies, before the Neolithic Age and the transition to agriculture, our ancestors were nomadic. It is thus difficult to find evidence of settlements dating before this historical time period.

The "first cities" (not fully settled) were built from 10000 to 8500 BC and were populated by a few thousand inhabitants. One of the first cities, Jericho, was created during the Neolithic Age (from 9000 BC) along with Ain Ghazal, Catal Hüyük and Khirokitia (Kostof, 1993). A priori, it seems difficult to find remains of older cities because, "Settlements or societies with no more than a few hundred members cannot sustain the degrees of specialization and sociopolitical power that we are accustomed to thinking of as urban" (Cowgill, 2004).

"Real cities" (fully settled according to Marcus, 1998), such as Uruk, emerged at around 3500 BC in Mesopotamia, but their population was still limited to thousands. Some Mesopotamian cities can be considered as city-states because of their particular organization, but the existence of regional integration is still in debate. In Egypt, it has been proven that the region was fully politically integrated from the Early-Dynastic period, between 3050 and 2700 BC.

The emergence of writing eased trade through registration and the invention of the wheel increased agricultural productivity while decreasing transportation costs. But, still, travel speed was limited. The modal share was restricted to either pedestrians or riding horses (Bairoch, 1991). Cities were dense and their radius amounted to a few kilometers; they grew to reach millions of inhabitants. In 1800, Beijing, populated by 2–3 million people, was the largest known city. After the Industrial Revolution, the population of Beijing was outnumbered by that of London.

1.2.1.2 History to the modern age

Technological progress enabled people to travel at higher speed across lands, seas and oceans in order to trade with neighbors at lower costs. As a result, cities enlarged. After the successive hegemonies of Mesopotomia, Greece, the Roman Empire and Constantinople, China became very powerful. The discoveries of the compass and the rudder foreshadowed China's technological advance. Thus,

China was able to carry out remote expeditions. During the fifteenth century, Zheng-He built 70 boats, which were larger than those of Christopher Colombus 70 years later. With 30,000 individuals on board, they explored East Africa, South Asia and the Middle East. These expeditions, and the large flotilla, prove that the Chinese Empire had high financial capacity and advanced marine technologies. Acemoglu *et al.* (2002) documented a positive correlation between the level of urbanization and the level of wealth. It is thus not surprising to find that cities in China were the largest until the Industrial Revolution took place in Europe. In contrast, over the entire period of 1300–1800, cities in Europe grew by only 20 percent (Bairoch, 1991) and subsequently grew at a higher speed due to the Industrial Revolution.

1.2.1.3 The Industrial Revolution

1.2.1.3.1 WESTERN EUROPE

This region (and Great Britain in particular) gained power during the nineteenth century, due to the Industrial Revolution. Countries that achieved this transition pattern of industrialization are richer today on average. As a matter of fact secured property rights for the entire population seems to be a necessary condition for the development of industrialization. Acemoglu *et al.* (2002) argue that the poorest colonies in 1500 are, on average, richer today than the richest colonies were in 1500. The colonists' treatment of these settlements explains this phenomenon. In the poorest colonies, colonists had incentives to create institutions with generalized property rights in order to promote growth, as in their homeland. By contrast, in the richest colonies, colonists used elites to extract as many local resources as possible. Due to property rights being secured for few elites, the populace had obviously no incentive to invest. Elites did not want to invest either, because they feared losing their power and advantages within the new capitalist system. However, the process of industrialization required the investment of a large part of the population. This condition was only satisfied in colonies which secured property rights for the populace, that is, in the poorest ones (in 1500).

The Industrial Revolution emerged in Great Britain, which was not among the most urbanized countries: Belgium, Italy, Netherlands and Portugal (Bairoch, 1991). The Industrial Revolution found its origins in the mechanization of spinning (following the invention of Arkwright's spinning frame in 1769), and the use of coal for the production of iron (with Darby's invention of the coke-fuelled blast furnace in 1709, expanded upon later during the nineteenth century), then in the steam engine of James Watt, used from 1790. Technical innovations, such as the steam engine, were the results of a very long process of accumulation, both in capital and knowledge, from the early age of societies. The invention of the wheel (3500 BC) and methods of irrigation generated surplus in the agricultural sector, allowing some citizens to focus only on intellectual production (i.e. the sciences). Knowledge has been stored over time through writing (3400 BC), which promoted technological advances. The steam engine, one of the major technological advances in history, allowed for the production of energy without the need for animate sources (either from animals

10 *André de Palma and Alexandre Guimard*

like cows or human labor). This enabled the development of public transportation (trains) as well as the mechanization of production, while staying independent from sources of water, in contrast to cotton mills.

During the nineteenth century, Great Britain began to be the fabric of the world. Agricultural, textile, as well as iron and steel production, largely increased. Iron and steel were necessary to produce machines, engines and railways, and to gradually construct buildings and, eventually, skyscrapers. The iron and steel industries needed to be located close to coalfields because transportation costs were still high despite the emergence of railways during the nineteenth century. Spinning industries were located close to train stations, because cotton was mainly imported from abroad. Furthermore, industries were looking for lower wages in small and rural areas, which explains why, during the Industrial Revolution, total populations largely increased in small and medium cities and not as much in large cities. In 1700—along with London—Norwich, Bristol, Newcastle and Exeter were the most populated cities in Great Britain, whereas Birmingham, Liverpool, Manchester and Leeds etc., were the major centers in the first phase of the Industrial Revolution (from 1700 to 1850). This did not apply to London, where the total population grew from 550 thousand in 1700 to 2,320 thousand in 1850.

It was possible for Great Britain to be the workshop of the world during the nineteenth century because the proportion of agricultural workers dropped from 75–80 percent in 1800 to 53–55 percent in 1910, concomitantly with agricultural revolutions. The first agricultural revolution started at the end of the seventeenth century, as a result of cultivation techniques imported from Netherlands. The second came after 1870, due to development of reapers, combines and fertilizers.

With the surge in urban density and poor sanitary conditions, diseases spread rapidly into the largest cities. During the nineteenth century, life expectancy was higher for those living in rural areas. The poorest were not able to afford public transportation (horse and wagon) at that time. During the first half of the nineteenth century, at least, the populace was located close to the factories, and entertainment trips were limited.

1.2.1.3.2 THE UNITED STATES

Many cities in the US were built during the nineteenth century and grew after World War II. Before 1945, cities mainly developed around harbors and railheads (examples of this are Boston and Detroit). Towards the end of the nineteenth century, street cars and trolleys allowed the highest income commuters to relocate farther away from the city center. The city thus expanded further in proximity to the train stations, developing into the "transit city." Moreover, motorized freight enabled firms to locate farther away from harbors and to benefit from lower rents. The first private car transportation was developed during the 1920s, but only the richest people could afford it. Such modes of transportation permitted them to locate between street-car centers, and cities began to spread more homogeneously. After the second half of the twentieth century, the automobile shaped the city structure; and the "transit city" was transformed into the "automobile city."[4]

1.2.1.4 Recent developments after World War II

1.2.1.4.1 WESTERN EUROPE

Many current city centers in Western Europe are similar to the walking city of the medieval period, which explains why population density is high close to the city hall, in contrast to US cities on average. Focusing on one country, i.e. France after World War II, people concentrated in urban cores such as in the Ile-de-France region (the administrative region where Paris is located), which was the most attractive in terms of net migration balance. Since 1970, the net migration balance has been negative (see the "Counter-urbanization" theory by Berry, 1976), concomitant with the accessibility of the private car. Currently, the net balance is still negative, but the Ile-de-France region remains attractive for young workers. In the last few years, the south-west and southern regions of France have attracted more and more people from all age brackets, except for the age bracket of 20–29 years in the south-west (Baccaïni, 2005). Within the most attractive regions, highly qualified workers in the age bracket of 30–59 years old accept lower wages, which can be explained because of better living conditions. Hence, differentials in wages may be used to assess the value of quality of life (Roback, 1982). As a matter of fact, in 2012—according to a CSA survey among Parisians who want to leave Paris—finding better living conditions is more important than lower living costs.[5] According to Godefroy (2011) the data from the SRCV survey of the French statistical institution (INSEE) show that there is a slight decrease in the level of general life satisfaction with city size. Actually, the level of average life satisfaction in Ile-de-France is relatively high because of its young population. People looking for a high quality of life and low rent may to some extent explain the trend between 1950 and 2000 in OECD countries, in which urban sprawl was massive and urban areas doubled in only 50 years (Kamal-Chaoui, 2010).

Urbanization is constantly increasing. One explanation is related to technological improvements in agriculture which push up the urban proportion. Currently, the volume effect is not so important, since the number of workers in agriculture is reaching a lower threshold. However, the proportion of the agricultural sector continued to decrease during recent decades, and dropped, for example, in France according to census data (INSEE)[6] from 8.0 percent in 1980 to 3.4 percent in 2007.

Rural areas face a number of problems, such as the problem of accessibility to local shops (see Figure 1.1). Their number decreased by −0.5 percent per year between 2002 and 2008. Many municipalities that face this issue the most are also the poorest. Altitude may explain accessibility, because of longer travel times. Altitude is also part of the natural advantages, and it must be correlated with revenues. In addition, the issue of accessibility to local markets is more of a problem in the poorest regions because businesses look for a large market to access. In contrast to rural areas, accessibility to local shops increased in large municipalities by 0.3 percent per year between 2002 and 2008, and by 1.5 percent in other cities. As a whole, in France, the model of large supermarkets has plateaued since the beginning of the twenty-first century. Between 1999 and 2007, the number of small grocery shops decreased at lower rates (−5.1 percent between 1993 and

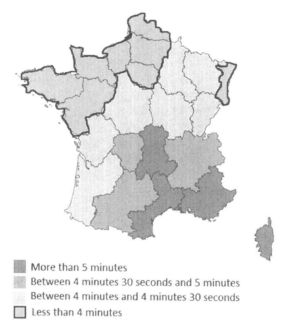

■ More than 5 minutes
Between 4 minutes 30 seconds and 5 minutes
Between 4 minutes and 4 minutes 30 seconds
☐ Less than 4 minutes

Figure 1.1 Accessibility to a local market.
Source: Solard (2010).

1999; −1.7 percent between 1999 and 2007 according to the INSEE).[7] In large and dense cities such as Paris, the number of local grocery shops is increasing, but it is not necessarily correlated with more competition. For example, the Casino brand in Paris has 60 percent of the total market share while Carrefour, the second largest, has only 20 percent of the market share (Authority for competition, in French: "Autorité de la concurrence").[8]

1.2.1.4.2 THE UNITED STATES

After 1945, the private car was more affordable for the middle classes, and people spread further away from the city center. Businesses and residents made strategic decisions to have access to roads. From that time on, instead of harbors, cities grew along highways. The phenomenon of cities expanding along the highways expanded even more in the 1970s, introducing the phenomena of "the edge cities" (Garreau, 1991). The urban sprawl grew concomitantly with the development of large shopping malls, and it largely affected the urban design of the US cities.

Even if the urban sprawl seems to be a transitional pattern due to the introduction of the private car as the main mode of transportation, it persisted over time. Between 1995 and 2005, the classic automobile cities such as Dallas, Denver and Atlanta, attracted increasing amounts of residents in the urban belt, becoming the champions of urban sprawl growth (Kamal-Chaoui, 2010). However, the phenomenon of urban sprawl is not a rule of thumb for all cities across the US, as some spread more than others.

Urban sprawl can be explained by city enlargement and the distribution of the added population within a city. For example, population growth in Los Angeles and NYC is quite homogeneous across the city, whereas in Dallas, Houston and Atlanta urban growth is preeminent in suburbs distanced 20–25 miles from the city hall. Additionally, strong disparities appeared across automobile cities such as Dallas, Houston, Phoenix and Atlanta. As an example, in Houston density is high close to the city hall, which is not the case for Dallas.

Furthermore, another explanation of urban sprawl is a new spatial distribution of existing households within the city towards the suburbs and away from the city hall. In Chicago, there are three major urban cores, the first at 6–7 miles, the second at 23–24 miles, and the last at 36 miles from the city hall, being a strong example of "polycentricism." The population located in the area of 6–7 miles distance from the city hall decreased between 2000 and 2010, while the population increased substantially in the third zone. The third zone overtook the second in terms of total population size. In Cleveland and Detroit, industrial plant shutdowns have had negative effects on the total population and the new spatial distribution of households towards the suburbs.

Many explanations may be used to explain the changes in the location of households and firms (between and within cities), as described above. Obviously, economic trends such as innovation, productivity and revenues are the major cause, but there exist also qualitative indicators. For example, quality of life and accessibility encourage residents and businesses to locate in specific areas.

Actually, there are other reasons for internal migration. Mortgage crises cause people to leave their homes and move from one city to another. This can substantially impact the shape of cities: those which are losing residents and others which host new households. In the US, between 2004 and 2007, residents had easy access to credit, and thus cities increasingly spread. From 2008–2009, defaults increased, as well as foreclosure rates, and it induced a high increase in the percentage of vacant homes in many cities across the country (among others, Florida and Nevada). This is dramatic in terms of urban development because, ex-post, there is an excessive urban sprawl. Houses were built, despite the fact that households were not affordable. Afterwards, new flows of households between cities were not necessarily globally optimal, since the benefits of the new host cities did not take into account the costs of cities which were losing residents. It would be necessary to think about a situation which is, at the intercity level, socially optimal. In particular, one may ask, is it optimal to build developments in new host cities such as Texas? These cities need new infrastructures and the destruction of open spaces, whereas, in other cities, policymakers have to face the problem of vacant homes.

1.2.1.4.3   FORMER SOCIALIST COUNTRIES

After the fall of the USSR in 1991, cities in former socialist countries fell into decline. Actually, transition was achieved a few years ago, or is in the process of

14 *André de Palma and Alexandre Guimard*

being achieved, in cities such as Sofia (Bulgaria), Tbilisi (Georgia) and Yerevan (Armenia). Mostly, the growth rate became positive between 2005 and 2010. Notice that Moscow did not suffer as much; between 1995 and 2000, the total population in Moscow grew at 1.67 percent per year.

1.2.1.4.4 EMERGING AND LESS DEVELOPED COUNTRIES

Since 1950, urban growth in developed countries has been very low compared to developing countries. In 1950, the total urban population in less developed countries was approximately equal to that in more developed countries. Since 1950, urban growth has been higher in less developed than in more developed countries. Since 1970, the total number of people living in cities has been higher in less developed countries than in more developed countries.

As an example, between 1950 and 2005, the urban proportion increased twice as much in China as in France (Kamal-Chaoui, 2010). Between 1990 and 1995, some cities in China increased by almost 20 percent per year. The population of Shenzhen, in 1990, was 875 thousand people, and grew at such levels that, in 2010, the city was populated by nine million inhabitants. As in other developed countries, some cities also declined in the last few years. For example, the total population of Pusan, in the Republic of Korea—one of the largest seaports in the world—decreased from 1995, because the net migration balance was negative—as indicated by Korean statistics.[9] The decrease in total population is slowing down, such that, in 2020, the population size will remain constant (UN, 2012).

Urban growth in China was more important along the coast. Between 1998 and 2004, all the cities which increased their share in China's gross domestic product (GDP) were on the coast (Kamal-Chaoui, 2010). However, at the same time, taking into account underestimated inflation in official data (Tsui, 2007), interprovincial inequality increased, especially between hinterlands and coastal cities (i.e. Shanghai and Shenzhen).

Urban growth in the largest cities is sometimes concomitant with more slums. In some countries, this situation has deteriorated during the last two decades. Wars and droughts are the major causes. In 2009, the proportion of urban slums reached 89.3 percent in Chad, 95.9 percent in the Central African Republic and 76.4 percent in Ethiopia. In Iraq, the proportion of urban slums jumped from 16.9 percent in 2000 to 52.8 percent in 2009; in Zimbabwe, it grew from 4 percent in 1990 to 24.1 percent in 2009.

In Rio de Janeiro, slums (*favelas*) were set up more than one century ago at the end of the nineteenth century. Slums expanded due to the rural exodus and flows of former soldiers. Shanty towns developed during the twentieth century, especially during 1940, then during the urbanization process in the second half of the century. Slums in Rio de Janeiro, as in other mega-cities, raise a number of important sanitary and security issues. These issues existed early in the history of *favelas*, at the beginning of the twentieth century (de Almeida Abreu and Le Clerre, 1994). Governments always tried to handle slums in order to raise the value of lands and/or promote the image of the city, for example in 1920 for the visit of the King of Belgium. All the attempts at renewal failed, as seen at the beginning of the twentieth century, or during the dictatorship in the 1970s. During the 1980s, the number of drug traffickers increased, and this raised even more of a problem of insecurity for residents. Between 1968 and 2005, education improved, however returns differentials from education between *favelas* and the developed areas of the city increased (Perlman, 2007). Fortunately, as a whole, the number of people living in slums is decreasing in Brazil. The proportion of slums dropped from 36.7 percent in 1990 to 26.9 percent in 2010 (UN Habitat, 2013); obviously, the latter rates are still unacceptable.

Globally, for two decades, sanitation has been getting better and better around the world. On average, the proportion of the urban population living in slums is decreasing significantly, especially in Asia. In China, between 1990 and 2009, the share dropped from 43.6 percent to 29.1 percent. The improvement is even more spectacular in India, where it dropped from 54.9 percent in 1990 to 29.4 percent in 2009. However, the proportion is still very high in a number of countries. For example, it is 61.6 percent in Bangladesh, 76.2 percent in Madagascar, and 62.7 percent in Nigeria.

1.2.2 Simple models of cities

Many researchers have studied tailored models to explain why cities are growing—some more than others—and in order to describe and predict the location of individuals and businesses among and within cities.

The first model of location is due to Von Thünen (1826). The bid rent, in other words, the willingness of farmers to pay for land rent, declines with distance from the city center because of higher transport costs. Some crops per unit of weight are more valuable than others, and the owner accepts the best bid. This model links rents to transportation costs, thus we have a location distribution of farmers within the rural area. The most productive crops are closer to the City Business District (CBD), and (all other things equal) the farmers, who incur higher travel costs (i.e. those who must maintain a low temperature for perishable products). In Figure 1.2, farmer type a has the highest bid rent (B_a) for all fields located at a distance lower than the distance d_a from the city hall. The crops produced by Farmer type a, (a per unit of weight, are highly valuable—the market price and transport costs are high). Farmer type b has the highest bid rent (B_b) for all fields located at a distance between the distances d_a and d_b. For locations farther away, farmer type c has the highest bid rent (B_c).

In Von Thünen's model, at equilibrium, the additional benefits for farmers to locate closer to the city center (lower shipping costs) are exactly offset by the additional costs (higher land rents).

The reasoning of comparing the marginal benefits and the marginal costs to locate closer to the city hall is the same for households. In 1964, Alonso developed the monocentric model, in which all jobs are located at the CBD, and residents locate in the surroundings. As explained in Anas *et al.* (1998), "the residential bid

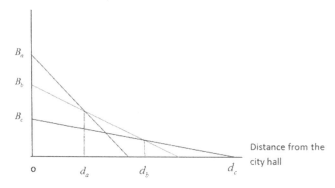

Figure 1.2 Bid rents function of distance from the city hall.
Source: Author's own construct.

rent $b(x, \bar{u})$ at location x is the maximum rent per unit land area that a household can pay and still receive utility $\bar{u}$". We have:

$$b(x, \bar{u}) = \max_{z,l} \left[\frac{Y - T(x) - z}{L} \right] st. u(z,l) \geq \bar{u}, \quad (1.1)$$

where, z is the amount of the numeraire good, L is the residential lot size, $T(x)$ is the commuting cost incurred by the resident located at distance x from the CBD, and Y is the total revenue of the individual, which covers expenditures (commuting costs, rents and the consumption of the numeraire good). At equilibrium, residents do not have any incentives to move closer or farther away from the city center. At equilibrium, the saving costs in transportation by locating closer to the city center are just equal to the additional costs in rents. We have:

$$\frac{db(x, \bar{u})}{dx} = -\frac{T'(x)}{L(y - T(x), \bar{u})} < 0$$

where $L(y - T(x), \bar{u})$ is a function solution of the maximization problem 1.1, and $T'(x)$ is the first derivative of the commuting cost. This equation is the Muth's condition.

The monocentric model with congestion was first introduced by Strotz (1965) and Mills (1967). A monocentric model, with congestion and endogenous roads investments, was used by de Lara et al. (2012) in order to simulate the impact of road pricing schemes on congestion and land use. Indeed, for a resident located at distance r, the travel cost $\tau(r)$ to get to the CBD is a function of the roads capacity, and the number of users. We have:

$$\tau(r) = \int_{\tau_C}^{r} c\left(\frac{N(x)}{L_T(x)}\right) dx,$$

where $c\left(\frac{N(x)}{L_T(x)}\right)$ represents the transport cost at distance x. The function c is assumed to satisfy $c(w) > 0$, $c'(w) > 0$, and $c''(x) > 0$ for all $w \geq 0$. Let $N(x)$ denote the number of households located further away than x from the city center, which is defined by a fixed radius r_c. Let $L_T(x)$ denote the amount of land devoted to transport at location x (control variable).

In a monocentric model, the location of businesses is fixed at the CBD. One explanation is that businesses are willing to pay higher rents than residents. This can be because firms may benefit more from concentration than residents. With large economies of scale and low transport costs (New Economic Geography) and/or agglomeration economies (urbanization and localization externalities, knowledge spillovers, etc.) businesses do have strong incentives to concentrate.

Internal economies of scale and transportation costs are the fundamental elements to explain concentration according to New Economic Geography. Firms in the manufacturing sector incur fix costs, which encourage them to concentrate activities at the same location, but they also want to be close to clients and to have a large market access, because of the existence of shipping costs. The core-periphery model (Lafourcade and Thisse, 2011) is useful to understand to what extent transportation costs are at the baseline of concentration *versus* dispersion, without considering the additional effects of input–output linkages, labor market pooling, knowledge spillovers and comparative advantages of classic international trade theories. Consider two sectors: the manufacturing sector and the agricultural sector. The agricultural sector is described by constant returns to scale, workers are immobile and there are no shipping costs in this sector. By contrast, the industrial sector is described by increasing returns to scale, and there are shipping costs. Each firm sells one type of differentiated output (no economies of scope). Firms have a market power that depends on the elasticity of substitution between varieties. Consumers have a preference for variety, which means that utility increases with the number of producers in the city core. Workers in the industrial sector are mobile between the two regions (the core and the periphery). Consider an increase in workers in one given region. This will induce a more than proportional increase of the share of industrial firms because more workers means more consumption, and firms benefit from economies of scale, which will attract even more firms (*the home market effect*). Thus, the given region will be more specialized in the industrial sector, which is not explained by comparative advantages. Prices will decrease because of more competition within the industrial sector (*the strategic effect*). Firms also need more labor, which causes nominal wages to increase (*the demand effect on the labor market*). Thus, even more people will move because first, they have a preference for variety and second, real wages increase. The flow of new dwellers will cause nominal wages to decrease in the labor market (*the supply effect*). Hence, the global effect on wages is undetermined. More competition in the urban core reduces the firms' mark-up, which constitutes a dispersion force. If transportation costs are sufficiently low, all firms will concentrate in one region, and especially in the urban core if firms have a larger market access. Low

18 *André de Palma and Alexandre Guimard*

transportation costs allow firms to ship their products at low costs to the immobile class of workers in the agricultural sector.

So far, we have not introduced input–output linkages. Concentration may be additionally enhanced by input–output linkages, labor market pooling and knowledge spillovers. In particular, Combes *et al.* (2012) found, for France—based on data for 341 employment areas, between 1994 and 2002—that firms in denser employment areas are on average 9.7 percent more productive than others in less dense employment areas. Among other explanations, firms may be more productive with the number of inputs suppliers. This is the case if the production function is a CES function type, as follows:

$$x = z_0^\alpha \left(\int_0^n z(w)^\rho dw \right)^{\frac{1-\alpha}{\rho}}.$$

The production x is a function of constant returns to scale in the homogeneous input z_0 and the differentiated inputs $z(w)$. The output elasticity of the homogeneous good is equal to α. Let ρ denote the degree of substitution between the differentiated inputs. The smaller inputs are substitutes, the more producers have a preference for variety and the more they are productive with the number of input suppliers.

In a model of individuals and activities location, consider the case where there are only knowledge spillovers to explain agglomeration economies. Firms share knowledge that is not internalized. A polycentrism pattern may appear if transportation costs are high enough relative to the degree of knowledge spillovers (Fujita and Thisse, 1997). But still, in all cities, as seen previously, the city center is denser and population density decreases with distance from the city hall (the same appears to be true for rents).

In addition, the number of large centers is smaller than the number of subcenters. The number of large cities is smaller than the number of medium and small cities. Those facts are addressed by the rank-size rule or Zipf's law. There seems to exist a kind of hierarchy of cities and urban centers in terms of city size and function. The central place theory of Christaller (1933) explains that cities at an upper level of the hierarchy are larger and more diversified. Moreover, the distance between large cities is longer than between small cities.

Individuals may choose to travel longer distances to get to a large market that holds a lot of diversified products. It allows them to buy uncommon goods, which they could not find among local merchants. Local merchants reversely sell common goods that are frequently bought by local residents. As explained by the law of retail gravitation (Reilly, 1931), the market area of a city increases with its size and with the ability to sell more products; thus we have:

$$d_{xb} = \frac{d_{ab}}{1 + \sqrt{\frac{P_a}{P_b}}},$$

where d_{ab} is the distance between the two cities a and b, and d_{xb} is the radius of the market area of the city b, which is increasing with its mass P_b and decreasing with the mass P_a of city a.

There also exist incentive mechanisms among firms that lead them to concentrate and sell differentiated products. First, Hotelling (1929), with the minimum product differentiation, explains that businesses tend to concentrate at the central urban core in order to catch more clients. Actually, with price competition and a quadratic transport cost function, it has been shown that firms have incentives to be strongly spatially differentiated (d'Aspremont et al., 1979). How much businesses will concentrate will depend on transportation costs compared to the level of product differentiation. It can be shown that when transportation costs are relatively low, and firms are differentiated, then firms tend to concentrate, that is, to be less spatially differentiated (de Palma et al. 1985).

To sum up, first, businesses have incentives to concentrate and sell differentiated products. Second, for non-differentiated and frequent products, many firms should also be homogeneously located over the urban area, which creates smaller sub-centers. This effect implies a distribution of cities in terms of city size and function; a hierarchy of cities in the sense of Christaller.

1.3 Regularities about the internal structure of cities

Businesses concentrate because they benefit from localized natural advantages, as well as agglomeration economies. The city size thus increases, and characteristics of the city change. Thus, the city can become more or less attractive through agglomeration forces versus dispersion forces. We will discuss below some regularities that are related to the internal structure of cities; in particular the scaling laws that link the size to the characteristics of cities.

1.3.1 The scaling laws

Cities are different sizes but obey, as a whole, scaling laws. Indeed, there are correlations between the size and a number of characteristics of cities, such as the population rank, energy consumption, expenditures in infrastructure, revenues per capita and crime. Only a few of them will be discussed in this chapter. Following Bettencourt et al. (2007), each city characteristic can be expressed as a power law function of its size as follows:

$$Y(t) = Y_0 N(t)^\beta \text{ with } \beta \geq 0, \tag{1.2}$$

where $N(t)$ is the city size at time t, $Y(t)$ denotes a characteristic of the city at date t (per capita income for example), and Y_0 is a normalization constant. If β is equal to 1, the given characteristic increases by 1 percent, with a one percent increase of the city size.

1.3.2 Urban sprawl

Land resources are obviously limited, which implies that an increase in the population size naturally involves urban sprawl. Marshall (2007) found, for the US cities, that the scaling rate is equal to 2, that is to say, an urban area increases twice as much as the population size (in percentage terms). When the city size increases by 1 percent, the population density decreases by 1 percent as well. By contrast, Fuller and Gaston (2009) found that larger cities are not denser.

In the monocentric models, larger cities are denser. When the city size increases, the urban boundary is moving away but the city is denser, rents are higher and they decrease more rapidly with the distance from the CBD. Thus, the polycentric urban structure of cities may explain why the urban area increases as much as city size, that is to say, why larger cities are not more compact. In a pure monocentric city, all jobs are centrally located. In a polycentric city, there are labor pools in suburbs as well. Hence, to evaluate the urban structure of the city, one may want to estimate the density of jobs and the population along the distance line from the city hall. Following Clark (1951), the urban density can be expressed as an exponential law, which is a function of distance from the center of the city:

$$D(r) = Ae^{-\gamma r},$$

where $D(r)$ is the density at distance r from the center of the city, γ is the density gradient, and $A = D(0)$ is the urban density at the center of the city. It follows the cumulative population size at a distance r from the city center (Clark (1951), Bussière (1972)). The population size at distance r from the city center is equal to the population density multiplied by the surface area. Yet, at distance r from the city hall, the surface area is infinitely small, equal to the perimeter $2\pi r$. Hence, the cumulative population size at distance r, $P(r)$, is given by the following integral:

$$p(r) = 2\pi \int_0^r r D(x) dx.$$

A positive density gradient indicates that density decreases with distance. The density gradient decreases over time (Muth, 1969; Mills, 1972) because cities spread from the city center. In addition, the density gradient differs between residents and firms. It is higher for firms, and it decreases over time. This means that firms are more centrally located and follow the de-concentration of people (Mieszkowski and Mills, 1993). The decentralization of jobs makes the city more and more polycentric, and it may then be important to estimate the density gradient in the more complex case of complementary sub-centers (Small and Song, 1994).

The urban shape mainly differs across cities. Indeed, as illustrated in Figure 1.3,[10] the urban population[11] of New York City is very concentrated close to the city hall, at a distance of 10 miles from the city hall. By contrast, in Atlanta, the urban population is more spread out, the pick of the population is farther away, at a distance of 20 miles from the city hall, and the population curve is smoother along the distance line. Moreover, by focusing on the proportion of jobs located

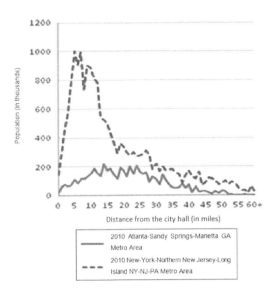

Figure 1.3 The distribution of residents in NYC and Atlanta.

Source: US Census Bureau, Patterns of Metropolitan and Micropolitan Population Change: 2000–2010, Population density profiles.

close to the city hall, as in Glaeser and Kahn (2001), one can easily notice that Chicago and Los Angeles are more polycentric than New York City. Indeed, in New York City, more than a quarter of total employment is at the city hall. On the contrary, in Los Angeles, almost all firms are located in the surroundings of the city hall. For all three cities, New York City, Los Angeles and Chicago, total employment is located at a distance below 25 miles from the city hall, since the cumulative distribution for that distance is equal to 100 percent. Furthermore, the proportion of commuting in total daytime population is largely lower in New York City than in Los Angeles.[12] In consequence, because New York City is more monocentric, one may expect that an increase in population size will produce a denser city.

1.3.3 *Congestion*

Congestion is a major issue for most of the largest cities because of the costs in terms of travel time and the harm from greenhouse gas emissions. The level of congestion, on average, depends on the shape (polycentricity and monocentricity) and the size of the city. Between 1982 and 2011, congestion increased in almost all cities. In Washington, DC in 2011, the yearly total for hours of delay per auto was 67 in comparison to 35 in Phoenix (Texas A&M Transportation Institute).[13]

In the monocentric city model, since all jobs are located at the CBD, an increase in the city size necessarily implies more congestion. Congestion encourages residents to either locate closer to the city hall or to leave the metropolitan

22   *André de Palma and Alexandre Guimard*

area for a smaller city. Investments in road infrastructure reduce congestion for those who are currently using their car, but it can also change the modal share. From 1956, large road investments in the US promoted car use as well as urban sprawl because travel speeds increased.

At the city level, based on the selection of major world cities (Ingram, 1999), the road network density (the road length per land area) is almost constant, which means that the increase in the length of the road network is possible due to the annexation of new land areas. This explanation seems reasonable, since urban land is very valuable, i.e. there is an important opportunity cost to increase the road network in cities. As a matter of fact, the saturation level of road network density in cities was estimated to be 23 kilometers of road per square kilometer of land area. Thus, even if the population size increases, the road network cannot extend above some levels. Yet, the road length per capita (in meters) is strongly correlated with urban density (population per square kilometers). As illustrated in Ingram (1999), if the urban density increases by 1 percent, the road length per capita decreases by 1 percent. Thus, when the urban density increases, traffic congestion should increase too.

According to Bettencourt *et al.* (2007), for infrastructures, and other material needs, the scaling parameter in Equation 1.2 is below 1 ($\beta < 1$). This means that roads do not develop in the same proportion as population size, and, on average, congestion increases with city size. It is what we observed for American cities between 1982 and 2011 (Texas A&M Transportation Institute). Indeed, in 2011, the average number of yearly hours of delay per auto was 52 for very large cities, whereas it was 37 hours for large cities, 28 for medium cities and 21 hours for small cities. Between 1982 and 2011, congestion increased in all the American cities, but more in larger cities than in smaller ones. In very large cities, the number of wasted hours per capita per year increased by 33 hours, whereas it increased by only 14 hours in small cities.

When the urban density increases congestion is more important, which encourages dwellers to choose public transportation, a two-wheel vehicle, or non-motorized modes of transportation (cycling or walking). It has been shown that car use, i.e. the number of car passengers multiplied by kilometers traveled, is correlated with the activity intensity, which is the number of persons and jobs per urban hectare. Newman and Kenworthy (2006) consider the 58 higher-income metropolitan areas around the world and show that this correlation is well fitted by a power law: $y = y_0 x^\beta$, where y is the measure of car use, y_0 a positive constant and β is the elasticity of car use with respect to activity intensity.[14] This coefficient β is negative, equal to -0.6612, which indicates that when the activity intensity increases by 1 percent, car use should decrease by 0.66 percent. In terms of values, the negative effect of the activity intensity on car use is very high for low values of the activity intensity (the slope of the curve is negative and steep), and it decreases with the activity intensity (the slope increases with the activity intensity). A similar power law can be observed when one regresses per capita private passenger transport energy use against urban density. Cities turn out to be clustered according to their geographical location, which indicates that among other factors, common history, demography, and culture also influenced the way that cities grew. For very low urban density, the car is the only means of transportation. Reversely, for very high urban density, it is more efficient for public transport to be developed. According to Newman and Kenworthy (1999), public transport usage increases concomitantly with urban density. Asian cities are very dense, and the proportion of public transportation is about 50 percent, in contrast to 10 percent, on average, in North American and Australian cities.

A denser city encourages dwellers to use public transport because of more traffic congestion. Policymakers may also want to invest in public transport in order to deal with congestion and air pollution, which are externalities that are not internalized by users. As a matter of fact, minimum urban density levels are required to develop large public investments in transportation (Cervero and Guerra, 2011) because the average capital cost per mile decreases with urban density, such as for light-rail and heavy-rail. One may thus expect, as an example, that denser cities have longer metro networks. As a matter of fact, when one regresses the length of metro networks on urban density the correlation is positive, but the variance is very large, and it increases with urban density, as illustrated in Figure 1.4.[15] Actually, it appears that the length of metro networks is strongly positively correlated with the GDP of cities, as illustrated in Figure 1.5.

1.3.4 Total and per capita city revenues

The first observable fact is that the richest countries do not have the richest cities in terms of total revenues. In 2012, the US was ranked first in terms of total GDP with 15,700 billion US dollars, above China (8,200), Japan (6,000), Germany (3,400),

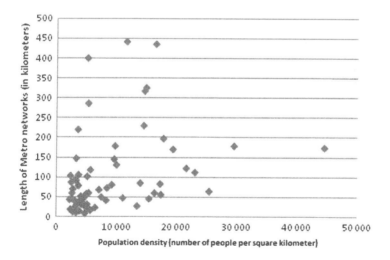

Figure 1.4 The length of metro networks vs. population density.
Source: Results for 67 World cities with data from Demographia (2005).

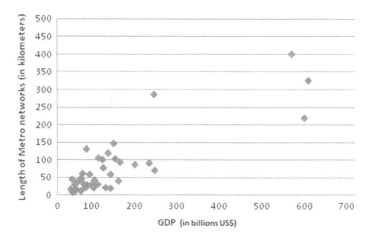

Figure 1.5 The length of metro networks vs. GDP of cities.

Source: Results for 67 cities from OECD countries with data from Demographia (2005), and OECD (2013).

France (2,600) and the United Kingdom (2,400). However, at the city level, New York City, the largest city of the US, was not ranked first in terms of total revenues. According to Dobbs *et al.* (2011), in 2008, New York City generated fewer revenues than Tokyo (1,406, and 1,479 billion US dollars respectively). Despite this, many American cities appeared at the top of the 2008 ranking. For example, Los Angeles and Chicago are ranked third and fourth, with 792 and 574 billion US dollars respectively.

Second, the wealth of a city is not purely correlated with GDP per capita.[16] As an example, in 2008, among OECD countries, the GDP per capita in Tokyo was relatively low: about 41,300 US dollars per year, in contrast to 73,300 for New York City, which was only ranked eighth. On average, residents from Edmonton and Calgary—in Canada—are the wealthiest people due to extractive industries.

Third, we observe that many large cities are within developing countries, which implies that revenues per capita and city size are negatively correlated. Nevertheless, on average, one of the most positive features relative to cities is that revenues per capita increase more than city size (in percentage). According to Bettencourt *et al.* (2007), increased city size increases people's interactions and the inherent inputs, such as revenues, increase more than proportionally. Thus, people may want to locate in larger cities. In addition, urbanization and revenues per capita are strongly positively correlated in history, which led Acemoglu *et al.* (2002) to use the level of urbanization as a proxy of the wealth of individuals (per capita income).

If, as a whole, revenues increase with city size, one may ask also about income inequality. The Kuznets curve predicts that revenue inequality increases with revenues and then decreases. Hence, if revenues increase with city size, inequalities should first increase and then decrease. In 1970, for US cities, it has been proved that revenue inequality increased with city size (Long *et al.*, 1977). In addition, the authors explained that the faster the city grows, the more revenue inequality increases. Revenue inequality may have negative impacts, such as on the level of crime (Thorbecke and Charumilind, 2002), which confirms the results of Bettencourt *et al.* (2007) who found that $\beta \geq 0$ in the equation linking crime and city size.

1.3.5 Internal structure of cities: potential scenarios

Cities are open systems that quickly evolve in terms of size and internal characteristics. Indeed, they interact with a changing environment, and attract more or fewer dwellers of different types over time. They all have their own urban growth pattern, but globally, due to regularities among cities, we can highlight global trends for the coming decades.

Sanitation and water access will be better on average. However, according to the UN (2012), the risk exposure to natural disasters is high, for example in East Asia. The major causes are soil erosion, monoculture, climate change which impacts the sea level, storms and desertification. Furthermore, we expect slums in overcrowded megalopolises to increase because of the growing flow of environmental refugees (Warner, 2010; Myers, 2002).

The number of private cars will increase in developing countries, because of the constant money budget (Schafer, 2000). This will imply more congestion and more greenhouse gas emissions, assuming that innovation cannot completely offset the increasing amount of cars. The increase in oil prices (Fournier *et al.*, 2013) will discourage people to commute by car, but this will depend on the price elasticity, which is estimated to be about -0.2, -0.3 for vehicle travel in the US (Litman, 2013). However, the price elasticity is also declining with revenues (Fournier *et al.*, 2013).

The largest cities will be more and more specialized by function (headquarters, finance, administrative support, etc.), but diversified in sectors with good access to financial services (Duranton and Puga, 2005). Competition among the world cities will keep increasing, with the goal of attracting highly skilled workers and headquarters. The world cities will have incentives to increase quality because their workers are mobile and are looking for a better place to live. By contrast, smaller cities, because they are specialized in less productive functions, need fewer skilled workers who are poorer and less mobile. Thus, competition among these cities may be less fierce, and they could have fewer incentives to invest in higher quality.

1.4 The distribution of cities

The population size of a city affects the number of its internal characteristics. Other regularities also appear among cities. First, the population size of a city is correlated with its rank in the country's or world's ranking of cities by population. Second, there are regularities in the spatial distribution of cities, since they develop more in some areas than in others.

26 André de Palma and Alexandre Guimard

1.4.1 The size distribution of cities

Cities have grown larger over time. In 1950 the largest city, New York City, accounted for a population of 12.34 million inhabitants. At that time, the difference between New York City and Tokyo was quite small, but by 1970, the total population of Tokyo largely exceeded that of NYC. In 2000, Tokyo was twice as large as New York City. In 2010, the total population in Tokyo was about 37 million people, but not twice as large as Delhi (ranked second).

In addition, in 2010, only three cities accounted for a population of between 20 and 30 million residents, and more cities (around 16) accounted for a population of between 10 and 20 million inhabitants. In 2010, almost all Chinese cities had a population below two million inhabitants (UN, 2012). According to Chan *et al.* (2008), the proportion of small and medium cities in China is much higher than in other countries around the world. The authors explain that this fact can be imputed from "central planning and political control" because it fostered investment in remote areas, whereas concentration should naturally appear with decreasing travel costs, economies of scale and agglomeration economies.

It can be easily shown that urban growth, both in India and China between 1990 and 1995, is dependent on city size. For China, especially, some cities grew very fast during this period (20 percent per year) because they benefited from being on the coast or "from the spillovers of industrial development from bigger cities" (Chan *et al.*, 2008). India has almost the same pattern and urban growth rates differ significantly across the cities, which confirms the results of McKinsey (Dobbs *et al.*, 2011). Between 2008 and 2025, population growth rates in medium cities are expected to be higher than in mega-cities (on average), even if the top three of the largest growth populations are in mega-cities (Beijing $= 5.5$ percent, Shanghai $= 5.2$ percent and Tokyo $= 3.3$ percent).

According to observable facts, first, the rank of given cities by population differs over time, thus some cities grow faster than others. Second, the population size of the largest city divided by that of the second largest city (as an example) is not constant over time. Third, the city size distribution differs across countries. In other words, small and medium cities grow faster in some countries than in others. Despite all these disparities, on average, researchers have found regularities (Ioannides and Overman, 2003). Indeed, on average, it has been proved that the logarithm of the rank of cities by population can be expressed as a linear function of the logarithm of the size of cities as follows:

$$\log r(s) = \log A - \xi \log S, \tag{1.3}$$

where S is the city size, $r(S)$ is the rank of the city of size S, A is a positive constant, and ξ is the elasticity of the rank with respect to the city size. The law above corresponds to Zipf's law when ξ is set to 1. Let S_t^i denote the normalized size of city i at date t, that is, the population of city i at date t divided by the total urban population at date $t(\sum_i S_t^i = 1, \forall t)$. Gabaix (1999a) has shown that if cities grow randomly with the same expected growth rate and variance, independent of the city size (Gibrat's law), at the steady state, Zipf's law is verified, and can be re-written as follows:

$$G(s) = \frac{a}{s^\xi}, \text{ with } \xi = 1, \qquad (1.4)$$

with $G(s)$ the counter-cumulative distribution function,[17] of normalized city sizes, s, and a being a positive constant. The counter-cumulative city size distribution function follows a power law, the city size distribution too. In other words, the probability of finding cities above a given population size decreases with the population size. There are many more small cities than large ones. Thus, rewriting Equation 1.4 in logarithm, it follows the rank-size rule of Equation 1.3, with a slope equal to -1 in the case of Zipf's law ($\xi = 1$). Zipf's law has been verified: when one regresses the logarithm of the ranks of cities by population on the logarithm of population sizes, the estimated straight line has a slope approximately equal to -1, and observations are close to the predictions, as illustrated in Figure 1.6. Consider now that, in Equation 1.3, A is normalized to the population of the largest city (S_{max}), and that ξ is set to 1, then, on average, the city size is approximately equal to the population of the largest city, divided by the rank of the city.

$$S = \frac{S_{max}}{r(s)}.$$

This latest equation implies that the ratio of the population sizes between two cities i and j is equal to the inverse of the ratio of the ranks as indicated in the following equation:

$$\frac{S_i}{S_j} = \frac{r(S_j)}{r(S_i)},$$

where S_i and $r(S_i)$ are, respectively, the population size and the rank of city i ($\forall i \neq j$).

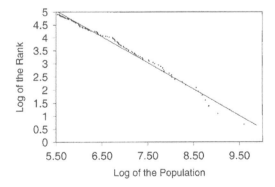

Figure 1.6 The rank-size rule for the 135 largest US metropolitan areas in 1991.
Source: Gabaix (1999b).

28 *André de Palma and Alexandre Guimard*

According to Zipf's law, as already exposed in Equation 1.4, the city size distribution follows a power law, or equivalently, the city size distribution is Pareto distributed. The first explanation is that each industry follows a Pareto distribution, and the sum of Pareto distributions is also a Pareto distribution.

Zipf's law is limited because, for some values of the parameter ξ in Equation 1.4, the city size distribution may have neither finite mean nor variance, or finite mean and no finite variance (Newman, 2005). Moreover, the expected growth rate and variance may depend on the city size, which contradicts Gibrat's law (Gabaix, 1999a). Even more problematic, it is not clear whether cities have the same growth rate distribution. Ioannides and Overman (2003) show that with a 95 percent confidence interval, Gibrat's law, and thus Zipf's law, cannot be rejected for a large range of cities. However, it appears that the smallest cities grow faster with smaller confidence intervals, thus leading the smallest cities to overtake the largest ones.

1.4.2 The spatial distribution of cities

The major growing cities between 1970 and 2011 were located in India and the east coast of China, as well as in West Africa (UN, 2012). It seems that being on the coast promoted urban growth, in the same way that "edge cities" grew in the US close to highways.

Coastal areas have natural advantages because firms can import and export at lower costs. Concentration may then be enhanced due to agglomeration economies, or due to increasing returns to scale associated with low transport costs, as explained by the New Economic Geography. Indeed, some firms may want to concentrate in coastal areas because of their natural advantages. These regions also attract mobile workers because of higher wages and a wider variety of goods. Hence, due to *the home market effect*, the manufacturing sector increases more than proportionally.[18] The only dispersion forces are relative to transport costs and the immobility of the working classes in the inland areas.

In addition, firms with large market access and access to suppliers are able to pay higher wages. Redding and Venables (2004) showed that access to the coast raises countries' income per capita by 60 percent.

The market access of coastal Chinese cities is higher than inland cities, but the European Union and the US are relatively far away. West Africa is closer to Europe and to the American east coast. The growing cities along the coast in China may be largely explained by access to suppliers: the Association of Southeast Asian Nations (ASEAN), Japan and the Republic of Korea. Except for the European Union, almost all the international suppliers are accessible on the coast.

1.5 Forecasts

The total population worldwide is constantly increasing, and urban population is increasing concomitantly. We now highlight the major demographic forecasts up to the end of the twenty-first century. Some regions and cities will grow very fast in contrast to others, such that economic forces should also change during the next decades.

1.5.1 Demographic perspectives and new economic forces

The world population should increase substantially during this century. In 2012, the US Census Bureau expected it to reach more than nine billion people before 2050. Even if the annual world population change is decreasing, the world population is still growing linearly because of the volume effect. This global trend hides strong disparities among countries.

1.5.1.1 Total population change up to 2050

Between 2011 and 2050, a large part of the total population growth will come from the middle- and low-income countries and will be in cities. As an example, between 2030 and 2050, the annual average rate of change in more developed countries will be 0.06 percent, whereas it will be 0.65 percent in less developed countries. Similarly, the urban population will grow by 0.29 percent per year in more developed countries, in contrast to 1.64 percent in less developed countries (UN, 2012).

The total population in India will largely grow, from 1.22 billion people in 2010 to 1.69 billion people in 2050. India will still have a positive but decreasing growth rate, from 1.31 percent in 2010 to 0.32 percent in 2045. India, in 2050, will be the most populated country in the world, above China and the US. This transition pattern must be compared to the large population change between 1950 and 2010. The total population multiplied by 3.29 in India between 1950 and 2010, and by 2.43 in China in the same period. Africa will still have a growing population. The population in Nigeria, for example, is expected to more than double before the middle of the century (2.5 times more people in 2050), to reach 390 million inhabitants in 2050. The total population in the US will continue to rise up until the end of the century. The US will still be ranked third in 2050, but Nigeria will then overtake the US.

If the population is forecast to rise in many countries, a transition pattern appears in many others. Most notably, the Chinese population will decrease, starting in 2035 (-0.14 percent between 2035 and 2040) and faster and faster (-0.23 percent between 2040 and 2045; -0.32 percent between 2045 and 2050), which is explained by the one-child policy, even if this policy has been relaxed by the government. The effect of this policy is illustrated by the evolution of the pyramid of ages.

The Japanese population will continue to decrease, but at higher rates (from -0.18 percent at this time, to -0.78 percent in 2045). The total population of the Russian Federation began to decrease 18 years ago in 1995. The conjecture is for about 108 million people in 2050, a decline of 38 percent of the total population since 1995. The total population of Germany also began to decrease a few years ago (2007), but at a lower rate. In 2050, France will be the most populated country in Europe—just above Germany—whereas, in 2010, the total population in Germany exceeded France by about 20 million people.

1.5.1.2 Total population between 2050 and 2100

The total population in India will begin to decrease and that in China will keep dropping (from 1.341 billion in 2010 to 941 million in 2100). More precisely, the total population of India will decrease before 2070. Nigeria should keep increasing at least until the end of the current century. In 2100, Nigeria will be the third most populated country in the world, before the US (fourth in 2100) and the total population aged 15–64 years old in 2100 will reach almost the same number as China. The total population in Russia will decrease during the century as in Japan, and Germany, among others.

The future decrease of the population in some countries can be currently explained by the vertical asymmetry of the pyramid of ages. Residents are ageing in China, as in Japan and most of the developed countries. In 2025, there will be two times more people over the age of 65 in Shanghai than in New York City. Tokyo will count ten million people in this age bracket (Dobbs *et al.*, 2011) out of an expected total population of 38.7 million inhabitants (UN, 2012). The fertility rate (expressed here as the average number of births per woman) in China is currently incredibly low—estimated to be at 1.53 between 2010 and 2015, but conjectured to increase to 1.77 at the middle of the century, which will still be below 2. In Nigeria, the pyramid of ages is very flat at the bottom. The fertility rate is currently very high in Nigeria (5.43) and conjectured to be at 4.86 in 2020–25. This rate should slightly decrease throughout the century, a decline due to the demographic transition, and to be around 2.20 at the end of the century, in other words, at a level acknowledged to be high in Europe (currently equal to the fertility rate of France). In India, total population will keep growing at least until 2050 because the fertility rate is conjectured to stay above 2 in 2020–25.

Obviously, the fertility rate will determine the number of people of working age in a country. In OECD countries, the number of people of working age (20–64 years old) over the number of persons of pensionable age (more than 65 years old) has been constantly decreasing over time since 1950. In 2050, almost all developed countries will tend to the ratio of 2. Turkey currently has a very high proportion of working-age people, but it will tend to the ratio of 2 at around 2050. The proportion of people at working age in developed countries should be divided by 2 on average between 2008 and 2050. The same pattern should also happen in China, according to the vertical asymmetry of its pyramid of ages. at around 2016–18, the number of working-age people (between 20 and 64 years old) should begin to decrease until at least 2100. The number of working-age people is constantly increasing in Nigeria, such that in 2100 there will be almost as many people at working age in China as in Nigeria.

1.5.1.3 *Demographic prospective in urban areas vs. rural areas*

This global trend at the national level has to be compared with what will happen at a more local level, that is to say, at the city level. In developed countries, the number of people living in rural areas will continue to decrease. In developing countries, the population living in rural areas has increased since 1950, but much less than in urban areas. By 2015, in developing countries, the number of people living in urban and rural areas should be equal, then it is expected that increasingly

Urbanization: an overview 31

fewer people will live outside cities. In developed countries, the equivalent shift of total population between cities and rural areas happened in around 1955.

The very low expected growth rate of the total population in China does not mean that cities will not keep growing, but rather that growth will continue at lower rates. Beijing will have a growth rate of almost 1 percent between 2020 and 2025, whereas it was 3.63 percent between 1990 and 1995. Beijing will not again, at least for the current century, be the largest city in the world. However, this fact has to be put in parallel with the growing share of the urban population in China. The urban share in China is expected to reach 61.9 percent in 2030, whereas it was 47 percent in 2010. Thus, it can be easily deduced that urban growth in China will come from the rural exodus. The rural proportion is decreasing more and more in China, from 1.62 percent in 2010 to −2.04 percent in 2045. That explains the growing number of large cities in China. No one city in China in 1990 had a population above eight million, whereas, in 2025, five cities will have more than ten million residents. The population in Shanghai will reach 20 million inhabitants in 2025. Between 1990 and 2025 the city size will be multiplied by 2.56. But urban growth in China is not in fact coming from the largest cities. In 1990, 33 cities had a population above one million, whereas 129 cities are expected to have at least one million inhabitants in 2025. As noted above, starting in 2035, the total population of China will decrease until the end of the century. In addition, the urban proportion will reach quite a high level in 2030 (61.9 percent) compared to the level of 1990 (26.4 percent). Thus, one has to wonder to what extent the rural exodus will be able to push up urban growth until 2100. Actually, the urban proportion of 61.9 percent is low compared to the level of urbanization in all developed countries, which is largely explained by the restrictive policies of the 1960s and 1970s. One may expect policymakers to relax the constraint of the *hukou* system if there are too many vacant buildings in cities in the future.

The urban growth decrease is lower in India than in China. In 1990, the average urban growth rate was 3.10 percent in India compared to 6.2 percent in China. Between 2045 and 2050, we expect urban growth to be 2.03 percent in India and 1.27 percent in China. Thus, until the middle of the century, the total population of India will keep growing as, also, will cities. The population in India will be biased towards the megalopolises. In 2025, three cities will account for a population that will exceed 20 million people (20.112 million in Kolkata, 25.810 million in Mumbai and 28.568 million in Delhi). The rural proportion will keep decreasing at higher rates, from −0.53 percent between 2010 and 2015 to −1.27 percent between 2045 and 2050. In India, urban growth will be due both to the total population growth and the rural exodus, which in the past explained 20–25 percent of total urban growth (Schaffar, 2010). Delhi will enlarge, but Tokyo will remain the largest city for a while. In 2010, it was forecast that the total population of Tokyo would increase slightly until 2030, despite the decrease in total population, because the country is still in the process of urbanization. It was also predicted that the level of urbanization would grow from 66.8 percent in 2010 to 73 percent in 2030.

32 *André de Palma and Alexandre Guimard*

Globally, since 1950, rural populations have decreased in developed countries. For example, in France, the urbanization level was 85.6 percent in 2010, which is high compared to Germany (73.8 percent) and the UK (79.6 percent). France will become more and more urbanized (91.8 percent in 2030). The same process of urbanization is happening in almost all countries around the world. However, we have to be careful about data because definitions of cities and urban areas vary over space and time. As an example, according to Lévy (2013), under some assumptions, France can be considered almost fully urbanized (96.05 percent of urban areas).

The large urban growth in China and India explains why Asia is responsible for 54 percent of total urban growth in the world. However, the share of urban growth attributable to Africa is constantly increasing, from 14 percent between 1950 and 2011 to 32.5 percent between 2011 and 2050, and a number of countries are strongly driving this global trend in Africa. As an example, the share of people living in urban areas will keep growing and at almost the same level as in China. In 2030, 63.6 percent of Nigerian people will live in cities. In Lagos, the yearly average growth rate is expected to be 3.2 percent between 2008 and 2025, which is the highest rate of medium-size cities (Dobbs *et al.*, 2011). Similarly, in 2011, the UN expected the average annual growth rate in Lagos to be 3.71 percent between 2011 and 2025. Those annual rates are especially high, but they have to be compared to the past growth rates of Chinese cities such as in Shenzhen (18.44 percent per year between 1970 and 1990, 11.89 percent per year between 1990 and 2011).

Lagos, in Nigeria, is growing even though the city is currently very dense. Indeed, in 2007, Lagos was the fourth densest city in the world. Similarly, Mumbai, in 2007, was the densest city and will keep growing relatively fast. The annual growth rate of these cities will slow down between 2010 and 2030, but total populations will still grow by 25 percent between 2010 and 2030. Is it possible to make more compact cities and ensure minimum quality of life? Naturally, already very dense cities will spread into the landscape, and will face the problem of congestion.

1.5.2 *Forecasts of GDP by city*

The urban proportion is increasing over time, thus one should know to what extent urban areas are more productive than rural areas (in terms of total GDP). Productivity in agriculture has largely increased due to technological advances and large crops, but it is difficult to be even more efficient in the developed countries since soil needs to generate itself. Productivity gains in industries located in small and medium cities, by contrast, are potentially unlimited due to technological innovations. One may expect urban GDP to rise faster than urban growth. Thus, one may think that urban GDP growth will be driven by the emerging world.

Globally, cities yield more revenue per capita than in rural areas. In 2007, half of the total population lived in rural areas, whereas they contributed to only 20 percent of total GDP worldwide. At the time of writing, the top 600 cities—by contribution to global GDP growth from 2007 to 2025—yield more than half of total GDP, while only a fifth of the total population live there. In 2025, these cities will yield even more revenue, nearly 60 percent of total GDP (Dobbs *et al.*, 2011).

So far, cities in developed countries contributed to 70 percent of total GDP, whereas cities in developing countries are responsible for only 14 percent of total GDP. However, total GDP growth mainly occurs in cities of developing countries. Such cities in emerging countries are overtaking cities in developed countries in their contribution to global GDP. Among the 136 new cities entering the top 600 (recall, by contribution to total GDP growth from 2007 to 2025), 100 were located in China, 13 in India, and 8 in Latin America.

The GDP of mega-cities will continue to increase. For example, between 2008 and 2025, the cumulative GDP growth of Shanghai and Mumbai will be almost 197 percent and 185 percent respectively. Smaller cities will also contribute considerably to global GDP growth. The small, medium and large cities in the emerging world will be responsible for 37 percent of total GDP growth, which is above the contribution of all developed cities in addition to the mega-cities of emerging countries (34 percent).

To sum up, even if global GDP is currently attributable to developed cities (70 percent), it will be driven by the medium-size cities of the developing world. Households in emerging countries will continue to benefit from this success. Population growth contributes only 22 percent to GDP growth in China, which is lower than in the US (37 percent). Thus, urban growth up to 2025 will largely increase the standard of living in emerging countries, and to a greater degree than in the US. Globally, the revenue per capita in the top 600 cities will increase by 2.7 percent per year, from 20,000 US dollars in 2007 to 32,000 US dollars in 2025.

1.5.3 The potential of Africa

According to the UN (2012) a larger proportion of urban growth originates in Africa (32.5 percent between 2011 and 2050, in contrast to 14 percent between 1950 and 2011). Africa, especially Nigeria, has natural advantages such as large liquefied natural gas and oil reserves and low wages. The number of working-age people in Nigeria is constantly increasing. In around 2100, the number of working-age people in Nigeria will be about the same as in China.

Furthermore, cities in Nigeria are closer to Europe, the east coast of the US and South America than China, thus the market access of West Africa is potentially high in addition to the growing local market.[19] Many entrepreneurs choose to invest in Africa, in Nigeria in particular, because the local market is increasing and wages are particularly low (Gu, 2009). Shen (2013) states that:

> Chinese OFDI is widely spread across Sub-Sahara Africa. However, some countries are more attractive than others to Chinese companies [...]. The top five recipient countries are Nigeria, South Africa, Zambia, Ethiopia and Ghana [...]. "Market access", primarily the local market but potentially also the export market, plays a predominant role in attracting private Chinese manufacturing firms to Africa.

34 *André de Palma and Alexandre Guimard*

One may expect that many Chinese plants will move to West Africa before the middle of the century, and even more so during the second half of the century. Indeed, in contrast to West Africa where the total working-age population will continue to increase at least until 2100, in China the number of working-age people will start to decrease by around 2016–18, which will induce wages to increase even more.

So far, China mainly exports to Hong Kong (ranked third), Japan (ranked fourth) and South Korea (ranked fifth). These countries are farther away from West Africa. Moreover, the main import partners of China[20] are the European Union,[21] Japan, South Korea, the US, Australia and Malaysia. Thus, by locating in Nigeria for example, these Chinese firms would have to find new suppliers. One may expect that these firms would substitute European and Brazilian inputs for inputs coming from East Asia to some extent. South America could also provide a large market demand for manufacturing goods produced in Africa. Notice, so far, that Brazil is ranked eighth supplier and thirteenth export partner of China.

Hence, one may expect economic forces to change in the next decades. Due to large economic potentials, cities in West Africa should continue to grow with the need to provide new public infrastructures, to guarantee accessibility to public goods, to ensure minimum open spaces per capita[22] and to control congestion and air pollution.

Since 2003, exports of manufactured goods from EU-27[23] to West Africa have constantly increased. Between 2009 and 2010, they increased by 18.98 percent, and represent 52 percent of total exports from EU-27.[24] Concomitantly with the economic development of Africa, one might expect that exports of manufactured goods, machinery and transport equipment will continue to increase, due to the geographical and political proximity of both regions.

1.6 Concluding comments

Urban issues reach a growing number of people over time. Since 2007, more than half of the total population worldwide has been located in cities, and the urban proportion will increase at least until the end of the century. In 2050, 70 percent of the total population will live in cities. Thus, the priority for policymakers is to ensure the best living conditions in cities for current generations—taking into account the welfare of future generations—and to monitor natural and industrial risk exposures. Living conditions may be evaluated in terms of GDP per capita, congestion, air and noise pollution, accessibility to local public goods and open spaces, urban sprawl, social equity and exclusion and security. Since cities are interdependent through externalities, such as air pollution, it seems necessary to handle a number of problems in a cooperative manner among policymakers around the world. The success of cities cannot be solely evaluated through total GDP, or even through GDP per resident, because it would limit the actual challenges in space and time, and to some groups of individuals. Many indicators have been built to evaluate cities, in terms of quality of life, social life, environmental friendliness and economic prosperity. Among others, the prosperity Index of

Urbanization: an overview 35

UN-Habitat highlights the main evaluation criteria: productivity, infrastructure, quality of life, equity and environmental sustainability, which are linked to the concept of Global Sustainability. For policymakers, all these targets can be contradictory, which explains how difficult it is to find compromises among social classes, generations, regions, and nations around the world, such as during climate change conferences. As explained by Trancik *et al.* (2013), "a global agreement on carbon emissions would be most effective at reducing the risks of climate change, but in the meantime a segmental approach can be helpful," involving "separate targeting of energy choices and energy consumption through regulations or incentives."

Notes

1 See www.ined.fr/fr/tout_savoir_population/atlas_population (last accessed on November 28, 2014).
2 See Marshall (1890), Arrow (1962), Romer (1986), and Porter (1990).
3 In particular, according to Brueckner (2000), "open space provides city dwellers with an easy escape from the frenetic urban scene and a chance to enjoy nature. Such open-space benefits, however, are not taken into account when land is converted to urban use."
4 See Newman and Kenworthy (2006) for a graphic representation of the transit city and automobile city.
5 See www.apce.com/cid134771/ces-franciliens-qui-revent-de-quitter-paris.html (last accessed on November 28, 2014).
6 See www.insee.fr/fr/themes/document.asp?ref_id=T11F172 (last accessed on November 28, 2014).
7 See www.insee.fr/fr/themes/document.asp?ref_id=ip1292 (last accessed on November 28, 2014).
8 See www.autoritedelaconcurrence.fr/user/standard.php?id_rub=417&id_article=1751 (last accessed on November 28, 2014).
9 In Pusan as well as in Seoul, "the numbers of move-out population are higher than those of move-in population" (Statistics of Korea, see, http://kostat.go.kr/portal/english/news/1/17/6/index.board?bmode=read&aSeq=273106&pageNo=&rowNum=10&amSeq=&sTarget=&sTxt= (last accessed on November 28, 2014)).
10 See www.census.gov/population/metro/data/pop_pro.html (last accessed on November 28, 2014).
11 Population in kilometer distance bands measured from city hall.
12 See www.census.gov/hhes/commuting/data/daytimepop.html (last accessed on November 28, 2014).
13 See http://mobility.tamu.edu/ums (last accessed on November 28, 2014).
14 At the denominator, total urbanized land includes "residential, commercial, industrial land, local parks and open spaces, plus roads and any other urban land uses, and excludes large areas of undeveloped land etc." Newman and Kenworthy (2006).
15 See http://mic-ro.com/metro/, and http://www.demographia.com/db-worldua.pdf (last accessed on November 28, 2014).
16 See http://measuringurban.oecd.org (last accessed on November 28, 2014).
17 $1 - F(s)$, with $F(s)$ as the cumulative distribution function.
18 The market size increases and firms benefit from economies of scale, which attract even more firms.
19 Currently, North Africa has a very large market access due to the proximity of Europe. In North Africa, in a perimeter of 4,000 kilometers, more than 20,000 billion dollars were produced, compared to only 4,000–5,000 billion dollars in West Africa

(see the interactive map on the INED website at: www.ined.fr/fr/tout-savoir-population/graphiques-cartes/cartes-interactives-population-mondiale/ (last accessed on December 12, 2014)).

20 See http://trade.ec.europa.eu/doclib/docs/2006/september/tradoc_113366.pdf (last accessed on November 28, 2014).

21 The balance of Trade of EU-27 with China is $-146,069$ million €, because the positive balance of Trade in services did not compensate for the large negative balance of trade in goods.

22 As discussed, Asian cities are already very dense. The same appears true for some cities in Africa, such as Lagos which was ranked fourth in terms of population density according to City Mayors Statistics. See http://www.citymayors.com/statistics/largest-cities-density-125.html (last accessed on November 28, 2014).

23 "The EU is a unique economic and political partnership between 27 European countries that together cover much of the continent." See: http://europa.eu/about-eu/basic-information/index_en.htm (last accessed on November 28, 2014).

24 See http://ec.europa.eu/trade/policy/countries-and-regions/regions/west-africa (last accessed on November 28, 2014).

Bibliography

Acemoglu, D., Johnson, S. and Robinson, J.A. 2002. Reversal of fortune: Geography and institutions in the making of the modern world income distribution. *The Quarterly Journal of Economics*, 117(4), pp. 1231–1294.

Aguiléra, A., L'Hostis, A. and Haon, S. 2013. Land use and transport interactions. *Technical Report, ERTRAC*.

Akiva, M.E.B. and Lerman, S.R. 1985. *Discrete Choice Analysis: Theory and Application to Predict Travel Demand*. Cambridge, MA: The MIT Press.

Anas, A., Arnott, R. and Small, K.A. 1998. Urban spatial structure. *Journal of Economic Literature*, 36(3), pp. 1426–1464.

Anas, A. and Lindsey, R. 2011. Reducing urban road transportation externalities: road pricing in theory and in practice. *Review of Environmental Economics and Policy*, 5(1), pp. 66–88.

Anas, A. and Liu, Y. 2007. A regional economy, land use, and transportation model. *Journal of Regional Science*, 47(3), pp. 415–455.

Anderson, S.P., de Palma, A. and Thisse, J.F. 1992. *Discrete Choice Theory of Product Differentiation*. Cambridge, MA: The MIT Press.

Anderson, S.P. and Renault, R. 2007. Advertising: the Persuasion Game. 2008 CESifo Conference Centre, Munich.

Arnott, R. 2004. Does the Henry George theorem provide a practical guide to optimal city size? *American Journal of Economics and Sociology*, 63(5), pp. 1057–1090.

Arrow, K.J. 1962. The Economic Implications of Learning by Doing. *Review of Economic Studies*, 29: pp. 155–173.

Baccaïni, B. 2005. "Enquêtes annuelles de recensement: résultats de la collecte 2004. Des changements de région plus fréquents qui bénéficient aux régions du sud et de l'ouest", Insee Première, n° 1028.

Bairoch, P. 1991. *Cities and Economic Development: From the Dawn of History to the Present*. Chigago, IL: University of Chicago Press.

Bakos, J.Y. 1997. Reducing buyer search costs: implications for electronic marketplaces. *Management Science*, 43(12), pp. 1676–1692.

Ballas, D. 2013. What makes a "happy city"?, *Cities*, 32: pp. S39–S50.

Bates, D.C. 2002. Environmental refugees? Classifying human migrations caused by environmental change. *Population and Environment*, 23(5), pp. 465–477.

Batty, M. 2012. Building a science of cities. *Cities*, 29: pp. S9–S16.

Batty, M. 2013. *The New Science of Cities*. Cambridge, MA: MIT Press.

Batty, M., Axhausen, K.W., Giannotti, F., Pozdnoukhov, A., Bazzani, A., Wachowicz, M., Ouzounis, G. and Portugali, Y. 2012. Smart cities of the future. *The European Physical Journal Special Topics*, 214(1), pp. 481–518.

Beaverstock, J.V., Smith, R.G. and Taylor, P.J. 1999. A roster of World cities. *Cities*, 16(6), pp. 445–458.

Begg, I. 1999. Cities and competitiveness. *Urban Studies*, 36(5–6), pp. 795–809.

Behrens, K. and Murata, Y. 2009. City size and the Henry George theorem under monopolistic competition. *Journal of Urban Economics*, 65(2), pp. 228–235.

Bento, A.M., Cropper, M.L., Mobarak, A.M. and Vinha, K. 2005. The effects of urban spatial structure on travel demand in the United States. *Review of Economics and Statistics*, 87(3), pp. 466–478.

Berry, B.J. 1976. *The Counterurbanization Process: Urban America Since 1970*. Beverly Hills, CA: Sage Publications.

Bertaud, A. and Malpezzi, S. 2003. The spatial distribution of population in 48 World cities: Implications for economies in transition, Washington, DC: World Bank.

Bettencourt, L., Lobo, J., Helbing, D., Kühnert, C. and West, G.B. 2007. Growth, innovation, scaling, and the pace of life in cities. *Proceedings of the National Academy of Sciences*, 104(17), pp. 7301–7306.

Bierlaire, M., de Palma, A. and Waddell, P. 2014. *Integrated Transport and Land Use Modeling for Sustainable Cities*. Lausanne: EPFL Press.

Brownstone, D. and Golob, T.F. 2009. The impact of residential density on vehicle usage and energy consumption. *Journal of Urban Economics*, 65(1), pp. 91–98.

Brueckner, J.K. 2000. Urban sprawl: diagnosis and remedies. *International Regional Science Review*, 23(2), pp. 160–171.

Brueckner, J.K., Thisse, J.F. and Zenou, Y. 1999. Why is central Paris rich and downtown Detroit poor? An amenity-based theory. *European Economic Review*, 43(1), pp. 91–107.

Brundtland, J. 1987. *Our Common Future*, Oxford: Oxford University Press.

Bussière, R. 1972. *Modèle de localisation résidentielle*. Paris: Annales du Centre de Recherche et d'Urbanisme.

Cervero, R. and Guerra, E. 2011. *Urban Densities and Transit: A Multi-dimensional Perspective*. University of California, CA: Institute of Transportation Studies.

Chan, K.W., Henderson, J.V. and Tsui, K.Y. 2008. Spatial Dimensions of Chinese Economic Development. In: *China's Great Economic Transformation*. Cambridge: Cambridge University Press.

Chandler, T. 1987. *Four Thousand Years of Urban Growth: An Historical Census*. Lewiston: St. David's University Press.

Chen, H., Lanzieri, G. and Mrkic, S. 2013. Principles and recommendations for a vital statistics system Revision 3. New York: The United Nation.

Christaller, W. 1933. *Die zentralen Orte in Suddeutschland*. Jena: Gustav Fischer.

Church, A., Frost, M. and Sullivan, K. 2000. Transport and social exclusion in London. *Transport Policy*, 7(3), pp. 195–205.

Clark, C. 1951. Urban population densities. *Journal of the Royal Statistical Society. Series A (General)*, 114(4), pp. 490–496.

Combes, P.P., Duranton, G., Gobillon, L., Puga, D. and Roux, S. 2012. The productivity advantages of large cities: Distinguishing agglomeration from firm selection. *Econometrica*, 80(6), pp. 2543–2594.

Cowgill, G.L. 2004. Origins and development of urbanism: Archaeological perspectives. *Annual Review of Anthropology*, pp. 525–549.

Dahlberg, M. and Gustavsson, M. 2008. Inequality and Crime: Separating the Effects of Permanent and Transitory Income. *Oxford Bulletin of Economics and Statistics*, 70(2), pp. 129–153.

d'Aspremont, C., Gabszewicz, J.J. and Thisse, J.F. 1979. On Hotelling's "Stability in competition." *Econometrica*, pp. 1145–1150.

de Almeida Abreu, M. and Le Clerre, G. 1994. Reconstruire une histoire oubliée. Origine et expansion initiale des favelas de Rio de Janeiro. *Genèses*, 16(1), pp. 45–68.

de la Barra, T. 1989. Integrated land use and transport modelling. Decision chains and hierarchies. s.l.: Number 12. *Cambridge Urban and Architectural Studies*.

de Lara, M., de Palma, A., Kilani, M. and Piperno, S. 2012. Congestion pricing and long term urban form: Application to Paris region. *Regional Science and Urban Economics*, Volume 43, pp. 282–295.

Demographia (2005) Demographia world urban areas: world agglomerations. Available at: http://www.demographia.com/ (last accessed on December 12, 2014).

Deneubourg, J.L. and Franks, N. 1995. Collective control without explicit coding: the case of communal nest excavation. *Journal of insect behavior*, 8(4), pp. 417–432.

de Palma, A., Ginsburgh, V., Papageorgiou, Y.Y. and Thisse, J.F. 1985. The principle of minimum differentiation holds under sufficient heterogeneity. *Econometrica*, pp. 767–781.

de Palma, A., Lindsey, R., Quinet, E. and Vickerman, R., 2011. *A Handbook of Transport Economics.*: Cheltenham: Edward Elgar Publishing.

de Palma, A., Motamedi, K., Picard, N. and Waddell, P. 2005. A model of residential location choice with endogenous housing prices and traffic for the Paris region. *European Transport*, 31: pp. 67–82.

de Palma, A., Picard, N., Angoustures, P. and Meyer, B. 2013. Etude sur les externalités des télécentres, s.l.: *PMP/ENS de Cachan.*

de Palma, A., Picard, N. and Waddell, P. 2007. Discrete choice models with capacity constraints: An empirical analysis of the housing market of the greater Paris region. *Journal of Urban Economics*, 62(2), pp. 204–230.

Dobbs, R., Smit, S., Remes, J., Manyika, J., Roxburgh, C. and Restrepo, A. 2011. *Urban World: Mapping the Economic Power of Cities*, New York: McKinsey.

Duranton, G. and Puga, D. 2005. From sectoral to functional urban specialisation. *Journal of Urban Economics* 57(2), pp. 343–370.

Echenique, M.H., Flowerdew, A., Hunt, J.D., Mayo, T.R., Skidmore, I.J. and Simmonds, D.C. 1990. The MEPLAN models of Bilbao, Leeds and Dortmund. *Transport Reviews*, 10(4), pp. 309–322.

Elzinga, D., Fulton, L., Heinen, S. and Wasilik, O. 2011. Advantage Energy: Emerging Economies, Developing Countries and the Private-Public Sector Interface, s.l.: OECD Publishing.

Feldman, M.P. and Audretsch, D.B. 1999. Innovation in cities: Science-based diversity, specialization and localized competition. *European Economic Review*, 43(2), pp. 409–429.

Fournier, J.M., Koske, I., Wanner, I. and Zipperer, V. 2013. The price of oil – will it start rising again?, s.l.: OECD Economic Department Working Paper No. 1031.

Fujishima, S. 2012. Evolutionary implementation of optimal city size distributions. *Regional Science and Urban Economics*, 43: pp. 404–410.

Fujita, M., Krugman, P.R. and Venables, A.J. 1999. *The Spatial Economy: Cities, Regions and International Trade*. Cambridge, MA: MIT Press.

Fujita, M. and Thisse, J.F. 1997. Economie géographique, problèmes anciens et nouvelles perspectives. *Annales d'Economie et de Statistique*, pp. 37–87.

Fuller, R.A. and Gaston, K.J. 2009. The scaling of green space coverage in European cities. *Biology Letters*, 5(3), pp. 352–355.

Gabaix, X. 1999a. Zipf's Law and the Growth of Cities. *The American Economic Review*, 89(2), pp. 129–132.

Gabaix, X. 1999b. Zipf's law for cities: an explanation. *The Quarterly Journal of Economics*, 114(3), pp. 739–767.

Gabaix, X. and Ioannides, Y.M. 2004. The evolution of city size distributions. *Handbook of Regional and Urban Economics*, 4: pp. 2341–2378.

Gaigné, C., Riou, S. and Thisse, J.F. 2012. Are compact cities environmentally friendly?. *Journal of Urban Economics*, 72(2), pp. 123–136.

Galster, G., Hanson, R., Ratcliffe, M.R., Wolman, H., Coleman, S. and Freihage, J. 2001. Wrestling sprawl to the ground: defining and measuring an elusive concept. *Housing Policy Debate*, 12(4), pp. 681–717.

Garreau, J. 1991. *Edge City: Life on the New Frontier*. New York: Doubleday, Anchor-Books.

Glaeser, E.L. and Kahn, M.E. 2001. Decentralized Employment and the Transformation of the American City, *Brookings-Whartoon Papers on Urban Affairs*, pp. 1–63.

Glaeser, E.L., Kallal, H.D., Scheinkman, J.A. and Shleifer, A. 1991. *Growth in Cities*. Cambridge, MA: National Bureau of Economic Research.

Glaeser, E.L. and Shapiro, J.M. 2002. Cities and warfare: The impact of terrorism on urban form. *Journal of Urban Economics*, 51(2), pp. 205–224.

Godefroy, P. 2011. *Satisfaction dans la vie: les personnes se donnent 7 sur 10 en moyenne*, Paris: INSEE.

Grimm, N.B., Faeth, S.H., Golubiewski, N.E., Redman, C.L., Wu, J., Bai, X. and Briggs, J.M. 2008. Global change and the ecology of cities. *Science*, 319(5864), pp. 756–760.

Gu, J. 2009. China's private enterprises in Africa and the implications for African development. *European Journal of Development Research*, 21(4), pp. 570–587.

Haag, G. 1990. *Transport: A Master Equation Approach*: *Urban Dynamics*. London: Routledge.

Hediger, W. 2000. Sustainable development and social welfare. *Ecological Economics*, 32(3), pp. 481–492.

Heilig, G.K. 2012. World Urbanization Prospects The 2011 Revision. *Presentation at the Center for Strategic and International Studies*.

Hotelling, H. 1929. Stability in Competition. *Economic Journal*, 39(153), pp. 41–57.

Ingram, G.L.Z. 1999. *Motorization and Road Provision in Countries and Cities*. Washington, DC: World Bank.

Ioannides, Y.M. and Overman, H.G. 2003. Zipf's law for cities: an empirical examination. *Regional Science and Urban Economics*, 33(2), pp. 127–137.

Jackson, K.T. 1996. All the World's a mall: Reflections on the social and economic consequences of the American shopping center. *The American Historical Review*, 101(4), pp. 1111–1121.

Jacobs, J. 1969. *The Economy of Cities*. New York: Random House.

Kahn, M.E. 2005. The death toll from natural disasters: the role of income, geography, and institutions. *Review of Economics and Statistics*, 87(2), pp. 271–284.

Kamal-Chaoui, L. 2010. Trends in Urbanisation and Urban Policies in OECD Countries: What Lessons for China? Washington, DC: OECD.

Kaplan, S. 1995. The restorative benefits of nature: toward an integrative framework. *Journal of Environmental Psychology*, 15(3), pp. 169–182.

Kellenberg, D.K. and Mobarak, A.M. 2008. Does rising income increase or decrease damage risk from natural disasters? *Journal of Urban Economics*, 63(3), pp. 788–802.

Kostof, S. 1993. *The City Shaped: Urban Patterns and Meaning Throughout History.* Boston, MA: Bulfinch Press.

Kwan, M.P., Dijst, M. and Schwanen, T. 2007. The interaction between ICT and human activity-travel behavior. *Transportation Research. Part A, Policy and Practice*, 41(2), pp. 121–124.

Lafourcade, M. and Thisse, J.F. 2011. *New Economic Geography: The Role of Transport Costs.* Handbook of Transport Economics.

Lanz, B. and Provins, A. 2011. Valuing local environmental amenity: using discrete choice experiments to control for the spatial scope of improvements, s.l.: CEPE Center for Energy Policy and Economics, ETH Zurich.

Lefèvre, B. 2009. Urban transport energy consumption: determinants and strategies for its reduction. An analysis of the literature. *Surveys and Perspectives Integrating Environment and Society*, Issue 2.3.

Lenz, B. and Nobis, C. 2007. The changing allocation of activities in space and time by the use of ICT-"Fragmentation" as a new concept and empirical results. *Transportation Research Part A: Policy and Practice*, 41(2), pp. 190–204.

Lévy, J. 2013. *Réinventer la France.* Paris: Fayard.

Lieber, E. and Syverson, C. 2011. *Online Vs. Offline Competition.* Peitz, M., Waldfogel.

Litman, T. 2013. Understanding transport demands and elasticities, s.l.: Victoria Transport Policy.

Loginova, O. 2009. Real and Virtual Competition. *The Journal of Industrial Economics*, 57(2), pp. 319–342.

Long, J.E., Rasmussen, D.W. and Haworth, C.T. 1977. Income inequality and city size. *The Review of Economics and Statistics*, 59(2), pp. 244–246.

Marchetti, C. 1994. Anthropological invariants in travel behavior. *Technological Forecasting and Social Change*, 47(1), pp. 75–88.

Marcus, J. 1998. The peaks and valleys of ancient states: An extension of the dynamic model. *Archaic States.* Sante Fe, NM: School of American Research Press, pp. 59–94.

Markusen, A. and Schrock, G. 2006. The distinctive city: divergent patterns in growth, hierarchy and specialisation. *Urban Studies*, 43(8), pp. 1301–1323.

Marshall, A. 1890. *Principles of Economics.* London: Macmillan.

Marshall, J.D. 2007. Urban land area and population growth: a new scaling relationship for metropolitan expansion. *Urban Studies*, 44(10), pp. 1889–1904.

Melo, P.C., Graham, D.J. and Noland, R.B. 2009. A meta-analysis of estimates of urban agglomeration economies. *Regional Science and Urban Economics*, 39(3), pp. 332–342.

Mieszkowski, P. and Mills, E.S. 1993. The causes of metropolitan suburbanization. *The Journal of Economic Perspectives*, 7(3), pp. 135–147.

Mills, E.S. 1967. An aggregative model of resource allocation in a metropolitan area. *The American Economic Review*, 57(2), pp. 197–210.

Mills, E.S. 1972. Studies in the structure of the urban economy. Baltimore, NJ: Johns Hopkins Press.

Mulligan, G.F. and Carruthers, J.I. 2011. Amenities, Quality of Life, and Regional Development. In: *Investigating Quality of Urban Life.* Springer, pp. 107–133.

Mumford, L. 1938. *The Culture of Cities.* New York: Harcourt Brace and Company.

Mumford, L. 1961. *The City in History*. New York: Harcourt, Brace and World, Inc.

Muth, R. 1969. *Cities and Housing*. Chicago, IL: University of Chicago Press.

Myers, N. 2002. Environmental refugees: a growing phenomenon of the 21st century. *Philosophical Transactions of the Royal Society of London. Series B: Biological Sciences*, 357(1420), pp. 609–613.

Newman, M.E. 2005. Power laws, Pareto distributions and Zipf's law. *Contemporary Physics*, 46(5), pp. 323–351.

Newman, P. and Hogan, T.S. 1987. Urban Density and Transport: A simple model based on three city types. *Transport Research Paper*, Issue 1/87.

Newman, P. and Kenworthy, J. 1999. *Sustainability and Cities: Overcoming Automobile Dependence*. Washington, DC: Island Press.

Newman, P. and Kenworthy, J. 2006. Urban design to reduce automobile dependence. *Opolis*, 2(1).

Newman, P. and Kenworthy, J.R. 1996. The land use-transport connection: An overview. *Land Use Policy*, 13(1), pp. 1–22.

OECD (2013) Demographia World Urban Areas, 9th edition. Available at: http://stats.oecd.org/ (last accessed on December 12, 2014).

Perlman, J.E. 2007. *Marginality from Myth to Reality, the Favelas of Rio de Janeiro 1968–2005*. Nyack: Mega-Cities Project.

Pfaffenbichler, P. 2003. *The strategic, dynamic and integrated urban land use and transport model MARS* (Metropolitan Activity Relocation Simulator). Institut für Verkehrsplanung und Verkehrstechnik der Technischen Universität Wien.

Picard, N., de Palma, A. and Inoa, I.A. 2013. *Discrete Choice Decision-Making with Multiple Decision Makers within the Household*. Mathematical Population Studies.

Porter, M.E. 1990. *The Competitive Advantage of Nations*. New York: Free Press.

Proost, S. and van der Loo, S. 2013. *Policy Insights and insights for Sustainability*. KU Leuven: European Commission.

Putman, S.H. 1991. DRAM/EMPAL ITLUP Integrated Tranportation Land-Use activity. Allocation models: general description. Philadelphia, PA: S.H. Putman Associates.

Redding, S. and Venables, A.J. 2004. Economic geography and international inequality. *Journal of International Economics*, 62(1), pp. 53–82.

Rees, W. and Wackernagel, M. 2012. Urban ecological footprints: why cities cannot be sustainable–and why they are a key to sustainability. *The Urban Sociology Reader*, p. 157.

Reilly, W.J. 1931. *The Law of Retail Gravitation*. New York: Published by the Author.

Roback, J. 1982. Wages, Rents, and the Quality of Life. *Journal of Political Economy*, 90(6), pp. 1257–1278.

Romer, P.M. 1986. Increasing Returns and Long Run Growth. *Journal of Political Economy*, Volume 94, pp. 1002–1037.

Rosenthal, S.S. and Strange, W.C. 2004. Evidence on the nature and sources of agglomeration economies. *Handbook of Regional and Urban Economics*, 4: pp. 2119–2171.

Scarpa, R., Campbell, D. and Hutchinson, W.G. 2007. Benefit estimates for landscape improvements: sequential Bayesian design and respondents rationality in a choice experiment. *Land Economics*, 83(4), pp. 617–634.

Schafer, A. 2000. Regularities in travel demand: an international perspective. *Journal of Transportation and Statistics*, 3(3), pp. 1–31.

Schaffar, A. 2010. Quelle est la nature de la croissance urbaine indienne? *Revue d'économie du dévelopement*, 24(2), pp. 101–120.

Shen, L.Y., Jorge Ochoa, J., Shah, M.N. and Zhang, X. 2011. The application of urban sustainability indicators – A comparison between various practices. *Habitat International*, 35(1), pp. 17–29.

Shen, X. 2013. Private Chinese investment in Africa: myths and realities. World Bank Policy Research Working Paper, Issue 6311.

Sicular, T., Ximing, Y., Gustafsson, B. and Shi, L. 2007. The urban-rural income gap and inequality in China. *Review of Income and Wealth*, 53(1), pp. 93–126.

Simmonds, D. 1999. The design of the DELTA land-use modelling package. *Environment and Planning B*, Volume 26, pp. 665–684.

Sjoberg, G. 1960. *The Preindustrial City: Past and Present*. New York: Free Press.

Small, K.A. and Song, S. 1994. *Population and Employment Densities: Structure and Change*. Société du Grand Paris, 2013. Le Nouveau Grand Paris: Société du Grand Paris.

Solard, G. 2010. Le commerce de proximité, *INSEE Premiere*, 1292: pp. 1–4.

Strotz, R.H. 1965. Urban Transportation Parables. *The Public Economy of Urban Communities* in J. Margolis, ed., Baltimore: Johns Hopkins University Press.

Thisse, J.F. 2012. *Avis du conseil scientifique sur l'évaluation socio-économique du schéma d'ensemble du réseau de transport public du Grand Paris*. Paris: Société du Grand Paris.

Thorbecke, E. and Charumilind, C. 2002. Economic inequality and its socioeconomic impact. *World Development*, 30(9), pp. 1477–1495.

Trancik, J.E., Chang, M.T., Karapataki, C. and Stokes, L.C. 2013. Effectiveness of a Segmental Approach to Climate Policy. *Environmental Science and Technology*.

Tsui, K.Y. 2007. Forces shaping China's interprovincial inequality. *Review of Income and Wealth*, 53(1), pp. 60–92.

Turok, I. 2004. Cities, regions and competitiveness. *Regional Studies*, 38(9), pp. 1069–1083.

UN-Habitat 2013. *State of the World's Cities 2012/2013: Prosperity of Cities*. London: Routledge.

United Nations. 1980. *Patterns of Urban and Rural Population Growth. Population Studies No. 68*. New York: United Nations Publications.

United Nations. 2012. *World Urbanization Prospects the 2011 Revision*. New York: United Nations Publications.

US Census 2004. Census 2000 urban and rural classification. US Department of Commerce, Bureau of the Census, Washington DC.

van den Bergh, J.C. and Verbruggen, H. 1999. Spatial sustainability, trade and indicators: an evaluation of the ecological footprint. *Ecological Economics*, 29(1), pp. 61–72.

van den Berg, P., Arentze, T. and Timmermans, H. 2013. A path analysis of social networks, telecommunication and social activity-travel patterns. *Transportation Research Part C: Emerging Technologies*, Volume 26, pp. 256–268.

van Lier, T., De Witte, A. and Macharis, C. 2012. The impact of telework on transport externalities: the case of Brussels Capital Region. *Procedia-Social and Behavioral Sciences*, 54: pp. 240–250.

Verhoef, E. 1994. External effects and social costs of road transport. *Transportation Research Part A: Policy and Practice*, 28(4), pp. 273–287.

Viscusi, W.K. 2009. Valuing risks of death from terrorism and natural disasters. *Journal of Risk and Uncertainty*, 38(3), pp. 191–213.

Von Thünen, J.H. 1826. *Der Isolierte Staat in Beziehung auf Landtschaft und Nationalokonomie, Hamburg*. (English translation by C.M. Wartenburg, von Thünen's Isolated State, Pergamon Press, Oxford.)

Warner, K. 2010. Global environmental change and migration: Governance challenges. *Global Environmental Change*, 20(3), pp. 402–413.

Wegener, M. 2004. Overview of land-use transport models. *Handbook of transport geography and spatial systems*, Volume 5, pp. 127–146.

White, E.V. and Gatersleben, B. 2011. Greenery on residential buildings: Does it affect preferences and perceptions of beauty? *Journal of Environmental Psychology*, 31(1), pp. 89–98.

Willis, H.H. 2007. Guiding resource allocations based on terrorism risk. *Risk Analysis*, 27(3), pp. 597–606.

Yuan, Y., Raubal, M. and Liu, Y. 2012. Correlating mobile phone usage and travel behavior – A case study of Harbin, China. *Computers, Environment and Urban Systems*, 36(2), pp. 118–130.

2 The hedonic value of urban quality of life

*Francesco Andreoli and
Alessandra Michelangeli*

2.1 Introduction

How often are questions such as "What does this city or neighborhood offer?" or "What does this city or this neighborhood offer *more* than the next city or neighborhood?" raised by potential landlords and tenants during the process of looking for a house? This is because landlords and tenants are interested not only in the housing-specific features of the unit they are going to buy or rent, but also the quality of the environment they acquire along with the house.

The proximity to good schools for children, the presence of parks, shops and sport facilities in the neighborhood, the low rate of unemployment and easy access to public transport are definitely "good" characteristics positively valued by potential buyers. Congestion, pollution, a high rate of unemployment and an unbalanced social mix are likely to be considered "bad" characteristics and adversely affect a potential inhabitant's evaluation of the neighborhood.

The above list of "goods" and "bads" is far from complete: the process of evaluating neighborhood quality is multidimensional in nature and involves a large set of environmental goods. Making residence choices, a potential dweller considers both local goods and "global" goods, common to all districts of the city, such as weather and altitude.

The potential dweller also looks at the opportunities provided by the local labor market in making his location choice. The unemployment rate, wage distribution and quality of jobs are all important factors. The mobility across labor markets, and therefore across cities, is strongly influenced by labor market conditions, although recent empirical evidence from the US has shown that "jobs follow people" rather than "people follow jobs" (Albouy and Stuart, 2014).

The answer to the two questions raised above depends crucially on the personal judgment of a city or on one of its neighborhoods which is mainly driven by global or local goods supply, housing quality and working conditions.

Local goods and services are distributed heterogeneously across urban areas: some areas have very good schools, but few green areas, others are well connected to the public transport network, but are overcrowded. This distributional heterogeneity means that different urban areas offer different living conditions to their inhabitants and, in the last analysis, different levels of *local quality of life*, corresponding to the well-being individuals experience from living in an area and consuming the goods it has to offer. Depending on the composition of the bundle of local goods offered, the choice of the neighborhood might reinforce or undermine the utility provided by a housing unit in isolation. This calls for an analysis of the distribution of goods and services, and the level of quality of life they generate, not only between cities, but also within each city. This chapter provides parallel considerations for the two dimensions.

In economic literature the most popular approach to measuring urban quality of life is the hedonic price method, based on an index measuring the monetary value of a bundle of local goods and services. The index is a measure of the utility provided by the composition of local goods available in the city where an individual lives. In technical jargon, city-specific characteristics with a positive impact on the individual's utility, such as leisure facilities, cultural infrastructure and school quality, are called amenities; those with a negative impact on the individual's utility (crowding, air pollution, noise, for example) are called disamenities.

The purpose of the discussion in this chapter is to present intuitively and informally the economics underlying the hedonic model, and to show how the model can be used to assess urban quality of life. It is measured by attaching a *value* to the bundle of (dis)amenities in each city or neighborhood, expressed in a counting unit that makes the measure comparable across urban areas, and in a metrics strictly related to changes in the individuals' utility.

The basic idea is very simple: if there is a richer supply of amenities in one city compared to another, the quality of life will be higher and the index will reach the highest value; the same applies for the evaluation of local quality of life at the level of neighborhoods. The most intuitive index of quality of life takes the form of budget constraint. For an urban area, the index is defined as the sum of the average quantities weighted by the implicit or hedonic prices of amenities. Disamenities have a negative value for the implicit price and decrease the index value. Implicit prices are conceptually derived from a theory on commodity differentiation developed by Lancaster (1966) and Rosen (1974). Different types of commodities are alternative bundles of utility-bearing characteristics. Under some assumptions, the characteristics specific to each bundle are individually evaluated by a hedonic price function that links the price of a commodity to its characteristics. Some years later, Rosen (1979) transposed the hedonic theory to an urban framework where cities were viewed as bundles of urban (dis)amenities. He ranked American cities on the basis of climate conditions, pollution, crime and market conditions. This work was followed by the PhD dissertation of Jennifer Roback, one of Rosen's students, in 1980 and a well-known article (Roback, 1982), where the theoretical model sketched by Rosen (1979) was refined and the index of urban quality of life, still in use today, was defined.

In this chapter, we first introduce and discuss the key ingredients of the hedonic method used to assess quality of life in urban areas (Section 2.2). Then, we show how the hedonic method has been integrated into a spatial equilibrium model, which explains the location choice of agents, i.e. consumers and businesses

46   *Francesco Andreoli and Alessandra Michelangeli*

(Section 2.3). Section 2.4 presents an extension of the hedonic methodology, where the standard measure of quality of life is integrated by welfare measures. Major data requirements and some specific aspects of empirical applications are presented in Section 2.5. Section 2.6 focuses on the relationship between quality of life and city size, described in depth in Chapter 6. Some concluding remarks about challenging problems and promising developments in the quality of life literature are set out in Section 2.7.

2.2   The value of (dis)amenities in a partial equilibrium model

The hedonic approach is a revealed preference method of valuation. Individuals reveal their preferences for a particular good by purchasing the good along with the characteristics it embodies. The price of the good is assumed to be a function of its characteristics. The function that relates price to characteristics is commonly referred to as the hedonic price function. As stated in the Introduction, Rosen (1974) first develops a partial equilibrium model where the hedonic price function emerges from the interaction between suppliers and demanders of a differentiated commodity. In empirical applications of the hedonic method, the market value of the good is the dependent variable of the hedonic price function, while the good's characteristics are independent variables. The estimated coefficient associated with each characteristic contributes to measuring the household's marginal willingness to pay for the characteristics, at the household's optimal choice. A typical good considered in hedonic analysis is housing, which comprises a set of utility-bearing characteristics distinguished in housing-specific attributes and local dis(amenities). When an individual chooses a housing unit to buy, implicitly he decides the best combination of housing-specific attributes and local amenities according to his preferences and the budget constraint he is under.

2.2.1   The nature of (dis)amenities

Valuing amenities is a difficult task because they are non-marketable goods. Most amenities are also public goods, such as green areas, clean air, policing, etc. and it is challenging to determine the social value of their production. Some are provided by the public as well as private sector, for instance educational and health services. Other amenities, such as recreational facilities, are provided privately at a price, which often fails to internalize the value of the externalities that they generate (the proximity of shops and reduction of search costs, but also pollution) so the price at which goods are sold does not account for the social value of these goods.

An important feature of amenities is that they produce local effects and their relocation is very costly: pupils can be assigned to publicly administrated schools according to the catchment area; air pollution and crowding are more intense in high-density areas; security is higher where police stations are located. The most striking example is public greenery: nature lovers are more likely to move to neighborhoods with huge green areas than wait for parks to be created where they now live.

2.2.2 The housing market

One of the markets where amenities are implicitly traded is the housing market. To understand how local amenities are capitalized in housing prices, imagine a representative individual with his own tastes in housing and a composite good representing all other goods. The consumer is endowed with a monetary budget to allocate to housing and the composite good. In the Rosen (1974) partial equilibrium model, work is not explicitly considered, as if this decision has already been taken. We will see later that Roback (1982) develops a model where housing and employment decisions are taken simultaneously. Nevertheless, the Rosen (1974) model does identify the forces in play behind the housing decision faced by the consumer. The way in which these forces are modeled is important in determining the value of amenities.

Housing and the composite good both produce utility for the consumer. There is, however, potentially an infinite number of different combinations of housing and composite goods that provide the same utility. Housing consumption involves a 0–1 choice: either the consumer buys the house, and consumes the rest of the money buying the composite good, or he does not. However, housing and other types of real estate properties are intrinsically differentiated products, and therefore no two units are identical. Therefore, the decision is not only whether to buy or not, or how much to pay, but also the amount of quality to buy, which is determined by housing-specific characteristics and local (dis)amenities. As a result, making the housing decision involves appreciating amenities. This has three consequences. First, different bundles of housing-specific characteristics and amenities can be ranked from the least to the most appreciated by the representative consumer. Second, there might be different amenity bundles, associated with the same housing-specific characteristics, that consumers consider as indifferent, i.e. the utility evaluation is the same across these bundles. This suggests that amenities are interchangeable. Finally, there are different combinations of amenities and composite goods that can be substituted one for the other at given substitution rates, such that the consumer has no preference for properties with similar characteristics but situated in neighborhoods offering different types and quantities of amenities.

Given the budget constraint, the consumer chooses the allocation to the composite good and housing attributes. Although all housing units are traded in the same market, usually identified at the city-level, there is no single, uniform price since housing enshrines different bundles of characteristics, making each unit unique. Rosen (1974) assumes a competitive market and the equilibrium price schedule is such that demand and supply for each housing unit meet.

2.2.3 The equilibrium price schedule

Consider again the case of a representative consumer in the housing market, and assume that the supply of housing units is fixed. Hence, house prices are entirely demand driven. The competitive market is in equilibrium if the representative consumer has no incentives to change his optimal choice about a given housing unit. This means that consumer utility should be equalized everywhere across neighborhoods. If it is not the case, the consumer would move to the most appreciated neighborhood, where greater utility is provided. Then, congestion would occur with a rise in the market price of properties in these neighborhoods. Prices rise until the number of bidders equates the number of available housing units in the neighborhood. At the point of equilibrium, utility should be equalized across the neighborhoods. Paraphrasing the words of Rosen (1979: 74), the housing market is "reminiscent of a 'voting with your feet' [Tiebout, 1956] criterion: each household's location choice maximizes its welfare and no family can be made better off by moving [to another neighborhood]."

The hedonic model assumes that consumers, who are price schedule takers, select the preferred housing unit by equalizing their marginal evaluation of each housing characteristic, including amenities, to the marginal value that the price schedule associates with each of these characteristics. The marginal value of a generic attribute k corresponds to the marginal change in house prices, which is associated with a marginal change in that attribute. Mathematically, this corresponds to the derivative of the hedonic price function with respect to the quantity of k. The marginal price depends on two components: on the one hand, the estimated parameters of the hedonic price function and, on the other, the quantity of the attribute k associated with each housing unit. It is this last component that determines the variability of the marginal price of the kth attribute across housing units. The price, also known as the hedonic price or implicit price of the kth attribute, identifies the marginal willingness to pay for access to an additional amount of that attribute.

The hedonic price function provides information on the marginal bids of the consumer for each amenity. The marginal bid of a generic amenity k is the maximum (minimum) amount of money that the consumer is willing to give up (accept) to consume an additional unit of amenity k, given the initial quantity of the same amenity he is already consuming, for a given level of income and utility. An example may be useful: consider a potential dweller for whom it is very important to buy a house near a green area. He can choose to buy one of three apartments on the same floor of the same building. The first apartment overlooks a very congested road, the second a small garden and the third a larger garden. In all other respects, the three flats are the same. Certainly, the consumer will prefer the second and third to the first, since he is willing to pay more to obtain some extra green space. The difference between the price schedule of the first and the second or the third flat gives an idea of the sign and magnitude of the hedonic price of the greenery. It is plausible, however, that the evaluation of every additional unit of green is always positive, but decreases with the quantity of green the potential dweller is actually consuming. So, if the marginal gain in utility he receives from the view of a larger garden is worth more than the additional price he has to pay for it, then the third apartment will be chosen, if not, the second will be preferred.

Actually, things are not so straightforward in empirical analysis. The price schedule is usually a non-linear relationship between house prices and housing-specific features and amenities. This means that marginal prices are not constant, but depend on the bundle chosen. Increasing one unit of green in an apartment in a neighborhood with lots of parks is less valuable than the same increase for a house in a built-up area.

Once the price schedule is estimated and marginal prices inferred, the hedonic model assumes that the equilibrium in the housing market is the result of the equilibrium in all the "submarkets" for amenities and housing-specific features. This means that housing equilibrium can be rationalized through the demand and supply of amenities and housing-specific features, and traditional models for consumer surplus can be used to assess the value of amenities and, in turn, the quality of life in an urban area.

2.3 The hedonic spatial equilibrium model

In Rosen (1979) the hedonic framework is used to assess the quality of life in urban areas. The model considers household and business location decisions in order to maximize utility and minimize costs, respectively. Household choices depend on the wage that one can earn living in a given city and the cost of living approximated by the cost of housing services. Households with a preference for amenity-rich areas will move to those areas, which are also the most expensive, and will be willing to earn lower wages to enjoy the higher (lower) level of amenities (disamenities):

> The combination of lower wages and higher housing prices is an implicit premium, or price, that households pay for choosing an urban area with more attractive amenities. It is this value of the local amenity bundle that Rosen and other urban economists call urban quality of life.
>
> (Blomquist, 2006: 485)

Conversely, households living in low-amenity areas will be compensated with higher wages and lower housing prices.

In equilibrium, no-one has an incentive to move, since the relocation costs are higher than the utility gains generated by moving. The representative household experiences the same level of utility in all cities, and unit production costs are equal to the unit production price.

Roback (1982) extends the model outlined above in a general equilibrium setting by considering the housing market in addition to the labor market, since the two markets are interconnected and both contribute to determining the full implicit price of amenities. A quality of life index is explicitly defined as the weighted sum of local amenities, where the weights are the amenity full implicit prices, obtained by the sum of the housing price differential and the negative of the wage price differential.

Since the pioneering work of Rosen (1979) and Roback (1982), additional refinements to this approach have been developed in different directions, both on theoretical and empirical grounds, to address the problem of the cost-of-living, tax

50 *Francesco Andreoli and Alessandra Michelangeli*

adjusted earnings, income other than source labor and the willingness to pay for amenities evaluated at the margin.

These issues are discussed separately, although recent work incorporates some of them into a single framework. For example, Albouy (2008) incorporates the first three of the above issues, i.e. cost-of-living, tax adjusted earnings, income other than source labor, in order to obtain much more sensitive estimates of quality of life.

2.3.1 Cost-of-living

In the earlier applications of the Rosen (1979) and Roback (1982) framework, amenities are capitalized in wages and housing rents. The only exception is the work of Gyourko *et al.* (1991), which includes locally traded goods other than housing as an observed amenity in the housing expenditure and wage equations. Gabriel *et al.* (2003) also capitalize amenities in cost-of-living other than housing. The standard approach is extended by using a three-equation system to estimate the capitalization of amenities in housing rents, wages and prices of local commodities excluding housing. Non-housing cost-of-living is measured using the American Chamber of Commerce Research Association's (ACCRA) index, although the authors acknowledge that it is not an ideal cost-of-living measure. They justify their choice by the lack of alternatives. The findings show that the compensating differential in the price of local consumption goods becomes a third component of the full price of amenities. Shapiro (2006) and Albouy (2008) also incorporate non-housing prices into their analysis, based on compensating differentials in the housing and labor markets. The ACCRA data are not used directly as in Gabriel *et al.* (2003), but are used to infer non-housing prices from housing prices. More specifically, non-housing prices are regressed on housing prices calculated from the ACCRA data. Albouy (2008) shows that, with this method, only 14 percent of the entire cost-of-living variation remains unexplained. However, Winters (2009) observes that the approach of Shapiro (2006) and Albouy (2008) does not allow for differences in non-housing prices between cities that are not correlated with housing prices. Instead of predicting non-housing prices on the basis solely of house prices, he suggests adding to the list of regressors census division dummies,[1] city size dummies, and amenities and not just house prices.

2.3.2 Tax-adjusted income other than labor source

In two recent papers, Albouy (2008) and Andreoli and Michelangeli (2014) consider all the disposable income for households instead of only labor income. Albouy (2008) develops a model where households are supposed to hold shares of land and capital which pay an income, which is independent of the households' location. Only the labor income varies across cities. The model conceived in this way is able to represent the situation of a potential migrant, who owns property outside the city to which he is moving and that he is likely to sell in order to move. In Andreoli and Michelangeli (2014) the willingness to pay for amenities depends explicitly on the share of income that remains for the consumption of all the other goods, represented by the composite good.

Moreover, Albouy (2008) recommends defining income as income after federal taxes, since empirical evidence for the United States shows that federal taxes are not correlated with federal expenditure.

2.3.3 Non-marginal prices for infra-marginal units of amenities

In empirical applications implicit prices are usually computed at the average quantities of the amenities in the sample area. They are then used as weights in the sum of the amenity quantities of each area to obtain the Roback (1982) quality of life index by area. The index calculated in this way provides an exact evaluation solely for the bundle with amenity average quantities computed on the overall sample areas. For all the other bundles specific to each sample area, the Roback (1982) index gives an approximated value of the quality of life, since the amenity quantities specific to each area are associated with the implicit marginal prices computed on the overall average quantities and not with the prices of infra-marginal units. In other words, the quality has no direct interpretation in terms of willingness to pay for bundles different from the overall average bundle, since marginal prices do not correspond to a proper evaluation of these units. As Roback acknowledges, the vector of marginal prices is used as weights for amenities and "merely shows the order of magnitude of expenditure in the average budget" (Roback, 1982: 1274). Andreoli and Michelangeli (2014) suggest a new value-adjusted quality of life index, providing the proper evaluation of infra-marginal units of amenities. The methodology relies on a hedonic welfare measurement model, presented in depth in the next section.

2.4 The value-adjusted quality of life index

The methodology put forward by Andreoli and Michelangeli (2014) considers a city for which quality of life is measured at the neighborhood level. The focus on a single city allows a simpler framework to be developed, where intercity differences in non-housing costs, intergovernmental transfers and local taxes can be neglected. Moreover, the labor market heterogeneity across neighborhoods is assumed to be negligible.

Suppose we are interested in assessing quality of life in the city and use the Roback (1982) index for the assessment. The index value is given by multiplying the implicit prices, calculated for the overall average quantities of the amenities in the city, by the average quantity of amenities in the city. Now suppose we are interested in measuring quality of life in neighborhood i of the city. The index value is given by multiplying the implicit prices, calculated as explained above, by the average quantities of amenities in neighborhood i. The index provides an approximate assessment of quality of life for the neighborhood, since it in all likelihood it differs in amenity quantities from the overall average bundle. The solution suggested by Andreoli and Michelangeli (2014) is to correct the Roback (1982) index with a term corresponding to the compensating benefit. The compensating benefit was first introduced by Luenberger (1996) in welfare analysis and thereafter used by Palmquist (2006) to evaluate environmental goods in a hedonic framework. To give an intuitive definition of this measure, suppose that the neighborhood i has fewer amenities than the average bundle. The compensating benefit corresponds to the amount of money that a representative consumer living in neighborhood i would like to accept as compensation for the poorer neighborhood in which he lives. Suppose now the opposite, i.e. neighborhood i is more endowed with amenities than the average bundle. The compensating benefit is the amount of money that the representative consumer is willing to give up in order to enjoy the richer bundle of amenities located in the neighborhood.

What about the case in which neighborhood i is more endowed with certain amenities and less with others? The compensating benefit is a monetary compensation if neighborhood i has a lower quantity of amenities which are more important for the consumer than the amenities whose quantity is higher; otherwise, the compensating benefit will represent the willingness to pay if neighborhood i has a higher quantity of amenities which are more important for the consumer. It is worth pointing out that the compensating benefit is the amount of money the consumer is willing to give up or (accept) for not moving from neighborhood i, since the utility is equal in all neighborhoods and coincides with the level of utility attained with the overall average bundle of amenities.

Once we have explained the compensating benefit in the quality of life assessment, we can ask how it can be modeled and estimated. The identification of the compensating benefit is based on the bid function, i.e the maximum (minimum) amount of money that the consumer is willing to give up (to accept) to consume a bundle of amenities different from the overall average bundle, given the consumer's income and without changing the level of utility. Actually, the bid function for the housing unit comprises housing-specific characteristics and amenities. The housing-specific characteristics are kept fixed at the sample overall average quantities so that bid functions associated with the different neighborhoods express the money evaluation for the bundle of amenities characterizing each neighborhood. We assume an Inverse Almost Ideal Demand System (IAIDS) specification for the bid function associated with each neighborhood. The IAIDS developed by Eales and Unnevehr (1994) is a model for consumer preferences, which allows the parametrical identification of the inverse demand for housing attributes as a function of consumer utility parameters, explicitly taking into account a set of restrictions on consumer taste, required by welfare analysis. The inverse demands are "almost ideal" because the underlying preferences are ideally crafted to generalize many other models used in applied analysis.

The compensating benefit for neighborhood i is the difference between the bid functions for amenities in neighborhood i and the bid function for the overall average quantities of the amenities in the city.

The new index, called the value-adjusted quality of life index, is the difference between the Roback (1982) index, calculated for the whole sample average amenity quantities, and the compensated benefit for this neighborhood.

We apply the value-adjusted quality of life index to the city of Milan, using a dataset on housing transactions between 2004 and 2010. The city is divided into 55 neighborhoods, identified by the public agency (Osservatorio del Mercato Immobiliare) providing data on housing transactions, internally homogeneous in terms of socio-economic and urban characteristics, availability and quality of public services. The quality of life is assessed on the basis of a set of eight amenities provided at neighborhood level and taken from public authority records. They are: environmental conditions measured by the amount of greenery in the neighborhood; educational services measured by the number of secondary schools per 10,000 inhabitants; public transport measured by the number of underground, and railway stations per 10,000 inhabitants; security measured by the number of police stations per 10,000 inhabitants; health services measured by the number of health centers per 10,000 inhabitants; facilities proxied by the number of pharmacies and Post Offices per 10,000 inhabitants; recreation measured by the number of cinemas, theaters, museums, art galleries, music academies and libraries per 10,000 inhabitants; the ethnic composition of the neighborhood measured by the percentage of Italians residents in the total population in the neighborhood.

Figure 2.1 compares the quality of life assessment obtained using the value-adjusted quality of life index with the assessment resulting from the standard approach.

Evidently, in both cases, neighborhoods with a high quality of life are predominantly located in the city-center. The scale measurement, however, is different. The value-adjusted quality of life index ranges from negative to positive values (from −14,432€ to 16,774€). The negative values represent the annual compensation that the household should receive for living in a more disadvantageous neighborhood compared to the city average. The positive values correspond to the amounts of money that the household is willing to pay to enjoy the amenities in the more endowed neighborhoods, compared to the city average. The Roback index (1982) provides only positive values (ranging from 2,368€ to 6,101€), which correspond to the implicit premiums that the household is willing to pay for access to the different bundles of amenities in the city neighborhoods.

The ranking of neighborhoods produced by the two indices are positively and significantly correlated, with Spearman's rank correlation coefficient equal to 0.6349.

2.5 Which amenities for the hedonic quality of life index?

The measurement of quality of life first requires the identification of the specific areas into which a given region is divided. It is commonly assumed that the measured quality of life is constant within each area, although it might be very different between areas. The size and composition of the bundle of amenities are chosen on the basis of the division. In most studies, the units analyzed are cities, regions or neighborhoods, whose territory is defined by administrative boundaries. In some works, statistical techniques are used to identify areas on the basis of functional rather than administrative criteria. Hiller and Lerbsy (2014), for example,

Figure 2.1 Comparison between the value-adjusted quality of life index and the Roback (1982) index.

Source: Andreoli and Michelangeli (2014).

measure quality of life in German cities and countries on the basis of the functional labor market and not administrative areas. These areas are determined by Kosfeld and Werner (2012) by factor analysis to commute data. The advantages of this territorial division are twofold: first, households both live and work in the functional labor market areas, so commuter costs can be safely ignored; second, the likelihood of parameter bias due to spatial autocorrelation in the ordinary least squares residuals is reduced.

Other works use more recent spatial techniques to account for spillover effects across areas capitalized into a proximity-based measurement setting for the amenities. Brambilla *et al.* (2013), for example, introduce the concept of available amenities defined as the quantity of amenities in the neighborhood where the individual dwells, plus a term indicating the presence of amenities in the surrounding areas, whose accessibility is a function of the distance between the neighborhood and its adjacent neighborhoods.

The difficulty in identifying the appropriate urban areas goes hand-in-hand with the difficulties in producing reliable measures of the amenities. Theory suggests that amenities should be measured in a way that fully captures how consumers view them. Objective measures are clearly the easiest to obtain. A general consensus exists within the literature on urban quality of life about the types of amenities that are most important to household location decisions and quality of life. We provide a descriptive list of the amenities encountered most commonly in applied research. This list is, however, far from complete.

2.5.1 *Climate*

Factors such as rainfall, humidity, heating degree days, cooling degree days, wind speed, sunshine, and so on, are all objectively measurable and frequently recorded indicators of climatic conditions. Like natural amenities, discussed below, in the terminology of Gyourko *et al.* (1991), climatic conditions are pure amenities, because they are non-produced public goods. Since the 1970s, empirical works on American cities have been strongly influenced by climate in location decisions. According to Glaeser *et al.* (2001), weather is the most important factor for population and house price rises at the county level in the United States. In other countries, the effect of climatic conditions is much more moderate. In Italy, for example, Colombo *et al.* (2012) show that economic and social amenities are the most important factors, explaining 24.2 and 24.5 percent of variations in housing prices, respectively. The contributions of other groups of amenities are lower: 20.7 percent for environmental amenities, 18.3 percent for services and, finally, just 12.3 percent for the climate.

Though empirical evidence has shown the relevance of climatic variables in describing residential patterns across cities, it is difficult to claim that climatic factors have any role in choosing a location within a city. At equilibrium, climatic factors should not be considered in determining utility differentials across neighborhoods, although climate might affect the level. Hence, climatic factors are irrelevant in a price schedule regression.

2.5.2 Natural amenities

Parks, coastlines, mountains, lakes, rivers and public greenery. Similarly to climatic variables, most of the natural amenities account for an important share of the differences in quality of life among regions or cities. In fact, the presence of one of these environmental amenities represents one of the attractions of the region, which affects not only house prices, but also the attractiveness of the labor market. This is particularly true of the tourist industry. Natural amenities, however, can also produce local effects on house prices across the neighborhoods of a city. The proximity-effect associated to public parks, highly regarded as leisure intensive facilities, offers the canonical (and probably best known) example of hedonic effect: in New York City, housing units directly overlooking Central Park, or in its proximity, command a dividend, which capitalizes the proximity to the park itself. As illustrated by Crompton (2001: Table 2), in the 20 years following the expansion of Central Park (around 1858), the value of the adjacent housing units rose tenfold, while on average house prices in Manhattan "merely" doubled during the period. Sometimes, what positively affects the price of nearby housing units, such as the presence of a river in a city, is a cost for other housing units located further away. In this case, it is complicated to separate the intrinsic value of natural amenities from the role played by their proximity, which should be evaluated separately.

2.5.3 The Environment

Air quality, local congestion, pollution. As for climate, these elements can be measured objectively. As for natural amenities, environmental quality is an important predictor of both housing and wages. Environmental amenities, however, differ from climate and natural amenities in at least two ways.

On the one hand, environmental amenities affect both house prices and wages, but in non-trivial directions. Pollution, for instance, is a by-product of manufacturing, but does not enter directly into the cost functions of companies. The more manufacturers pollute the environment, the higher wages they pay to compensate workers for the dangerous environment they create. This also impacts on house prices, since pollution depreciates the local environment. For this reason, the contribution of pollution to local quality of life cannot be reliably estimated, according to Berger et al. (2008), working on the measurement of quality of life in Russia.

On the other hand, environmental quality is relevant not only for cross-regional comparisons, but also local analysis: pollution and congestion indicate proximity to production areas, which in turn means lower commuting costs for local residents. We therefore expect these variables to have a negative impact on the housing price schedule and a positive, compensatory impact on the wage schedule.

2.5.4 Local fiscal conditions: taxes and public services

2.5.4.1 Taxes

Gyourko and Tracy (1989) and Gyourko et al. (1991) were the first to extend the Rosen (1979) and Roback (1982) models to explicitly take into account fiscal conditions as an important factor affecting the location decisions of households and businesses. In their first work (Gyourko and Tracy, 1989), they argue that differences between cities in tax rates and publicly produced services may be capitalized into wage rates as well as land rents. This is empirically verified using a sample of workers from 125 cities in 46 states, taken from the 1980 Current Population Survey. Seven fiscal variables are included in the analysis to measure the following local fiscal conditions: state income taxes; state corporate tax rates; government services, i.e. police, fire, health and educational services. It turns out that local fiscal conditions explain almost as much of the variations in wages as do worker characteristics. High income taxes act as a disamenity, reducing the attractiveness of the city. High corporate income taxes reduce wage rates. Yu and Rickman (2013) interpret this result as suggesting that higher corporate income taxes reduce company profitability and, accordingly, labor demand and nominal wages.

In their second work (Gyourko et al., 1991), the analysis of fiscal conditions is extended to consider not only wage differentials across cities but also home rent differentials. Data and variables are almost the same as in Gyourko and Tracy (1989). The results confirm the importance of fiscal conditions in explaining housing and wages differentials across cities, accounting for about 21 percent of the explained variation in house prices and about 47 percent of the measured variation in wages.

2.5.4.2 Public services

Transport infrastructure, the quality of schools, healthcare and public safety are the parameters most frequently used in hedonic studies. Perhaps even more significantly, most commercial websites for real estate agents provide information on a house for sale about its proximity to public services, suggesting that these services are an important feature of a neighborhood.

In local quality of life measurement at the neighborhood level, the presence of public services impacts strongly on prices, since they represent valid alternatives to expensive goods available on the private market. At the neighborhood level, not only the quantity but also the quality of public services plays a role in the price schedule. While the quantity can be measured simply through objective indicators, and attractiveness can be identified by proximity to the services, their quality can hardly be verified empirically. The fact that very similar houses placed on different sides of some of the best-known boulevards of central Paris are sold at significantly different prices due to belonging to separate school catchment areas (as shown by Fack and Grenet, 2010), is clear evidence that school quality indeed plays a role. In virtually all hedonic price analysis, the quantity of public services is considered as an amenity.

At the regional and urban level, only aggregate quantity measures for public service provision are taken into account, such as the number of underground or bus stops, the number of educational facilities or the average student/teacher ratio, the available number of beds in healthcare facilities or the number of doctors, and the number of police stations and policemen per inhabitant or the frequency of violent crimes. As shown by Colombo *et al.* (2014), these variables alone account for a sizable part of the variation in house prices across Italian provinces. The same variables are scaled at the local level to account for the contribution of public services to cross-neighborhood variations in quality of life (see Brambilla *et al.*, 2013), where the equity component underlying the distribution of these public services is also an important issue.

Unlike environmental and natural resources, public services are produced by a public provider. Hence, location, quantity and quality depend on the political objectives of the urban planner, while financing might be regulated by local or national taxation. Equity issues arise when the wealthy begin to create segregated communities with higher taxes and better public services, especially schools. The "voting with your feet" model of Tiebout (1956) describes this type of dynamic, which might reproduce income inequality in terms of opportunity and access inequality. Where financing is based on national taxation, equity concerns persist: richer landlords offer higher prices for housing units located in neighborhoods with better public services. This has an impact on quality of life if the value of public services incorporates the social costs associated with the uneven distribution across neighborhoods of a city. On the assumption that equal access to amenities is a primary goal of society, Brambilla *et al.* (2013) estimate, for instance, that the standard quality of life index for the city of Milan should be reduced by 28 percent because of the unequal access to public services across neighborhoods.

2.5.5 *Cultural and recreational opportunities*

In a popular article by Glaeser *et al.* (2001), cultural and recreation amenities are called consumption amenities. In this work the authors demonstrate the importance of consumption amenities for quality of life in 19 metropolitan areas in the US, as well as for London and Paris. Following these authors, in particular cultural infrastructure such as restaurants, art museums, or movie cinemas increase quality of life in a city and attract additional residents. Other studies (e.g. Berger *et al.*, 2008) indicate the increasing importance of cultural amenities in developed countries as well as in transition economies such as Russia and China.

2.5.6 *Population density*

Population density is often included to measure urban-scale amenities and disamenities that are partially or totally unobservable. The positive effects associated with density are effectively illustrated by Glaeser *et al.* (2001). First, in high-density cities, commuting distances and transport costs are lower than in low-density cities. The fact that transport costs are relatively low creates benefits not only for commuting, but also for leisure (hobbies and friends). Second, it is easier and less costly for workers to find or change a job in dense labor markets. Third, high-density cities offer a rich variety of services and goods that have substantial scale economies, such as numerous restaurants, opera companies, art museums and so on. Scale economies imply that each of these goods has a critical mass of customers that enable the business to make a reasonable profit. However, the literature also highlights problems related to population density, increased traffic congestion and air pollution, high rents and more generally a high cost-of-living.

Given that population density creates both advantages and disadvantages, it is rather difficult to predict the net effect of density on quality of life. In Rosen (1979), density turns out to be a negative effect on individual utility, and crime and pollution explicitly enter into the hedonic regression. The interpretation of this result is that the cost-of-living effect outweighs the positive effects of density, such as the reduction of commuter costs and a wider variety of consumption activities that are not available in more sparsely populated cities because of weak demand for those goods. Roback (1982) considers population size, population growth rate and population density as amenities. The first two have a strong positive effect, while the latter is not statistically significant.

Some recent works examine the inverse causal relationship between density and quality of life, i.e. density is not a factor in quality of life, but quality of life, together with worker productivity, determines population density. Rappaport (2008) develops a calibrated general equilibrium model, which demonstrates that differences in consumption amenities across urban areas can cause differences in density. Empirical findings show that cross-sectional variations in quality of life account for approximately one-fifth of the cross-sectional variations in population density. Albouy and Stuart (2014) develop a model where amenities and population density are jointly determined. They argue that quality of life dominates job location and turns out to be the most important factor in determining the concentration of people in an urban area. Leknes (2014) puts forward an alternative methodology to investigate the endogenous relationship between population density and quality of life. The methodology relies on a quasi-natural experiment, where the exogenous spatial distribution of mineral resources across Norwegian regions is used to predict the current population size. The results show a statistically significant positive effect of regional population size on quality of life. The findings can be interpreted as economies of scale in providing goods and services that offset disamenities such as crime, noise, air pollution and traffic.

2.5.7 The socio-economic composition of the population

Some studies consider amenities infrequently used in the literature to assess quality of life. For example, Colombo *et al.* (2014) measure the quality of life in Italian provincial capitals and include the unemployment rate in the set of amenities, as it is an important factor in individual well-being and social conditions. The results show that the unemployment rate is the amenity with the greatest impact on quality of life in absolute terms. An increase by one standard deviation in this variable implies a decrease of about 2,400€ in the value of the quality of life index—2.5 times more than violent crime and almost 5 times more than air pollution.

Assessing the quality of life in the city of Milan, Brambilla *et al.* (2013) and Andreoli and Michelangeli (2014) consider the ethnic composition of the neighborhoods as an amenity. In the former, the ethnic composition is measured by the ratio of Italian/foreign residents in the neighborhoods of the city. More specifically, the numerator is the number of Italians in the generic neighborhood *i* and the denominator is the number of foreigners in the same neighborhood plus the number of foreign people living in the adjacent neighborhood, weighted by the inverse of the squared Euclidean distance between neighborhood *i* and each adjacent neighborhood. This variable approximates the probability that Italian residents in neighborhood *i* interact with immigrants living in neighborhood *i* and in the adjacent neighborhoods. In the latter, the ethnic composition variable is simply the percentage of Italian residents by neighborhood. More interestingly, Andreoli and Michelangeli (2014) test the endogeneity of the Italian percentage, which may be due to reverse causation and/or an omitted variable. The former occurs when the ethnic composition of a neighborhood is affected by the value of housing in that neighborhood. To be more specific, immigrants tend to live in those areas where housing prices are lower that the city average. The sample correlation coefficient between the immigrant ratio and housing prices is -0.2083, meaning that the presence of immigrants in a neighborhood is inversely related to the value of houses. The latter occurs when other variables, in addition to ethnic composition and other covariates included in the specification of the hedonic price function, affect the market value of houses. If the ethnic composition is correlated with these unobserved factors, the correlation between ethnic composition and housing prices may just be picking up the correlation between the unobserved factors and housing prices. Endogeneity is verified by the gravity model approach developed by Card *et al.* (2008) and Saiz and Wachter (2011), according to which ethnic composition is predicted via the settlement patterns in previous periods. The predicted ratio is used as an instrument to test the endogeneity of the Italian percentage by applying the Hausman test. The ethnic composition of neighborhoods does not turn out to be endogenous to the simultaneous value of housing prices, since the null hypothesis of no endogeneity for the Italian percentage is not rejected.

In addition to the variable measuring urban amenities, a set of covariates about houses, workers, occupation and industry have to be included in the hedonic wage and housing regressions to prevent local amenities erroneously picking up the effects of structural differences between cities for housing rents and wages.

In relation to the empirical specification of the hedonic price function, theory offers very few insights. A linear specification is easy to estimate, but assumes that the marginal prices of amenities are independent one from the other and from the quantity of amenities. This artificially imposes constraints on the tastes of the representative consumer. Moreover, a linear price function assumes that any sort of arbitrage activity is allowed. But housing units and jobs are indivisible and differentiated products; both are comprised of a bundle of attributes that cannot be untied. For these reasons, the hedonic price function is assumed to be non-linear. The log-linear form is the most used specification in this strand of literature. Recent works use spatial econometric models to explicitly take into account the spatial interrelation that most likely characterizes housing units and jobs.

2.6 Quality of life and city size: the role of the cost of living

From the outset of literature on urban quality of life, a recurring question has been whether quality of life is specifically related to city size. The first works—Berger *et al.* (1987), Blomquist *et al.* (1988), Gyourko *et al.* (1991)—find a significant negative relationship between quality of life and city size, measured by population. Burnell and Galster (1992), focusing in particular on the work of Berger *et al.* (1987), argue that this result is due to the choice of amenity variables. Environmental variables favor smaller areas, while recreational and cultural variables are more frequent in larger areas. If the former are included in the hedonic model and the latter are excluded—as in the above mentioned works[2]— the ranking of cities according to quality of life is biased in favor of smaller areas. Moreover, Burnell and Galster (1992) observe that Berger *et al.* (1987) ignore the industrial structure of the cities they investigate and underplay cost of living. As illustrated in Chapter 6, there is a positive correlation between industrial structure and city size, and industry generally leads to higher wages in larger urban areas. Since industrial structure is not included in the model, the wage effect attributable to industrial structure is picked up partly by environmental variables that are also related to population size. Thus the coefficients of the environmental variables for larger cities overestimate the true effect of environmental deterioration, with downward pressure on quality of life scores in larger areas. Regarding the cost of living, Berger *et al.* (1987) estimate housing and wage equations separately. They employ a wage equation where nominal wages, instead of real wages, are regressed on a set of amenity variables, as well as individual human-capital characteristics and employment characteristics. Cost of living—which, is positively correlated with city size—is then excluded from the wage equation. This suggests that the estimated wage effect of amenity variables related to city size would be greater than if cost-of-living differences were included in the model. Recently, Albouy (2008) has returned to the issue and stated that previous studies on quality of life place too much weight on wage differences and too little on cost-of-living differences across cities. Thus in large cities, characterized by high wages and a high cost of living, real incomes are overestimated and quality of life is underestimated. As explained in Section 2.3, Albouy (2008) adjusts the Roback (1982) index to take into account the cost of living, tax adjusted earnings and income other than source labor, and applies the new methodology to 290 metropolitan areas in the United States, observed in 2000. He considers a certain number of amenities divided into two groups: the first are climate and natural amenities, which are exogenous to the city population; the second group contains amenities that depend on the city

62 Francesco Andreoli and Alessandra Michelangeli

inhabitants. The results show the lack of any relationship between quality of life and city size.

2.7 Concluding remarks: challenging problems and promising developments in the quality of life literature

The hedonic quality of life index is an attractive and compelling methodological tool for assessing quality of life in urban areas. In a single value, it summarizes all the domains affecting individual well-being—from climate to environmental and socio-economic factors, as well as public goods, services and infrastructure— and allows different areas to be ranked according to the quantity and quality of amenities offered to its inhabitants. This ranking might prove useful to policy makers who want to identify problematic areas where action needs to be taken. The hedonic prices associated with (dis)amenities allow the magnitude of the effect of each dis(amenity) on quality of life to be quantified. This too is useful for policy makers aiming to establish which groups of amenities require action.

This chapter presents some important recent contributions to this strand of literature. Nevertheless, some research questions remain open. On the one hand, most of the studies on quality of life are based on data on amenities at the city level, and the index is calculated for the city as a whole, without differentiating the index value by neighborhood, or some other territorial division. On the other hand, studies of a single city assess the distribution of quality of life across city neighborhoods, but in general do not provide a comparison between cities. This is because it is very difficult to obtain detailed data for more than a single city.

Increased awareness at the institutional level of the importance of making available an adequate level of statistical and regularly updated information is desirable. It is especially important for countries or regions undergoing rapid urbanization, where cities are increasingly gaining relevance as independent administrative centers. So-called urban "smart growth," advocated by European policy makers, includes among its priorities the sustainability of the process, which involves offering a decent, if not equal, quality of life to everybody in the city, regardless of location. To discover the implications of the distribution and redistribution of amenities for the "smart growth" of a city, local policy makers need access to adequate statistical information.

The future challenge for the analysis of urban quality of life consists in adapting the tools provided by the literature for policy analysis. The hedonic index is necessarily an *ex post* evaluation tool to assess quality of life, using observed quantities of (dis)amenities and information drawn from the labor and housing markets to infer the implicit prices associated with the (dis)amenities. Suppose that the local government of a city implements a policy to increase the variety and quantity of amenities in the poorer neighborhoods of the city. The hedonic quality of life index cannot measure the change in quality of life in these neighborhoods, since the implicit prices are a proxy for the current distribution of amenities within the city. But the methodology introduced by Andreoli and

Michelangeli (2014), is a promising way to evaluate *ex ante* the effect on quality of life of policies that modify the distribution of amenities across and within urban areas. Instead of fixing the hedonic prices, which change endogenously with the distribution of amenities, these authors suggest fixing the tastes of the representative consumer and then evaluating the change in welfare from the perspective of this consumer. The underlying hypothesis is that tastes are unaffected by policy and an individual's residential choice does not change. A promising avenue for future research consists in conceptualizing the value-adjusted quality of life index within the hedonic equilibrium framework to develop appropriate *ex ante* evaluation criteria for the distribution and redistribution of quality of life at the local level.

Notes

1 The eight census division dummies are: Middle Atlantic, East North Central, West North Central, South Atlantic, East South Central, West South Central, Mountain, Pacific.
2 Berger *et al.* (1987) consider six variables measuring climatic conditions, six environmental variables and only one variable for central city location, measured as the proportion of individuals in the standard metropolitan statistical area (SMSA) living in the central city, to capture access to entertainment and the arts. Blomquist *et al.* (1988) consider six variables measuring climatic conditions, six environmental variables, a dummy variable indicating the proximity to a coast, the teacher–pupil ratio, and a violent crime variable. Gyourko *et al.* (1991) consider weather, environmental, and fiscal variables and the metro area size, measured by the population of the SMSA as an amenity proxy.

Bibliography

Albouy, D. (2008) "Are Big Cities Really Bad Places to Live? Improving Quality-of-Life Estimates across Cities," NBER Working Paper No. 14472.

Albouy, D. and Stuart, B. (2014) "Urban Population and Amenities," NBER Working Paper No. 19919.

Andreoli, F. and Michelangeli, A. (2014) "Welfare Measures to Assess Urban Quality of Life," Working Paper No. 278, University of Milano-Bicocca, Department of Economics.

Berger, M. C. and Blomquist, G. C. (1988) Income, opportunities, and the quality of life of urban residents. In M. G. H. McGeary and L. E. Lynn, Jr. (eds.), *Urban Change and Poverty*, Washington, DC: National Academy Press, pp. 66–101.

Berger, M., Blomquist, G. and Sabirianova, K. (2008) "Compensating differentials in emerging labor and housing markets: Estimates of quality of life in Russian cities," *Journal of Urban Economics*, 63, pp. 25–55.

Berger, M., Blomquist, G. and Waldner, W. (1987) "A revealed-preference ranking of quality of life for metropolitan areas," *Social Science Quarterly*, 68, pp. 761–778.

Blomquist, G. (2006) "Measuring Quality of Life." In R. Arnott and D. McMillen (eds.), *A Companion to Urban Economics*, Oxford: Blackwell-Synergy, pp. 483–501.

Blomquist, G., Berger, M. and Hoehn, J. (1988) "New estimates of quality of life in urban areas," *American Economic Review*, 78(1), pp. 89–107.

Brambilla, M., Michelangeli, A. and Peluso, E. (2013) "Equity in the city: on measuring urban (ine)quality of life," *Urban Studies*, 50(16), pp. 3205–3224.

Burnell, J. D. and Galster, G. (1992) "Quality-of-life measurementents and urban size: an empirical note," *Urban Studies*, 29(5), pp. 727–735.

Card, D., Mas, A. and Rothstein, J. (2008) "Tipping and the dynamics of segregation," *Quarterly Journal of Economics*, 123(1), pp. 177–218.

Colombo, E., Michelangeli, A. and Stanca, L. (2012) *Città italiane in cerca di qualità. Dove e perché si vive meglio*, Università Bocconi Editore.

Colombo, E., Michelangeli, A. and Stanca, L. (2014) "La Dolce Vita: hedonic estimates of quality of life in Italian cities," *Regional Studies*, 48(8), pp. 1404–1418.

Crompton, J. L. (2001) "The Impact of Parks on Property Values: A Review of the Empirical Evidence," *Journal of Leisure Research*, 33(1), pp. 1–31.

Eales, J. S. and Unnevehr, L. J. (1994) "The inverse almost ideal demand system," *European Economic Review*, 38(1), pp. 101–115.

Ezzet-Lofstrom, R. (2004) "Valuation of metropolitan quality of life in wages and rents," *Cityscape: A Journal of Policy Development and Research*, 7(1), pp. 23–37.

Fack, G. and Grenet, J. (2010) "When do better schools raise housing prices? evidence from Paris public and private schools," *Journal of Public Economics*, 94(1–2), pp. 59–77.

Gabriel, S. A., Mattey, J. P. and Wascher, W. L. (2003) "Compensating differentials and evolution of quality of life among US states," *Regional Science and Urban Economics*, 33, pp. 619–649.

Glaeser, E. L., Kolko, J. and Saiz, A. (2001) "Consumer city," *Journal of Economic Geography*, 1, pp. 27–50.

Gyourko, J. and Tracy, J. (1989) "The importance of local fiscal conditions in analyzing local labor markets," *Journal of Political Economy*, 97(5), pp. 1208–1231.

Gyourko, J., Kahn, M. and Tracy, J. (1991) "The structure of local public finance and the quality of life," *Journal of Political Economy*, 99(4), pp. 774–886.

Gyourko, J., Kahn, M. and Tracy, J. (1999) Quality of life and environmental comparisons. In: E.S. Mills and P. Cheshire (eds.), *The Handbook of Applied Urban Economics*, vol. 3, Amsterdam: Elsevier, pp. 1413–1454 .

Heckman, J. J., Matzkin, R. and Nesheim, L. (2010) "Nonparametric Identification and Estimation of Nonadditive Hedonic Models," *Econometrica*, 78(5), pp. 1569–1591.

Henderson, J. V. (1982) "Evaluating consumer amenities and interregional welfare Differences," *Journal of Urban Economics*, 11(1), pp. 32–59.

Hiller, N. and Lerbsy, O. (2014) "The capitalization of non-market attributes into regional housing rents and wages: evidence on German functional labor market areas", Discussion Papers No. 71, Center of Applied Economic Research Munster (CAWM), University of Munster.

Kosfeld, R. and Werner, A. (2012) "Deutsche Arbeitsmarktregionen – Neuabgrenzung nach den Kreisgebietsreformen 2007–2011," *Raumforschung und Raumordnung*, 70, pp. 49–64.

Lambiri, D., Biagi, B. and Royuela, V. (2007) "Quality of life in the economic and urban economic literature," *Social Indicators Research*, 84, pp. 1–25.

Lancaster, K. J. (1966) "A new approach to consumer theory," *Journal of Political Economy*, 74(2), pp. 132–157.

Leknes, S. (2014) "Causal evidence of quality of life and population size using historical mines," Working Paper No. 1/2014, Department of Economics, Norwegian University of Science and Technology.

Luenberger, D. G. (1996) "Welfare from a benefit viewpoint," *Economic Theory*, 7(3), pp. 445–462.

Palmquist, R. B. (2006) "Property value models." In: K. G. Maler and J. R. Vincent (eds.), *Handbook of Environmental Economics*, vol. 2, Amsterdam: Elsevier, pp. 763–819.

Rappaport, J. (2008) "Consumption amenities and city population density," *Regional Science and Urban Economics*," 38, pp. 533–552.

Roback, J. (1980) *The Value of Local Urban Amenities: Theory and Measurement*, PhD dissertation, University of Rochester.

Roback, J. (1982) "Wages, Rents, and the Quality of Life," *Journal of Political Economy*, 90(6), pp. 1257–1278.

Rosen, S. (1974) "Hedonic prices and implicit markets: Product differentiation in pure competition," *Journal of Political Economy*, 82(1), pp. 34–55.

Rosen, S. (1979) "Wage-based indexes of urban quality of life," pp. 74–104. In: P. Mieszkowsi and M. Stratzheim (eds.), *Current issues in urban economics*, Baltimore, NJ: John Hopkins Press.

Saiz, A. and Wachter, S. (2011) "Immigration and the neighborhood," *American Economic Journal*, 3(2), pp. 169–188.

Shapiro, J. M. (2006) "Smart cities: quality of life, productivity, and the growth effects of human capital," *Review of Economics and Statistics*, 88(2), pp. 324–335.

Tiebout, C. M. (1956) "A pure theory of local expenditures," *The Journal of Political Economy*, 65(5), pp. 416–424.

Winters, J. V. (2009) "Wages and prices: Are workers fully compensated for cost of living differences?," *Regional Science and Urban Economics*, 39(5), pp. 632–644.

Yu, Y. and Rickman, D. S. (2013) "US state and local fiscal policies and non-metropolitan area economic performance: A spatial equilibrium analysis," *Papers in Regional Science*, 92(3), pp. 579–597.

3 Measuring urban quality of life

A life satisfaction approach

Luca Stanca

3.1 Introduction

Urban quality of life is a multi-dimensional concept that is defined and measured in many different ways in the social sciences. Sociologists, psychologists and economists, in particular, have adopted different statistical methods for evaluating and comparing quality of life in cities and metropolitan areas (see e.g. Diener and Suh, 1997; Blomquist, 2007; Lambiri *et al.*, 2007; D'Acci, 2014, for comprehensive reviews). In this chapter, we present a recently developed method to measure urban quality of life, the life satisfaction approach, with an application to Italian cities.

The most common method for measuring quality of life is the social indicators approach (Allardt, 1973; Erikson and Sharpe, 1987; Noll, 2004). Within this framework, a large set of indicators is identified as capturing the key dimensions of quality of life. The different indicators are then aggregated into a single index of quality of life by means of explicit or implicit weights (e.g. Commission of the European Communities, 1999, 2009, 2010; European Environment Agency, 2009; OECD, 2011). The main problem with this approach, commonly adopted by sociologists, is that it can be viewed as paternalistic. Both the selection of the underlying component indicators and, more importantly, the choice of the values for the corresponding weights, are to a large extent arbitrary.

An alternative approach, commonly adopted by psychologists, is based on subjective (self-reported) evaluations (see e.g. Diener, 1984; Myers, 1993; Diener *et al.*; 1999, Argyle, 2001). Within this framework, individuals are directly asked to rate their own quality of life, either overall or with respect to specific domains. The main advantage of this approach is that it does not require a preliminary definition of what variables are relevant for quality of life. The main problem, however, is that subjective measurement suffers from several types of biases. Ultimately, it may provide a measurement of the characteristics of the individuals living in a given place that affect perceived quality of life, rather than the actual quality of the place itself.

Among economists, the most popular approach is the hedonic price method. Within this framework, agents reveal their preferences for the bundle of attributes that characterize urban areas through their location decisions. The underlying assumption is that households and firms compete to locate in areas characterized by different levels of amenities and disamenities. In equilibrium, households are willing to pay higher housing prices, or accept lower wages, in order to locate in cities characterized by better amenities. Monetary valuations of local amenities can therefore be obtained from the marginal response of housing prices and wages to the presence of specific local amenities or disamenities. The main advantage of the hedonic price method is that the weights attributed to different amenities are derived from the agents' preferences, rather than the researcher's. Its main draw-back, however, is that it is based on the assumption of spatial equilibrium, which is unlikely to be met in practice. In addition, the hedonic price method is based on the unrealistic assumption of zero transaction and moving costs (see, e.g. Gyourko *et al.*, 1999; Van Praag and Baarsma, 2005; Bayer *et al.*, 2009, for a discussion).

More recently, the Life Satisfaction Approach has been proposed as an alter-native method for the valuation of non-market goods (Frey, 2008) and, more specifically, for environmental valuation (Ferreira and Moro, 2010; Frey *et al.*, 2010). This method is based on the assumption that local amenities (or dis-amenities) contribute to determine individual overall well-being. Self-reported life satisfaction, used as a proxy for subjective well-being, is thus modeled as a function of local amenities, while controlling for individual socio-demographic and economic characteristics. The resulting estimates are used to obtain a valu-ation of amenities in terms of well-being (Moro *et al.*, 2008). In addition, they can provide a monetary valuation derived from the marginal rate of substitution between income and individual amenities (Frey and Stutzer, 2002; Di Tella and MacCulloch, 2006).

The main advantage of the Life Satisfaction Approach is that it is not based on hypothetical decisions, as for instance in the contingent valuation method, so that it does not suffer from biases related to the virtual setting of the decision, social desirability or strategic behavior. In addition, the Life Satisfaction Approach does rely on the assumption of spatial equilibrium, as in the hedonic price method. While the hedonic price method provides indirect estimates of agents' prefer-ences, as inferred from equilibrium prices in housing and labor markets, the Life Satisfaction Approach aims at providing a direct measurement of preferences. On the other hand, the Life Satisfaction Approach relies crucially on the assumption that life satisfaction provides an appropriate proxy for utility and that it satisfies restrictive properties, such as cardinality and interpersonal comparability (Frey, 2008). It is commonly argued, instead, that self-reported well-being does not pro-vide a good proxy for individual utility, due to cognitive biases related to ordering effects, question wording and difference in scales (e.g. Bertrand and Mullainathan, 2001).

Several authors have investigated the life satisfaction value, and the corre-sponding monetary value, of environmental characteristics such as air pollution, weather, aircraft noise, local amenities and even environmental attitudes. In this chapter, we present an application of the Life Satisfaction Approach to measure quality of life in Italian cities. We use individual-level data for the 103 Italian province capitals to estimate the value of local amenities and construct a life

68 *Luca Stanca*

satisfaction index of quality of life. The analysis provides a ranking of Italian cities along several dimensions of quality of life (weather, environment, services and socio-demographic characteristics). In addition, it allows us to compare the results for the overall quality of life index based on the Life Satisfaction Approach with quality of life indices based on alternative approaches.

The chapter is structured as follows. Section 3.2 briefly sets the context, while Section 3.3 discusses previous studies using the Life Satisfaction Approach. Section 3.4 describes the data and methods, while Sections 3.5 and 3.6 present the results. Section 3.7 concludes with a brief discussion of the main findings and the implications of the analysis.

3.2 The economics and happiness revolution

Following the seminal contribution by Easterlin (1974), in the past three decades a growing number of studies have investigated the effects of demographic, social and economic conditions on subjective well-being, measured as self-reported levels of happiness or life satisfaction (see Blanchflower, 2008; Dolan *et al.*, 2008, for recent reviews). In this section, we briefly review this literature, in order to provide the context of the recently developed Life Satisfaction Approach to the measurement of quality of life.

The key empirical finding that originated in the literature on economics and happiness, generally referred to as the Easterlin paradox, can be summarized as follows: while across individuals and countries higher income results in higher happiness, over time income growth is not associated with higher happiness levels (Easterlin, 1974; Blanchflower and Oswald, 2004b; Stevenson and Wolfers, 2008). Among the many different interpretations of this paradox, it is possible to identify four main explanations based on hedonic, aspirational, positional and relational mechanisms. Intuitively, the common theme in all these explanations is that improvements in economic conditions are accompanied by changes in some other dimension of life that offset the impact on perceived well-being. This general idea is captured by the treadmill metaphor: while our material conditions improve, some other change occurs at the same time in the opposite direction, so that, similarly to the position of a runner during a treadmill workout, our life satisfaction remains unchanged.

The explanation based on the hedonic treadmill relates to habituation. In this view, changes in life circumstances only have temporary effects on subjective well-being. Subjects rapidly return to their baseline levels of well-being, which are largely determined by personality factors (Kahneman, 1999; Argyle, 2001; Lucas *et al.*, 2004). The satisfaction treadmill is based instead on changing aspirations (see Stutzer, 2004; Frey *et al.*, 2005; Bruni and Stanca, 2006). Subjective well-being depends on the gap between material achievements and aspirations. To the extent that aspirations rise together with income, subjective satisfaction may remain unchanged, even as income rises (Kahneman, 2000). The positional treadmill refers to the fact that people tend to compare their material conditions with those of some reference group. As a consequence, utility depends on relative,

Life satisfaction approach 69

rather than absolute, income. More recently, the relational treadmill has been proposed as an additional explanation for the income–happiness paradox: over time, the effect on happiness of better economic conditions is offset by lower consumption of relational goods (see, for example, Bruni and Stanca, 2008; Gui and Stanca, 2010).

Early studies in the economics and happiness literature focused on the effects of microeconomic conditions on well-being, while controlling for sociodemographic characteristics, factors related to personality and the external context. Income is generally found to be positively and significantly related to well-being across individuals and across countries (see Clark *et al.*, 2008, for a review). However, the effect is relatively small and diminishing. The evidence also indicates that being unemployed has a large negative effect on well-being (see, for example, Clark and Oswald, 1994; Winkelmann and Winkelmann, 1998) that goes well beyond the effects of income loss. Stanca (2010) investigates the spatial pattern of the effects of economic conditions on subjective well-being, using a large sample of individuals from 81 countries. The effect of income on well-being is found to be significantly stronger in countries with lower GDP per capita and higher unemployment rates. The effect of unemployment on well-being is instead significantly stronger in countries with higher GDP per capita and higher unemployment rates.

A number of studies have focused instead on the effects of macroeconomic conditions on individual well-being, indicating that both unemployment and inflation have significant adverse effects on individual happiness. Di Tella *et al.* (2001, 2003), using Eurobarometer data for 12 nations between 1975 and 1991, showed that subjective well-being is negatively related to both aggregate unemployment and inflation. Wolfers (2003), using Eurobarometer data for 16 nations, found that subjective well-being is negatively affected by macroeconomic volatility (the amplitude of business cycles).

The Life Satisfaction Approach has been used to shed light on the effects of a number of individual domains beyond economic conditions (see Scoppa and Ponzo, 2010, for an analysis based on Italian individual-level data). As for demographic characteristics, the literature generally finds a U-shaped relationship between age and happiness (Blanchflower and Oswald, 2004a; Easterlin, 2006; Ferrer-i-Carbonell and Gowdy, 2007). A second stylized fact is the existence of a positive gender happiness gap: ceteris paribus females report higher happiness than males (see Alesina *et al.*, 2004). However, this gap has fallen sharply in the past decades (Stevenson and Wolfers, 2008, 2009; Plagnol and Easterlin, 2008).

Regarding socially acquired characteristics, education is found to have a small but positive net effect on well-being (Blanchflower and Oswald, 2004b; Stutzer, 2004), similarly to health conditions and religious beliefs and activities. As for the effect of parenthood, Stanca (2012) finds that, in a large sample of individuals from 94 countries, having children has a negative effect on well-being. Conditioning on age, gender, marital status and education only partially helps to interpret this finding (see also Haller and Hadler, 2006; Hansen, 2012). The negative effect

70 *Luca Stanca*

of parenthood on well-being is explained by a large adverse impact on financial satisfaction, which on average dominates the positive impact on non-financial satisfaction.

Recent studies have also measured the value of social relations in terms of subjective well-being. Using a large sample of individuals from the World Values Survey, Bruni and Stanca (2008) show that relational goods have a significant and quantitatively relevant effect on life satisfaction. Interestingly, this effect is found to be stronger for social relations that are personalized and non-instrumental, such as active involvement in charities, church- and art-related volunteering activities, as opposed to unions, parties and environmental organizations. Following a similar approach, Becchetti *et al.* (2008, 2012) and Ateca-Amestoy *et al.* (2013) extend the analysis to different samples and data sets. Overall, these studies provide support to the relational treadmill.

3.3 Life satisfaction, environmental valuation and quality of life

In recent years the Life Satisfaction Approach has been extended to measure the economic value of several non-market goods. A large number of authors have used the Life Satisfaction Approach for environmental evaluation. Within this literature, the well-being effects of pollution have received great attention. Welsch (2002, 2006) investigates the effect of air pollution on well-being across nations, providing a monetary valuation of pollutant emissions. Ferreira *et al.* (2012), Rehdanz and Maddison (2005), Luechinger (2009, 2010) and Levinson (2012) find a significant negative relationship between air pollution and happiness. MacKerron and Mourato (2009) study the effects of air quality on the well-being of individuals living in the London area. Using spatially disaggregated data, they find that air pollution, both objective and perceived, has a significant negative effect.

Van Praag and Baarsma (2005) study the effects of aircraft noise on individuals living near the Amsterdam airport area, showing that well-being is negatively affected by perceived noise but not by objective noise (see also Rehdanz and Maddison, 2005). Brereton *et al.* (2008) investigate the effects of water pollution and proximity to wastelands in Ireland. Ambrey and Fleming (2013) and Smyth *et al.* (2008) investigate the impact of urban green on life satisfaction in Australian cities. Bertram and Rehdanz (2014) study the effect of the area of green space surrounding a respondent's home in Berlin.

Rehdanz and Maddison (2005) study the effects of climate on well-being in a panel of 67 countries, showing that well-being is positively related to higher temperatures in winter and lower temperatures in summer. They also find that rainfall reduces happiness, while daylight (proxied by latitude) does not affect subjective well-being. Within countries, Frijters and van Praag (1998) find that Russian households dislike cold winters and hot summers and rainfall is negatively associated with well-being, while daylight has a positive effect. Brereton *et al.* (2008) and Ferreira and Moro (2010) study the relationship between weather and individual well-being, finding that a warmer climate has a significant positive impact on subjective well-being. Ferrer-i-Carbonell and Gowdy (2007) examine the effects of environmental attitudes, finding that higher sensitivity to environmental issues is negatively related to subjective well-being. More recently, using European data on reported life satisfaction, Murray *et al.* (2013) find that individuals located in areas with lower than average levels of sunshine and higher than average levels of relative humidity are less satisfied with their lives.

In closely related studies, Moore and Shepherd (2006) and Frey *et al.* (2009) study the well-being effects of fear of crime and terrorism, respectively. The former study, based on UK data, indicates that a substantial increase in household income is required to offset the threat of physical violence. The latter study shows that a resident of Northern Ireland would be willing to pay between 26 percent and 37 percent of his income for a reduction in terrorist activity to a level that prevails in the more peaceful parts of the country. A resident of Paris would be willing to forego between 4 percent and 8 percent of his income. More recently, the Life Satisfaction Approach has been used to measure the monetary cost of commuting time (Frey and Stutzer, 2008), natural disasters such as floods (Luechinger and Raschky, 2009) and droughts (Carroll *et al.*, 2009), and wars (Frey, 2012). Several studies find significant effects of city characteristics, such as perceived crime, on subjective well-being (Lelkes, 2006). City size has also been found to negatively affect subjective well-being (see, for example, Piper, 2013). Florida *et al.* (2013) study the determinants of the happiness of cities. Using metropolitan-level data from the 2009 Gallup Healthways Survey, they find that human capital plays a key role for the happiness of cities.

A smaller number of studies use the Life Satisfaction Approach to measure the monetary value of social relations. Clark and Oswald (2002) estimated the monetary value of life events, showing that, relative to being single, marriage is worth about £75,000 a year for a representative individual in the United Kingdom. More recently, Powdthavee (2008) adopted a similar approach to estimate the monetary value of interactions with friends, relatives and neighbors. The findings, based on the British Household Panel Survey, indicate that an increase in the level of social involvement is worth up to £85,000 a year in terms of life satisfaction.

Stanca (2009) uses the Life Satisfaction Approach to construct composite indicators of quality of relational life. Implicit valuations estimated from microeconometric life satisfaction equations are used to weigh scores on several dimensions of relational life. The method is applied to a large sample of individuals from 94 countries, producing composite indicators that focus on three dimensions of interpersonal relations: friends, family and society. Overall, the results indicate that, at the individual level, better economic conditions are associated with higher quality of interpersonal relationships. Colombo and Stanca (2014) use the hedonic approach to measure the monetary price of social relations capitals in Italian cities, focusing on time spent with friends, active participation in associations and frequency of going out for leisure activities. Based on the estimated price of relational amenities, they construct monetary indices of quality of relational

72 Luca Stanca

life. The findings indicate that individuals are willing to pay a positive and significant monetary price to live in cities where people spend more time with their friends.

In a paper closely related to the present work, Moro *et al.* (2008) use subjective well-being to estimate the implicit price of local amenities and construct a quality of life index for Irish regions. Also related to the present work, Oswald and Wu (2010) use a large sample of individuals from the Behavioral Risk Factor Surveillance System to study the consistency between subjective and objective indicators of well-being. They find a strong and significant relationship between quality of life, as measured by hedonic indices, and subjective well-being across states in the United States.

3.4 Data and methods

Our analysis is based on two data sets covering 103 Italian provinces, corresponding to NUTS 3 level (Nomenclature of Territorial Units for Statistics). We focus on cities defined as the municipalities of province capitals. The unit of analysis is therefore the municipal area of province capitals.

The first data set provides city-level information about local amenities. Information on local amenities and characteristics for the municipalities of the 103 Italian provinces for the period 2001–2010 has been collected from the Italian National Statistical Office (ISTAT) and other sources. Our analysis focuses on the same set of city-level amenities analyzed in Colombo *et al.* (2014). This set includes 12 amenities that can be divided into four different domains: climate, environment, services and society (see Colombo *et al.*, 2014, for details, definitions and summary statistics).

Climate is measured by maximum temperature in January, precipitation (monthly average) and humidity (maximum in July). The environmental domain is based on both physical features of the territory (percentage of green areas in the city and a dummy variable indicating a coastal city) and pollution (number of air-polluting agents). Indicators of quality of services focus on education (teacher–pupil ratio), culture (an index of cultural infrastructure, capturing several dimensions of the city's cultural offerings, such as museums, cinemas, theaters, etc.), and transport infrastructure (a multi-modal indicator of accessibility by air, train or car). The society domain refers to socio-economic conditions of cities, as measured by crime rate, population density and unemployment rate. The unemployment rate is included among the amenities, since it is an important determinant of social conditions and individual well-being, over and above its pure economic costs (see Roback, 1982; Buettner and Ebertz, 2009).

The second data set, providing individual-level information about well-being and socio-demographic characteristics, is the survey Aspects of Daily Life, conducted annually by the Italian Statistical Office (ISTAT, 2010) on a rotating sample of about 19,000 households (50,000 individuals) per year. This survey, which is part of the *Multiscopo* integrated system of social surveys, is designed to be

Life satisfaction approach 73

Table 3.1 Individual characteristics, descriptive statistics

	Mean	*St.Dev.*	*Min.*	*Max.*	*N.*
Life satisfaction	7.01	16.70	0	10	31168
Age	45.28	23.16	15	106	36311
Male	0.47	0.50	0	1	36314
Married	0.47	0.50	0	1	34559
Separated	0.05	0.23	0	1	34559
Divorced	0.03	0.17	0	1	34559
Widowed	0.09	0.29	0	1	34559
Couple with children	0.50	0.50	0	1	36311
Couple without children	0.20	0.40	0	1	36311
Single male with children	0.02	0.12	0	1	36311
Single female with children	0.10	0.30	0	1	36311
Upper education	0.16	0.37	0	1	34559
Lower education	0.49	0.50	0	1	34559
Work: Unemployed	0.09	0.28	0	1	31797
Work: Housewife	0.15	0.36	0	1	31797
Work: Student	0.08	0.28	0	1	31797
Work: Unable	0.01	0.10	0	1	31797
Work: Retired	0.23	0.42	0	1	31797
Work: Other	0.02	0.12	0	1	36314
Year 2010	0.34	0.47	0	1	36311
Year 2011	0.33	0.47	0	1	36311
Year 2012	0.33	0.47	0	1	36311

Source: Istat (2010).

representative of the Italian population at province level. The survey provides detailed information on several aspects of the daily life of individuals and families, ranging from family relations to household characteristics, health and lifestyle. We consider three annual waves (2010, 2011 and 2012), as the life satisfaction variable was not present in the survey in previous years. Table 3.1 presents descriptive statistics. The overall sample is equally distributed into the three annual waves. Life satisfaction is available for about 31,000 individuals, with an average value of 7.01 in the sample.

Life satisfaction is measured on a scale between 1 and 10, based on the following question: "At present, how satisfied are you with your life as a whole?" This variable is available for 92 cities, and the average value in the overall sample is 7.01. Over time, average life satisfaction was 7.11 and 7.12 in 2010 and 2011, while it fell to 6.79 in 2012. Figure 3.1 displays the geographic distribution of average life satisfaction across Italian cities in each of the three years. Satisfaction with life is generally higher in northern cities, while relatively similar in the remaining parts of the country.

Table 3.2 reports the city ranking for average life satisfaction in the overall sample. Life satisfaction is highest, on average, in Mantova (8.04), Savona (7.77), and Como (7.68), while it is lowest, in Viterbo (6.11), Enna (6.17) and Oristano (6.33). Roma has a relatively row rank (66), while Milano is in the upper part of

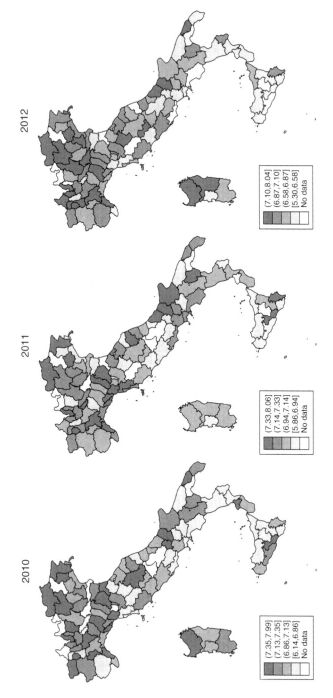

Figure 3.1 Life satisfaction across cities, by year.

Source: Author's own construct.

Table 3.2 Life satisfaction, city ranking

Ranking	City	Life satisfaction
1	Mantova	8.04
2	Savona	7.77
3	Como	7.68
4	Bolzano	7.59
5	Ravenna	7.58
6	Brindisi	7.56
7	Chieti	7.49
8	Alessandria	7.48
9	Biella	7.48
10	Lodi	7.43
11	Trento	7.39
12	Treviso	7.38
13	Verbania	7.38
14	Campobasso	7.35
15	La Spezia	7.35
16	Modena	7.34
17	Foggia	7.31
18	Trieste	7.29
19	Udine	7.29
20	Sassari	7.29
21	Massa	7.29
22	Aosta	7.28
23	Parma	7.27
24	Lecco	7.25
25	Padova	7.25
26	Matera	7.23
27	Varese	7.21
28	Nuoro	7.19
29	Bologna	7.18
30	Siracusa	7.16
31	Gorizia	7.15
32	Pesaro	7.15
33	Caltanissetta	7.14
34	Pavia	7.13
35	Milano	7.12
36	Rimini	7.11
37	Perugia	7.10
38	Vicenza	7.09
39	Cremona	7.07
40	Rovigo	7.07
41	Lecce	7.07
42	Macerata	7.07
43	Lucca	7.06
44	Vercelli	7.06
45	Brescia	7.05
46	Reggio Emilia	7.05
47	Terni	7.05
48	Potenza	7.04
49	Pordenone	7.04
50	Grosseto	7.03
51	Firenze	7.03
52	Verona	7.03

(*Continued*)

Table 3.2 (Continued)

Ranking	City	Life satisfaction
53	Ascoli Piceno	7.02
54	Asti	7.02
55	Prato	7.01
56	Genova	6.99
57	Cagliari	6.96
58	Salerno	6.95
59	Forli	6.95
60	Teramo	6.94
61	Venezia	6.94
62	Torino	6.94
63	Bergamo	6.94
64	Ferrara	6.92
65	Vibo Valentia	6.92
66	Roma	6.91
67	Arezzo	6.91
68	Cuneo	6.89
69	Novara	6.88
70	Imperia	6.86
71	Pisa	6.86
72	Reggio Calabria	6.85
73	Livorno	6.85
74	Ancona	6.82
75	Benevento	6.81
76	Pistoia	6.80
77	Siena	6.79
78	Messina	6.78
79	Rieti	6.77
80	Piacenza	6.76
81	Trapani	6.75
82	Catania	6.73
83	Napoli	6.72
84	Isernia	6.70
85	Pescara	6.70
86	Frosinone	6.69
87	Catanzaro	6.67
88	Avellino	6.65
89	Caserta	6.63
90	Cosenza	6.63
91	Palermo	6.61
92	Bari	6.59
93	Agrigento	6.53
94	Crotone	6.53
95	Latina	6.43
96	L'Aquila	6.40
97	Ragusa	6.40
98	Oristano	6.33
99	Enna	6.17
100	Viterbo	6.11
101	Belluno	
102	Sondrio	
103	Taranto	

Source: Istat (2010).

Life satisfaction approach 77

the ranking (35). Life satisfaction data are not available for Belluno, Sondrio and Taranto.

Our analysis is based on the Life Satisfaction Approach, as described in detail in Frey *et al.* (2010) and Moro *et al.* (2008). We estimate the parameters of an empirical specification, where the self-reported life satisfaction of an individual in a given city is assumed to be a linear function of a set of city-specific amenities and a set of individual characteristics. The quality of life index is then obtained by computing the predicted life satisfaction in each city for a representative agent with average individual characteristics. The quality of life index thus changes across cities because of the different endowments of amenities, which are weighted using the corresponding estimated life satisfaction prices.

The set of urban amenities/disamenities was described in the previous section. Cities' unobserved heterogeneity is also controlled for by including population size and a dummy for region capitals. It is important to observe that the choice of the explanatory variables is crucial in constructing Life Satisfaction Approach quality of life indices. Rankings may be sensitive to the variables included. Therefore, the results should be taken with caution, because the rankings obtained may reflect data availability.

Individual characteristics include gender, age, marital status (single, married, separated, divorced, widowed), type of family (couple with children, couple

Table 3.3 Well-being and individual characteristics

Individual characteristics	OLS	Ordered logit
Male	−0.42*	−0.04*
Age	−0.25**	−0.03**
Age squared	0.00**	0.00**
Married	2.88**	0.33**
Separated	0.93	0.11
Divorced	0.07	0.02
Widowed	0.67	0.08
Couple with children	1.44**	0.18**
Couple without children	2.39**	0.28**
Single male with children	−0.34	−0.08
Single female with children	−1.72**	−0.18**
Upper education	2.19**	0.26**
Lower education	−2.16**	−0.23**
Work: Unemployed	−7.43**	−0.82**
Work: Housewife	−1.13*	−0.14**
Work: Student	1.60*	0.21**
Work: Unable	−12.66**	−1.18**
Work: Retired	0.34	0.03
Work: Other	−7.22**	−0.77**
R-squared	0.07	0.02
Number of observations	30873	30873

Source: Istat (2010).

78 Luca Stanca

without children, single male with children, single female with children, single without children), education level (upper, medium, lower) and employment status (employed, unemployed, housewife, student, unable to work, retired, other). Year dummies are also included to account for time-fixed effects.

The resulting specification is estimated by either ordinary least squares or ordered logit, in order to allow for the ordinal nature of the dependent variable. The estimation sample includes about 31,000 observations. In order to ease the interpretation of coefficient estimates, the dependent variable (life satisfaction) is multiplied by 10. Robust standard errors are clustered at the city level in order to allow for within-city correlation and explanatory variables that are both at the individual and the city level.

Based on the estimated weights described above, a life satisfaction quality of life index is obtained by computing the predicted life satisfaction in each city for a representative agent with average individual characteristics. Similarly, domain-specific indices are obtained by focusing only on differences in the corresponding component variables, while setting all other amenities at their average value.

Table 3.4 Well-being and local amenities, net effects

Factors affecting well-being	OLS	Ordered logit
Precipitation	0.00	0.00
	(0.01)	(0.00)
Temperature	−0.23	−0.04*
	(0.13)	(0.02)
Humidity	0.05	0.00
	(0.06)	(0.01)
Coast	0.77	0.13
	(0.64)	(0.08)
Green areas	−0.02	0.00
	(0.02)	(0.00)
Air pollution	0.06	0.01
	(0.10)	(0.01)
Teacher–pupil ratio	0.66**	0.09**
	(0.19)	(0.02)
Transport infrastructure	−0.01	0.00
	(0.01)	(0.00)
Culture infrastructure	0.01**	0.00**
	(0.00)	(0.00)
Violent crime	−0.12	−0.01
	(0.14)	(0.02)
Urban density	−0.04	−0.01
	(0.17)	(0.02)
Unemployment rate	−0.05	−0.01
	(0.06)	(0.01)
R-squared	0.07	0.02
Number of observations	30873	30873

Source: ISTAT and other sources, as detailed in Section 5.3.

3.5 The life satisfaction value of amenities

Table 3.3 presents the results for the baseline specification, focusing on demographic and socio-economic individual characteristics. The results are generally consistent with the literature. Ceteris paribus, males are on average less satisfied with their life than females. Age has an inverted U-shape effect on life satisfaction. Married people are significantly more satisfied with their life than singles, and the difference is large (2.9 points on a 1–100 scale) and strongly significant. Being separated, divorced or widowed does not imply significant differences in life satisfaction with respect to being single. Interestingly, couples with children are less satisfied with their lives than couples without children (Stanca, 2012). Similarly, among single parents, the negative effect of having children is stronger for females than for males, so that only females with children are significantly less satisfied with their life than single parents without children. Education has a significant positive effect on life satisfaction, while unemployment has a very large and strongly significant negative effect.

Table 3.4 reports coefficient estimates for the full set of amenities entered jointly, so that the coefficients represent the net effect of individual amenities on well-being. The results are virtually unchanged across the two estimation methods. Focusing on the ordinary least squares results, local amenities are jointly strongly significant ($p < 0.01$). Individually, life satisfaction is significantly higher in cities where the teacher–pupil ratio is higher ($p < 0.01$) and cultural infrastructure is higher ($p < 0.01$). In the ordered logit results, temperature is also significant, although with a negative coefficient. Estimates for all other amenities do not always have the expected sign, but are not statistically significant.

In order to provide a consistency check, Table 3.5 reports ordinary least squares estimates obtained by entering each amenity separately. The coefficients can therefore be interpreted as the gross effects of individual amenities on well-being. The results indicate that, controlling only for individual characteristics, life satisfaction is significantly lower, on average, in cities where temperature or unemployment are higher, and in cities located on the coast. Life satisfaction is, instead, lower in cities where the teacher–pupil ratio is higher.

3.6 Quality of life in Italian cities

Figure 3.2 displays the geographic distribution of the overall life satisfaction quality of life index. Quality of life displays a clear spatial pattern, as it is generally higher in cities in the north of Italy and lower in cities in the south of Italy and the main islands (Sicilia and Sardinia). The map also shows a clustering pattern, as neighboring cities are characterized by similar levels of the quality of life index.

Table 3.6 reports the city-ranking for the life satisfaction quality of life index. The results indicate that amenities account for substantial variation in life satisfaction quality of life. The cities with the highest quality of life are Bolzano and Trento, with an index of 7.55 and 7.46, respectively. Considering that the average quality of life in the sample is 7.16, these results indicate that, on average, the

Table 3.5 Well-being and local amenities, gross effects

Factors affecting well-being	(1)	(2)	(3)	(4)	(5)	(6)	(7)	(8)	(9)	(10)	(11)	(12)
Precipitation	0.02 (0.01)											
Temperature		−0.26** (0.06)										
Humidity			0.01 (0.06)									
Coast				−1.11* (0.51)								
Green areas					−0.05 (0.03)							
Air pollution						0.19 (0.10)						
Teacher-pupil ratio							0.57* (0.28)					
Transport infrastructure								0.01 (0.01)				
Culture infrastructure									0.01 (0.00)			
Violent crime										0.03 (0.13)		
Urban density											−0.16 (0.09)	
Unemployment rate												−0.11** −0.03
R-squared	0.07	0.07	0.07	0.07	0.07	0.07	0.07	0.07	0.07	0.07	0.07	0.07
Number of observations	30873	30873	30873	30873	30873	30873	30873	30873	30873	30873	30873	30873

Source: ISTAT and other sources, as detailed in Section 5.3.

Life satisfaction approach 81

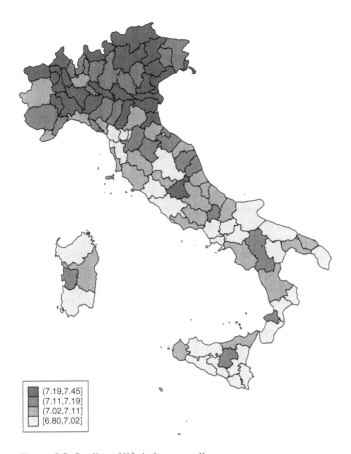

Figure 3.2 Quality of life index, overall.

Source: Author's own construct.

quality of life of individuals living in cities with the best bundle of amenities is estimated to be about 5 percent higher than individuals living in cities with average levels of amenities. At the bottom of the ranking are large cities of the south, such as Palermo (6.93), Roma (6.94) and Napoli (6.98).

Figure 3.3 displays the geographic distribution of the life satisfaction quality of life indices for each of the four life domains being considered. A clear north–south divide can be observed in the weather and society domains, where cities in the north generally display higher quality of life. This geographic pattern is less clear-cut for the environment and services domains.

Table 3.7 reports pair-wise correlations of the life satisfaction quality of life indices, overall and by domain. The overall index is strongly and significantly correlated with the weather, society and services domains, while only weakly related to the environment domain.

Table 3.6 Quality of life (overall), city ranking

Ranking	City	Quality of life
1	Bolzano	7.55
2	Trento	7.46
3	Trieste	7.40
4	Verbania	7.37
5	Vercelli	7.37
6	Treviso	7.35
7	Gorizia	7.34
8	Cremona	7.33
9	Venezia	7.33
10	Novara	7.32
11	Pavia	7.32
12	Rovigo	7.31
13	Ferrara	7.30
14	Alessandria	7.30
15	Rieti	7.29
16	Modena	7.29
17	Aosta	7.29
18	Piacenza	7.29
19	Lodi	7.29
20	Padova	7.28
21	Sondrio	7.28
22	Asti	7.28
23	Como	7.28
24	Udine	7.28
25	Vibo Valentia	7.28
26	Varese	7.27
27	Vicenza	7.27
28	Biella	7.27
29	Isernia	7.26
30	Mantova	7.26
31	Pordenone	7.26
32	Belluno	7.26
33	Enna	7.26
34	Firenze	7.25
35	Verona	7.25
36	Savona	7.24
37	Lecco	7.24
38	Macerata	7.23
39	Bergamo	7.23
40	Bologna	7.23
41	Potenza	7.23
42	Reggio Emilia	7.22
43	Ravenna	7.22
44	Imperia	7.22
45	Arezzo	7.21
46	Milano	7.20
47	Cuneo	7.19
48	Nuoro	7.19
49	Frosinone	7.19
50	Livorno	7.19
51	Messina	7.19
52	Forli	7.19

Table 3.6 (Continued)

Ranking	City	Quality of life
53	Oristano	7.19
54	Cosenza	7.19
55	Avellino	7.18
56	La Spezia	7.18
57	Rimini	7.18
58	Ascoli Piceno	7.17
59	Terni	7.17
60	Pesaro	7.17
61	Parma	7.17
62	Siena	7.16
63	Caserta	7.16
64	Brescia	7.16
65	Lucca	7.16
66	Latina	7.16
67	Trapani	7.16
68	Benevento	7.15
69	Brindisi	7.14
70	Campobasso	7.14
71	Salerno	7.14
72	Pescara	7.13
73	Genova	7.13
74	Cagliari	7.13
75	Grosseto	7.13
76	Viterbo	7.13
77	Torino	7.12
78	Perugia	7.12
79	Reggio Calabria	7.12
80	Chieti	7.12
81	Matera	7.12
82	Taranto	7.11
83	Lecce	7.11
84	Teramo	7.11
85	Ancona	7.11
86	Prato	7.11
87	Catanzaro	7.11
88	Sassari	7.09
89	Crotone	7.09
90	Siracusa	7.09
91	Ragusa	7.09
92	Pistoia	7.08
93	Massa	7.08
94	L'Aquila	7.07
95	Foggia	7.07
96	Pisa	7.04
97	Bari	7.03
98	Agrigento	7.02
99	Catania	7.01
100	Caltanissetta	7.00
101	Napoli	6.98
102	Roma	6.94
103	Palermo	6.93

Source: ISTAT (2010).

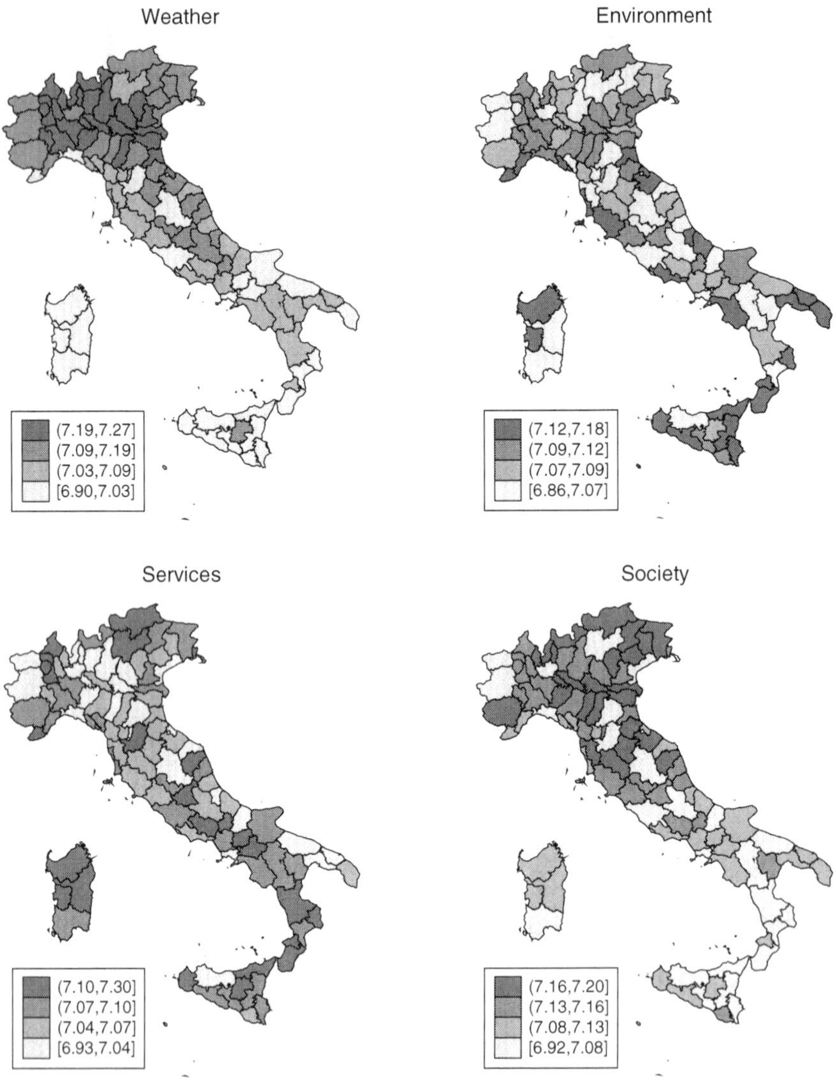

84 *Luca Stanca*

Figure 3.3 Quality of life, individual domains.

Source: Author's own construct.

Table 3.7 also reports, in the bottom part, pair-wise correlations between the life satisfaction quality of life indices and the corresponding indices obtained by Colombo *et al.* (2014), using the hedonic price approach. It should be observed that the correlation between the life satisfaction indices and the hedonic price overall quality of life indices is low (0.03) and not statistically significant ($p = 0.08$).

Table 3.7 QoL indices, pairwise correlations

QoL indices	(1)	(2)	(3)	(4)	(5)	(6)	(7)	(8)	(9)
QoL LSA (1)									
QoL LSA - Weather (2)	0.77								
	(0.00)								
QoL LSA - Environment (3)	0.11	−0.04							
	(0.26)	(0.69)							
QoL LSA - Services (4)	0.32	−0.09	0.21						
	(0.00)	(0.35)	(0.03)						
QoL LSA - Society (5)	0.56	0.70	0.29	0.13					
	(0.00)	(0.00)	(0.00)	(0.19)					
QoL HP (6)	0.02	0.03	−0.15	−0.33	0.12				
	(0.87)	0.76	0.13	0.00	0.24				
QoL HP - Weather (7)	−0.73	−0.90	0.32	0.22	−0.45	−0.15			
	(0.00)	(0.00)	(0.00)	(0.02)	(0.00)	(0.12)			
QoL HP - Environment (8)	−0.45	−0.50	0.18	−0.01	−0.35	0.27	0.51		
	(0.00)	(0.00)	(0.07)	(0.91)	(0.00)	(0.01)	(0.00)		
QoL HP - Services (9)	0.22	0.38	−0.28	−0.37	0.03	0.64	−0.55	−0.24	
	(0.02)	(0.00)	(0.00)	(0.00)	(0.73)	(0.00)	(0.00)	(0.01)	
QoL HP - Society (10)	0.65	0.74	−0.31	−0.25	0.58	0.51	−0.83	−0.49	0.55
	(0.00)	(0.00)	(0.00)	−(0.01)	(0.00)	(0.00)	(0.00)	(0.00)	(0.00)

Source: ISTAT (2010).

3.7 Conclusions

Research on economics and happiness has generally provided several important policy implications (see, for example, Layard, 2005; Frey, 2008). This chapter presented an application of the Life Satisfaction Approach to measure and compare urban quality of life. Focusing on Italian cities, we used micro-level data for subjective well-being and individual characteristics, together with city-level data on local amenities, to estimate the well-being valuation of local amenities. We obtained implicit prices for local amenities within four domains: weather, environment, services and society. These implicit prices were used to construct quality of life indices for the municipalities of the 103 Italian provinces.

It is important to observe that there are several difficulties in applying the Life Satisfaction Approach to value environmental amenities, as it crucially relies on the assumption that life satisfaction provides an appropriate proxy for utility, while satisfying cardinality and interpersonal comparability. Nevertheless, our analysis provides an important step towards a direct measurement of the value of local amenities and urban quality of life.

Our analysis provided a ranking of Italian cities along several dimensions of quality of life. We found that quality of life is higher in medium-sized cities located in the north, while generally lower in larger cities in the south. The quality of life of individuals living in cities with the best bundle of amenities is about 5 percent higher than individuals living in cities with average levels of amenities. We also compared the results for the quality of life index based on life satisfaction

86 *Luca Stanca*

with quality of life indices based on alternative approaches. Interestingly, the results indicate that the life satisfaction QoL index is only weakly correlated with a hedonic QoL index based on the same set of amenities. This indicates that market prices and subjective well-being may provide different valuations of local amenities.

Bibliography

Allardt, E. (1973) *Individual Needs, Social Structures, and Indicators of National Development*, Beverly Hills, CA: Sage Publications.

Alesina, A., Di Tella, R. and MacCulloch, R. (2004) "Inequality and Happiness: Are Europeans and Americans Different?," *Journal of Public Economics*, 88, pp. 2009–2042.

Ambrey, C. L. and Fleming, C. M. (2013) "Public Greenspace and Life Satisfaction in Urban Australia," *Urban Studies*, pp. 1–32.

Argyle, M. (2001) *The Psychology of Happiness*, New York: Taylor & Francis.

Ateca-Amestoy, V., Aguilar, A. and Moro-Egido, A. (2013) "Social Interactions and Life Satisfaction: Evidence from Latin America," *Journal of Happiness Studies*, 108(3), pp. 453–490.

Bayer, P., Keohane, N. and Timmins, C. (2009) "Migration and Hedonic Valuation: The Case of Air Quality," *Journal of Environmental Economics and Management*, 58(1), pp. 1–14.

Becchetti, L., Pelloni, A. and Rossetti, F. (2008) "Relational Goods, Sociability, and Happiness," *Kyklos*, 61, pp. 343–363.

Becchetti, L., Giachin Ricca, E. and Pelloni, A. (2012) "The Relationship betweeen Social Leisure and Life Satisfaction: Causality and Policy Implications," *Social Indicators Research*, 108(3), pp. 453–490.

Bertram, C. and Rehdanz, K. (2014) "The Role of Urban Green Space for Human Well-being, Institute for New Economic Thinking," Working Paper no. 1911.

Bertrand, M. and Mullainathan, S. (2001) "Do People Mean What They Say? Implications for Subjective Survey Data," *American Economic Review*, 91(2), pp. 67–72.

Blanchflower, D. G. (2008) "International Evidence on Well-Being," NBER Working Paper, no. 14318.

Blanchflower, D. G. and Oswald, A. J. (2004a) "Money, sex and happiness: An empirical study," *Scandinavian Journal of Economics*, 106(3), pp. 393–415.

Blanchflower, D. G. and Oswald, A. J. (2004b) "Well-being Over Time in Britain and the USA," *Journal of Public Economics*, 88, pp. 1359–1386.

Blomquist, G. (2007) "Measuring Quality of Life," in Arnott, R. and McMillen, D. (eds.), *A Companion to Urban Economics*, Oxford: Blackwell-Synergy, pp. 483–501.

Brereton, F., Clinch, J. P. and Ferreira, S. (2008) "Happiness, Geography and the Environment," *Ecological Economics*, 65, pp. 386–396.

Bruni, L. and Stanca, L. (2006) "Income Aspirations, Television and Happiness: Evidence from the World Values Survey," *Kyklos*, 59(2), pp. 209–225.

Bruni, L. and Stanca, L. (2008) "Watching alone: Relational Goods, Television and Happiness," *Journal of Economic Behavior and Organization*, 65(3–4), pp. 506–528.

Buettner, T. and Ebertz, A. (2009) "Quality of Life in the Regions: Results for German Countries," *Annals of Regional Science*, 43, pp. 89–112.

Carroll, N., Frijters, P. and Shields, M. A. (2009) "Quantifying the Costs of Drought: New Evidence from Life Satisfaction Data," *Journal of Population Economics*, 22, pp. 445–461.

Clark, A., Frijters, P. and Shields, M. A. (2008) "Relative Income, Happiness and Utility: An Explanation for the Easterlin Paradox and Other Puzzles," *Journal of Economic Literature*, 46(1), pp. 95–144.

Clark, A. E. and Oswald, A. J. (1994) "Unhappiness and Unemployment," *Economic Journal*, 104, pp. 648–659.

Clark, A. and Oswald, A. (1996) "Satisfaction and Comparison Income," *Journal of Public Economics*, 61(3), pp. 359–381.

Clark, A. and Oswald, A. (2002) "A Simple Statistical Method for Measuring How Life Events Affect Happiness," *International Journal of Epidemiology*, 31(6), pp. 1139–1144.

Colombo, E. and Stanca, L. (2014) "Measuring the Monetary Value of Social Relations: A Hedonic Approach," *Journal of Behavioral and Experimental Economics*, 50, pp. 77–87.

Colombo, E., Michelangeli, A. and Stanca, L. (2014) "La Dolce Vita: Hedonic Estimates of Quality of Life in Italian Cities," *Regional Studies*, 48(8), pp. 1404–1418.

Commission of the European Communities (1999) *Evaluation of Quality of Life in European Regions*, Committee of the Regions – EU, Brussels.

Commission of the European Communities (2009) *GDP and Beyond, Measuring Progress in a Changing World*, Brussels.

Commission of the European Communities (2010) *Survey on Perceptions of Quality of Life in 75 European Cities*, Brussels.

D'Acci, L. (2014) "Monetary, Subjective and Quantitative Approaches to Assess Urban Quality of Life and Pleasantness in Cities (Hedonic Price, Willingness-to-Pay, Positional Value, Life Satisfaction, Isobenefit Lines)," *Social Indicators Research*, 115, pp. 531–559.

Di Tella, R., MacCulloch, R. J. and Oswald, A. J. (2001) "Preferences over Inflation and Unemployment: Evidence from Surveys of Happiness," *American Economic Review*, 91(1), pp. 335–341.

Di Tella, R., MacCulloch, R. J. and Oswald, A. J. (2003) "The Macroeconomics of Happiness," *The Review of Economics and Statistics*, 85(4), pp. 809–827.

Di Tella, R. and MacCulloch, R. J. (2006) "Some Uses of Happiness Data in Economics," *Journal of Economic Perspectives*, 20(1), pp. 25–46.

Diener, Ed (1984) "Subjective Well-Being," *Psychological Bulletin*, 95(3), pp. 542–575.

Diener, E. and Suh, E. M. (1997) "Measuring Quality Of Life: Economic, Social and Subjective Indicators," *Social Indicators Research*, 40, pp. 189–216.

Diener, E., Suh, E. M., Lucas, R. E. and Smith, H. L. (1999) "Subjective Well-Being: Three Decades of Progress," *Psychological Bulletin*, 125(2), pp. 276–302.

Dolan, P., Peasgood, T. and White, M. (2008) "Do We Really Know What Makes Us Happy? A Review of the Economic Literature on the Factors Associated with Subjective Well-Being," *Journal of Economic Psychology*, 29, pp. 94–122.

Easterlin, R. A. (1974) "Does Economic Growth Improve the Human Lot?," in David, P. A. and Reder, M. W. (eds.), *Nations and Households in Economic Growth: Essays in Honor of Moses Abramovitz*, New York: Academic Press, pp. 89–125.

Easterlin, R. (2006) "Life Cycle Happiness and its Sources. Intersections of Psychology, Economics and Demography", *Journal of Economic Psychology*, 27, pp. 463–482.

Erikson, R. and Sharpe, M. E. (1987) *The Scandinavian Model. Welfare States and Welfare Research*, New York: M. E. Sharpe.

88 Luca Stanca

European Environment Agency (2009) *Ensuring Quality of life in Europe's Cities and Towns*, Report no. 5/2009.

Ferreira, S. and Moro, M. (2010) "On the Use of Subjective Well-being Data for Environmental Valuation," *Environmental and Resource Economics*, 46, pp. 249–273.

Ferreira, S., Moro, M. and Clinch, J. P. (2006) "Transaction Costs and Hedonic Valuation: The Case for a Life Satisfaction Approach," Working Paper, Planning and Environmental Policy Series, University College Dublin.

Ferreira, S., Akay, A., Brereton, F., Cunado, J., Martinsson, P. and Moro, M. (2012) "Life Satisfaction and Air Quality in Europe", IZA Discussion Paper 6732, Institute for the Study of Labor, Bonn, Germany.

Ferrer-i-Carbonell, A. and Gowdy, J. M. (2007) "Environmental Degradation and Happiness," *Ecological Economics*, 60(3), pp. 509–516.

Florida, R., Mellander, C. and Rentfrow, P. (2013) "The Happiness of Cities," *Regional Studies*, 47(4), pp. 613–627.

Frank, R. (2005) "Does Absolute Income Matter?," in Bruni, L. and Porta, P. (eds.), *Economics and Happiness: Framing the Analysis*, Oxford: Oxford University Press, pp. 145–165.

Frey, B. S. (2008) *Happiness: A Revolution in Economics*, Cambridge, MA: MIT Press Books.

Frey, B. S. (2012) "Well-being and war," *International Review of Economics*, 59(4), pp. 363–375.

Frey, B. S. and Stutzer, A. (2002) "What Can Economists Learn From Happiness Research?," *Journal of Economic Literature*, 40(2), pp. 402–435.

Frey, B. S. and Stutzer, A. (2008) "Stress that Doesn't Pay: The Commuting Paradox," *Scandinavian Journal of Economics*, 110(2), pp. 339–366.

Frey, B. S., Benesch, C. and Stutzer, A. (2005) "Does watching TV make us happy?," Institute for Empirical Research in Economics, University of Zurich, Working Paper no. 241.

Frey, B. S., Luechinger, S. and Stutzer, A. (2009) "The Life Satisfaction Approach to Valuing Public Goods: The Case of Terrorism," *Public Choice*, 138(3), pp. 317–345.

Frey, B., Luechinger, S. and Stutzer, A. (2010) "The Life Satisfaction Approach to Environmental Valuation," *Annual Review of Resource Economics*, 2(1), pp. 139–160.

Frijters, P. and van Praag, B. M. S. (1998) "The Effects of Climate on Welfare and Well-being in Russia?," *Climate Change*, 39, pp. 61–81.

Gui, B. and Stanca, L. (2010) "Happiness and Relational Goods: Well-being and Interpersonal Relations in the Economic Sphere," *International Review of Economics*, 57(2), pp. 105–118.

Gyourko, J., Kahn, M. and Tracy, J. (1999) "Quality of Life and Environmental Comparisons," in E. S. Mills and P. Cheshire (eds.), *Handbook of Applied Urban Economics*, vol. 3, Amsterdam: Elsevier, pp. 1413–1454.

Haller, M. and Hadler, M. (2006) "How Social Relations and Structures can Produce Happiness and Unhappiness: An International Comparative Analysis," *Social Indicators Research*, 75, pp. 169–216.

Hansen, T. (2012) "Parenthood and Happiness: A Review of Folk Theories versus Empirical Evidence," *Social Indicators Research*, 108, pp. 29–64.

ISTAT (2010) *La vita quotidiana nel 2008 - Indagine multiscopo annuale sulle famiglie, Aspetti della vita quotidiana*, Rome.

Kahneman, D. (1999) "Objective Happiness", in Kahneman, D., Diener, E. and Schwartz, N. (eds.), *Well-Being: Foundations of Hedonic Psychology*, New York: Rassel Sage Foundation, pp. 3–25.

Kahneman, D. (2000) "Experienced Utility and Objective Happiness: A Moment-Based Approach", in Kahneman, D. and Tversky, A. (eds.), *Choices, Values and Frames*, New York: Cambridge University Press, pp. 1–26.

Lambiri, D., Biagi, B. and Royuela, V. (2007) "Quality of Life in the Economic and Urban Economic Literature," *Social Indicators Research*, 84, pp. 1–25.

Layard, R. (2005) *Happiness: Lessons from a New Science*, New York: Penguin.

Lelkes, O. (2006) "Knowing What is Good for You: Empirical Analysis of Personal Preferences and the 'objective good'," *Journal of Behavioral and Experimental Economics*, 35(2), pp. 285–307.

Levinson, A. (2012) "Valuing Public Goods Using Happiness Data: The Case of Air Quality," *Journal of Public Economics*, 96, pp. 869–880.

Lucas, R. E., Clark, A. E., Georgellis, Y. and Diener, E. (2004) "Unemployment Alters the Set-Point for Life Satisfaction," *Psychological Science*, 15(1), pp. 8–13.

Luechinger, S. (2009) "Valuing Air Quality Using the Life Satisfaction Approach," *Economic Journal*, 119, pp. 482–515.

Luechinger, S. (2010) "Life Satisfaction and Transboundary Air Pollution," *Economic Letters*, 107, pp. 4–6.

Luechinger, S. and Raschky, P. A. (2009) "Valuing Flood Disasters Using the Life Satisfaction Approach," *Journal of Public Economics*, 93, pp. 620–633.

MacKerron, G. and Mourato, S. (2009) "Life Satisfaction and Air Quality in London", *Ecological Economics*, 68, pp. 1441–1453.

Moore, S. C. and Shepherd, J. P. (2006) "The Cost of Fear: Shadow Pricing the Intangible Costs of Crime," *Applied Economics*, 38(3), pp. 293–300.

Moro, M., Brereton, F., Ferreira, S. and Clinch, J. (2008) "Ranking Quality of Life Using Subjective Well-being Data," *Ecological Economics*, 65(3), pp. 448–460.

Murray, T., Maddison, D. and Rehdanz, K. (2013) "Do Geographical Variations In Climate Influence Life-Satisfaction?," *Climate Change Economics*, 4(1), pp. 1–21.

Myers, David G. (1993) *The Pursuit of Happiness*, London: Aquarian.

Noll, H. H. (2004) "Social Indicators and Quality of Life Research: Background, Achievements and Current Trends," in Genov, N. (ed.), *Advances in Sociological Knowledge over Half a Century*, Paris: International Social Science Council, pp. 151–181.

OECD (2011) *Compendium of OECD Well-being Indicators*, Paris: OECD.

Oswald, A. J. (1997) "Happiness and Economic Performance," *Economic Journal*, 107(445), pp. 1815–1831.

Oswald, A. and Wu, S. (2010) "Objective Confirmation of Subjective Measures of Human Well-being: Evidence from the USA", *Science*, 327(5965), pp. 576–579.

Piper, A. T. (2013) "Europe's Capital Cities and the Happiness Penalty: An Investigation Using the European Social Survey," MPRA WP no. 47793.

Plagnol, A. and Easterlin, R. (2008) "Aspirations, Attainments, and Satisfaction: Life Cycle Differences Between American Women and Men," *Journal of Happiness Studies*, 9, pp. 601–619.

Powdthavee, N. (2008) "Putting a Price Tag on Friends, Relatives, and Neighbours: Using Surveys of Life-Satisfaction to Value Social Relationships," *Journal of Behavioral and Experimental Economics*, 37(4), pp. 1459–1480.

Rehdanz, K. and Maddison, D. (2005) "Climate and happiness", *Ecological Economics*, 52, pp. 111–125.

Roback, J. (1982) "Wages, Rents, and the Quality of Life," *Journal of Political Economy*, 90(6), pp. 1257–1278.

Scoppa, V. and Ponzo, M. (2010) "An Empirical Study of Happiness in Italy," *Journal of Behavioral and Experimental Economics*, 39(1), pp. 89–99.

Smyth, R., Mishra, V. and Qian, X. (2008) "The Environment and Well-Being in Urban China," *Ecological Economics*, 68, pp. 547–555.

Stanca, L. (2009) "With or Without You: Measuring the Quality of Relational Life Throughout the World," *Journal of Behavioral and Experimental Economics*, 38, pp. 834–842.

Stanca, L. (2010) "The Geography of Economics and Happiness: Spatial Patterns in the Effects of Economic Conditions on Well-Being," *Social Indicators Research*, 99(1), pp. 115–133.

Stanca, L. (2012) "Suffer the Little Children: Measuring the Effects of Parenthood on Well-Being Worldwide," *Journal of Economic Behavior and Organization*, 81(3), pp. 742–750.

Stevenson, B. and Wolfers, J. (2008) "Economic Growth and Subjective Well-Being: Reassessing the Easterlin Paradox," *Brookings Papers on Economic Activity*, Economic Studies Program, The Brookings Institution, 39(1), pp. 1–102.

Stevenson, B. and Wolfers, J. (2009) "The Paradox of Declining Female Happiness," *American Economic Journal: Economic Policy*, 1(2), pp. 190–225.

Stutzer, A. (2004) "The Role of Income Aspirations in Individual Happiness," *Journal of Economic Behavior and Organization*, 54(1), pp. 89–109.

Van Praag, B. M. S. and Baarsma, B. E. (2005) "Using Happiness Surveys to Value Intangibles: The Case of Airport Noise," *Economic Journal*, 115, pp. 224–246.

Welsch, H. (2002) "Preferences over Prosperity and Pollution: Environmental Valuation Based on Happiness Surveys," *Kyklos*, 55(4), pp. 473–494.

Welsch, H. (2006) "Environment and Happiness: Valuation of Air Pollution Using Life Satisfaction Data," *Ecological Economics*, 58(4), pp. 801–813.

Winkelmann, L. and Winkelmann, R. (1998) "Why Are the Unemployed So Unhappy? Evidence from Panel Data," *Economica*, 65(257), pp. 1–15.

Wolfers, J. (2003) "Is Business Cycle Volatility Costly? Evidence from Surveys of Subjective Well-Being," *International Finance*, 6(1), pp. 1–26.

4 Cities, equity and quality of life

Marco Giovanni Brambilla,
Alessandra Michelangeli and
Eugenio Peluso

4.1 Introduction

The past few decades have seen an enormous surge in economic growth, but in some countries this phenomenon has been accompanied by a daunting degree of inequality, in various forms: widening income gaps and greater poverty in many cities. According to the 2008/2009 State of the World's Cities Report by UN-Habitat (2008),[1] Africa and Latin America have extremely high levels of urban inequality compared to European and Asian cities. Notably, Latin American and Caribbean cities are among the most unequal in the world, with Brazilian and Colombian cities topping the list, closely followed by some cities in Argentina, Chile, Ecuador, Guatemala and Mexico. In Europe, countries with relatively high income inequality include Greece, Ireland and Italy, with a Gini coefficient[2] of between 0.32 and 0.33, and Portugal with 0.36 and the United Kingdom and Spain at 0.34. In North America, the largest cities in the United States tend to be more unequal than small cities. In this regard, major metropolitan areas, such as Atlanta, New Orleans, Washington DC, Miami and New York have the highest levels of inequality in the country.

Scholars, political institutions and development agencies are in full agreement that excessive inequality not only hampers poverty reduction and economic growth, but also disrupts the normal functioning of an urban system. As a consequence, equity concerns have been moving up the development agendas of international organizations, since a virtuous cycle can be triggered when prosperity thrives on equity. In the words of UN-Habitat: "when equity is embedded in urban development strategies, efficiency is enhanced, asset utilisation becomes optimal, productivity improves and social cohesion is strengthened" (UN Habitat, 2013: 4).

The aim of this chapter is to investigate the most puzzling issues relating to the concept of equity at the urban level. We first argue why excessive inequality can be harmful for the development of an urban community (Section 4.2). We then discuss some methodological difficulties arising in assessing urban inequality, related to the spatial dimension of the problem (Section 4.3). Specifically, we discuss the Modifiable Areal Unit Problem (MAUP) and its leading consequences when an inequality measure is decomposed into a component within and

92 *Marco Giovanni Brambilla et al.*

between groups. In Sections 4.4, 4.5 and 4.6, we seek a link between different research fields, to analyze the effect of urban policies on quality of life. We then contrast the main equity criteria used in planning, urban economics and social justice theory, showing that the assessment of urban quality of life can be remarkably enriched from both the conceptual and methodological sides by incorporating equity criteria developed in planning literature and some recent advances in multidimensional welfare assessment. We also show that some concepts developed in different fields such as equality of opportunities and territorial justice can be reconciled when the focus of the analysis is on the quantity and the location of urban facilities. We end the chapter by examining the role of preferences on urban quality of life. More precisely, we examine the aggregation problem behind the provision of urban facilities. After a quick overview of voting models, where both the size and the location of urban facilities are decided by aggregating citizens' preferences through majority rule, we present a novel approach to embedding citizens' preferences into quality of life indices (Sections 4.7 and 4.8).

4.2 Why is excessive inequality bad for cities?

Kuznets-type development models consider a rise in inequality as an inescapable consequence of economic growth in developing countries. Dual models, which study the rural–urban migration process by focusing on rural and urban labor market balances, consider the presence of unemployment and the formation of an informal sector at the urban level as an endogenous consequence of rational migration choices and claim that wage inequality at the urban level is an essential component of labor market equilibrium with migration (Harris and Todaro, 1970). The empirical evidence for a positive correlation between urbanization and inequality has been found also in US cities (Nielsen and Alderson, 1977). Glaeser *et al.* (2009) cite many studies that consider a moderate degree of inequality as an acceptable and even desirable component of economic development at the urban level. The presence of poor people in a city, certainly a symptom of urban inequality and of the presence of informal markets, also demonstrates that a city can attract people as a place worth living in to improve one's status (Glaeser, 2011). Similarly, an increase in skills distribution, making a location socially more unequal by increasing the share of highly educated citizens, can stimulate urban growth. Benabou (1993), Reynolds (1997) and Anas (2008) are in favor of some degree of economic mixing at the urban level, as this gives to the less fortunate examples of successful behavior and more opportunities for employment.

On the other hand, in democracies, Persson and Tabellini (1994) found a negative relation between inequality and growth at the country level; to some extent this result can be transferred to urban contexts because drivers of urban growth coincide with those at the country level (e.g. schooling).

Other studies show that inequality hampers growth via numerous channels. Datt and Ravaillon (1992) claimed that inequality can offset the gains from growth for the poor, such as in Brazil in the 1980s. Birdsall (1996) compared Latin America's slow growth rate with the "East Asian miracle" since the 1960s, explaining part of growth rate differentials in terms of different savings rates caused by high inequality in Latin America. Alesina and Rodrik (1994) investigated the negative effects on growth of the potential political conflict generated by calls for redistribution in excessively unequal countries. Excessive inequality rates can also lead to corruption (You and Khagram, 2005; Uslaner, 2011) and hamper the correct functioning of the judicial system (Begovic, 2006). Several empirical studies carried out mainly on US cities show that cities with high inequality are more subject to social problems including crime, social decay, under-employment, educational atrophy and unhappiness. Kelly (2000), for example, finds a significantly strong relationship between violent crime and inequality in US counties studied in the early 1990s. The literature on crime puts forward at least three theories to explain the relationship between inequality and crime. The first is the strain theory, formulated by Merton (1938), according to which the higher the inequality among individuals, the stronger the sense of frustration of the poorest and hence the propensity to commit crimes. The second is the theory of social disorganization put forward by Shaw and McKay (1942), which asserts that the crime rate increases where social control is weak. The factors that threaten the stability and order of an urban society through the weakening of social control are poverty, ethnic heterogeneity, residential mobility and family instability (Shaw and McKay, 1942; Kornhauser, 1978). The third is the economic theory of crime developed by Becker (1968) and later by Ehrlich (1973) and Block and Heineke (1975). They argue that the poor in highly unequal cities have low expectations of returns from legal activities and may decide to allocate part of their time to criminal activities in order to increase their income. Kelly (2000) provides an explanation of property crime based on the economic theory of crime, whilst arguing that violent crime is a clear expression of the theory of social disorganization and stress theory.

The relationship between inequality and happiness, understood as the degree of subjective satisfaction, is frequently debated. Alesina *et al.* (2004) show that unequal cities are more unhappy, especially in Europe. In a couple of recent papers, Glaeser *et al.* (2009; 2014) argue that unequal metropolitan areas tend to be happier, while segregation has negative effects on the subjective evaluation of personal well-being. It should be recalled that segregation increases inequality between groups of citizens and reduces within-group inequality, because the more educated (or wealthier) tend to be located together in the same city or in the same neighborhoods of a city and to live separated from the less educated (or poorer).

In the same way, the Urban Age Programme (2009) emphasized that the spatial proximity of rich and poor may intensify the feeling of relative deprivation and injustice felt by the poor. The social tension that may emerge can lead to a vicious circle in which the rich retreat from the rest of the city, creating enclaves and stigmatizing the poor as criminals.

After reviewing some major problems related to the high level of inequality, it is worth recalling the international alert line established by UN-Habitat (2008). This line corresponds to a Gini coefficient value of 0.4 as "the threshold at which cities and countries should address inequality as a matter of urgency" (UN-Habitat, 2008: 51). Above this threshold inequality can have drastic consequences

94 *Marco Giovanni Brambilla et al.*

Table 4.1 Interpreting the Gini coefficient

Gini coefficient value	What it means
0.6 or above	Extremely high levels of inequality, not only among individuals, but also among social groups (known as "horizontal inequality"). Wealth concentrated among certain groups at the exclusion of the majority. High risk of social unrest or civil conflict.
0.5–0.59	Relatively high levels of inequality, reflecting institutional and structural failures in income distribution.
0.45–0.49	Inequality approaching dangerously high levels. If no remedial actions are taken, could discourage investment and lead to sporadic protests and riots. Often denotes weak functioning of labor markets or inadequate investments in public services and lack of pro-poor social programs.
0.40	International alert line—inequality threshold
0.3–0.39	Moderate levels of inequality. Healthy economic expansion accompanied by political stability and civil society participation. However could also mean that society is relatively homogeneous – that all groups are generally rich or poor – and, therefore, disparities are not reflected in income or consumption levels.
0.25–0.29	Low levels of inequality. Egalitarian society often characterized by universal access to public goods and services, alongside political stability and social cohesion.

Source: UN-HABITAT Monitoring and Reseach Division (2008).

of an economic (lack of investment), social (protests and riots) and political (civil conflicts) nature. In addition to listing the negative consequences of excessive inequality, UN-Habitat posits some reasons for high inequality, e.g. the poor functioning of labor markets, inadequate investments in public services and institutional and structural failures in income distribution (see Table 4.1).

A Gini coefficient lower than the threshold indicates that cities and countries have an even distribution of resources (for values of the Gini coefficient between 0.25 and 0.29) or moderate levels of inequality (for levels between 0.3 and 0.39).

Can we trust these results based on thresholds for the degree of inequality or could inequality indices such as the Gini coefficient be misleading when the spatial dimension of the problem is significant? In the next section, we review the main difficulties that arise from the prominence of the spatial dimension in inequality and assessment. A limited number of articles have addressed this issue from the theoretical standpoint, despite the huge amount of applied literature on inequality breakdowns among population subgroups, where subgroups often coincide with inhabitants of cities or regions, on the basis of geographical divisions of the territory.

4.3 Inequality and space

Per-capita gross domestic product (GDP) was the main measure of human development and well-being of a country before multidimensional approaches,

Cities, equity and quality of life 95

in particular those based on social indicators,[3] started to spread throughout the United States and the rest of the world in the early 1950s. Both unidimensional and multidimensional approaches have developed several indices to measure well-being inequality. Below, we focus on income inequality, first presenting some basic properties that a good inequality index must enshrine, then discussing the main conceptual problems that arise when the spatial dimension of inequality is taken into account.

An inequality index is a function mapping each income vector into a real number. Its main properties, sometimes formally stated as axioms, can be summarized as follows:

- *Unitary range.* The index values range from 0 to 1.
- *Anonymity.* It does not matter who is earning the income; permutations of incomes among individuals do not change the index value.
- *Scale invariance.* An equally proportional change of income for statistical units does not change the index value.
- *Principle of transfers (or Pigou-Dalton principle).* Any transfer from a rich to a poor individual, preserving the rank of the two individuals in the income distribution, reduces the degree of inequality.
- *Replication invariance.* If one income vector is obtained from another by repeating the incomes of the latter a finite number of times, the inequality index does not change.

The first two properties—unitary range and anonymity—are self-evident. Scale invariance is a suitable property when comparing income vectors in different currencies. However, in the case of a hypothetical economic growth process in which all incomes in a given country increase proportionally, scale invariance becomes debatable, since all the absolute distances between individual incomes increase. Consequently, it cannot be said that the inequality index does not change. The Pigou-Dalton axiom is probably the most important property an inequality index should satisfy, since it registers a decrease in inequality when the distance among any two incomes (even at the top of the distribution) decreases. Finally, replication invariance enables inequality comparisons among groups containing a different number of individuals.

In regional and urban analysis, a good inequality index should take into account the spatial dimension of inequality, so as to be able to distinguish the part of income inequality depending on the location of individuals in a given area from income inequality depending on the income distribution within the areas they live in. A suitable methodology frequently used to capture the spatial heterogeneity of inequality is given by subgroup decomposition techniques. The territory is divided into a finite number of areas that contain subgroups of the statistical population under examination. We might be interested, for example, in measuring inequality in a country divided into many cities, and for each city we measure the income of its inhabitants. The index measuring the total inequality between individuals, given by I, could be decomposed into two components: a within component, W, which accounts for inequality within each city, and a between component, B, accounting for inequality between cities. The spatial component of inequality coincides with the between component and the related measure of the inequality is given by the ratio B/I. This ratio measures the share of total inequality determined by the spatial heterogeneity between urban areas. If $W = 0$ then individuals living in the same city have equal incomes, and all differences in income are due to the spatial dimension measured by B. If, in the opposite case, $B = 0$, then all cities are characterized by the same average income and inequality is due only to the heterogeneous income distribution within cities.

The Gini index, perhaps the inequality index most commonly used by political institutions and international organizations, satisfies all the four axioms presented above, but cannot be broken down perfectly into the between and within components, unless a specific condition is met, i.e. the relative position of each statistical unit in the subgroup is exactly the same in the total income distribution.

The indices in the Generalized Entropy class satisfy the four axioms and are decomposable. The term "entropy" derives from thermodynamics and measures disorder. In income inequality literature, entropy means deviation from perfect equality. The formula of such a class of indices is given by the following equation:

$$E(\alpha) = \frac{1}{n(\alpha^2 - \alpha)} \sum_{i=1}^{n} \left[\left(\frac{y_i}{\bar{y}} \right)^{\alpha} - 1 \right], \tag{4.1}$$

where n is the total number of statistical units; y_i is the amount of income of another monetary variable observed for the statistical unit i; $\bar{y}$ is the average income; α is the parameter that determines the specific form of the index belonging to the Generalized Entropy class. The most used Generalized Entropy indices are: mean logarithmic deviation, also called Theil's second measure, for which $\alpha = 0$; Theil index with $\alpha = 1$; one-half of the squared coefficient of variation with $\alpha = 2$. For positive and increasing values of α, the index becomes more sensitive to what happens to the upper tail of the income distribution.

Focusing on the between component, an interesting issue, conceptually, is the behavior of this component when the number of areas changes. Let n be the number of individuals and m the number of areas in which individuals are located. Shorrocks and Wan (2005) investigate this issue proving that spatial inequality, measured by B, cannot increase (if anything it decreases) whenever two areas are combined, i.e. the division becomes less fine and m decreases. For the opposite case, that of a finer division (m increases), Shorrocks and Wan (2005) conjecture that the between component, on average, is larger. In other words, if we consider a division with $m' > m$ groups the between component could increase, but also could decrease, depending on the specific spatial configuration. However, if we consider all the possible divisions with $m' > m$ we can safely expect an increase of the between component. Figure 4.1 illustrates a simple case of eight individuals living in two areas (see panel (a)). The numbers represent the income endowments of individuals. The average income is 6.5 for the lower bound triangle, and 3.5 for the upper bound triangle. An index decomposable in the two components, between and within, has a strictly positive between component since the average incomes differ by area.

Suppose we reorganize the territory into four areas and in each area we locate two individuals, as in panel (b). According to the Shorrocks and Wan (2005) conjecture, the between component of the index should increase. Instead it decreases to zero, since the average income is 5 for each area, the spatial inequality is absent and the overall inequality is exclusively due to the inequality within each area. The conjecture states that, considering all the possible divisions of the populations across $m' > m$ subgroups (and not only that illustrated in panel (b) of Figure 4.1), the average value of the between components B is expected to increase.

Shorrocks and Wan (2005) also show that, for a given number of areas m, the between component reaches its maximum value when individuals are located such that their incomes do not overlap between areas, as in Figure 4.2.

From these examples it is clear that measures of spatial inequality crucially depend on how spatial data are organized. In the next paragraph we explore this

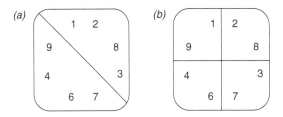

Figure 4.1 Income endowments of eight individuals living in two areas (panel (a)) or in four areas (panel (b)).

Source: Author's own construct.

Figure 4.2 Case of individuals located such that their incomes do not overlap between areas.

Source: Author's own construct.

98 *Marco Giovanni Brambilla et al.*

problem, which can affect the assessment of other phenomena such as segregation, poverty and quality of life.

4.3.1 The Modifiable Areal Unit Problem

The bias introduced by different admissible divisions of a territory on the spatial component of inequality can be seen as a special case of the Modifiable Areal Unit Problem (MAUP). Spatial data comprises information on location and measures of attributes. Three types of spatial data are usually available: geostatistical, area and point pattern data. Geostatistical data provide observations at fixed locations (e.g. pollution measured in different stations). Area data provide information for regions or given areas. Point pattern data concern the spatial arrangements of points in situations where their location is of interest (e.g. household addresses). Area data represent the most common type of spatial data, and areas can be designed historically, politically or in a number of arbitrary ways. The unit of spatial analysis is modifiable and the results of quantitative analysis applied to such data (from correlation and regression analysis, gravity-type spatial interaction models, inequality and segregation assessment to ecology, epidemiology and many other fields) can dramatically change, introducing a strong bias in inference processes that can drive incorrect policy decisions in important sectors such as schooling, public transport, health services and so on.

Gehlke and Biehl brought this issue to light in the 1930s (Gehlke and Biehl, 1934), studying bias on spatial autocorrelation. The increasing use of computers explains the renewed interest in this phenomenon at the end of the 1970s, when Openshaw and Taylor (1979) introduced the term MAUP, providing the example of the correlation coefficient between Republican voting and the share of old people living in Iowa. According to the criterion used to aggregate counties, they showed that the correlation coefficient could range from -0.97 to $+0.99$. In a subsequent work, Openshaw and Rao (1995) computed correlation coefficients ranging from -1.00 to $+1.00$ between the unemployment rate and the share of households without a car in Merseyside.

The MAUP problem has two different aspects:

- *the scale effect* consisting in the major differences obtained by changing the size of the areas. Generally, correlation increases for bigger units and effects on spatial inequality are illustrated in the previous paragraph;
- *the zonation effect* which depends on how the territory under examination is divided up, even at the same scale.

These definitions concern the geographical division and are not exhaustive where the population division is also relevant to the research objectives. In general, the population is not homogeneously distributed in the territory and the change in population size in each area does not necessarily go hand-in-hand with the change in size of the areas. The implications of this aspect on inequality deserve specific investigation.

Cities, equity and quality of life 99

Although the increasing availability of GIS data provides a powerful tool to develop more accurate techniques:

> currently, no general solutions exist. Some scholars suggest that the zoning problem is simpler because it can be treated as a data interpolation or transformation problem (Fisher and Langford, 1995). For scale effect, one approach is to develop relatively scale-insensitive analytical techniques. This approach has had limited success so far and the solutions are subject-dependent (e.g., Tobler, 1989; Wong, 2001).
>
> (Wong, 2004: 575).

4.4 Equitable cities: measurement issues

The negative effects of inequality, shown in Section 4.2, induce scholars, institutions and political actors to rethink urban systems to promote the equitable development of cities, where equitable means what "a society considers appropriate to the needs, status and contribution of its various members" (Peyton Young, 1994). We turn from the undimensional approach, where income is a proxy of individual well-being, and give an initial definition of an equitable city in terms of quality of life. The latter is essentially a multidimensional concept that requires dealing with some important issues presented below.

We start from the simplest configuration where equity and equality coincide. A city is equitable if inhabitants enjoy the same level of quality of life, wherever they live within the city. We therefore need to establish when a neighborhood, characterized by different bundles of amenities, ensures equivalent liveability. Consider the simple example of a city divided into two neighborhoods, A and B, where quality of life is determined by two amenities, public infrastructures and climate conditions. Any ranking generated by comparing each amenity at any time is incomplete, whenever we observe less infrastructure and better climate in A than in B. It appears natural to aggregate the different determinants of quality of life in a single index, in order to produce a complete ranking. This procedure, used largely in the social sciences, requires the choice of different weightings for the various urban amenities. This choice often relies on pragmatic criteria or statistical methods that are rarely justified by theoretical models or axiomatic theories. The most common procedure consists in attaching the same weight to each amenity, if necessary resorting to the counting approach in the case of binary variables. As we saw in Chapter 2, the hedonic quality of life index, developed by Rosen (1979) and Roback (1982), is a valuable exception, since the weightings coincide with the implicit prices assigned to the amenities and are determined by a spatial general equilibrium model for the location decisions of individuals and firms.

The aggregation process becomes much more cumbersome when more than two determinants of quality of life are considered. Suppose we aim to evaluate quality of life in a city using the hedonic quality of life index *à la* Roback (1982), and consider the following four amenities: public greenery, shopping facilities, hospitals and recreational facilities. The statistical population comprises a large number of

100 *Marco Giovanni Brambilla et al.*

housing units,[4] and variables measuring the different amenities are given by the distance between each housing unit and the nearest of each amenity. To calculate the index at the city level, these distances are averaged across housing units. This procedure neglects the degree of association in the distribution of amenities within the statistical population. By association we mean any relationship between variables that renders them statistically dependent. Suppose a group of housing units is located near some amenities (public greenery and shopping facilities) and far from others (hospital, recreational facilities), while another group of units is located far from public greenery and shopping facilities and near hospitals and recreational facilities. The hedonic quality of life index calculated for this city does not change if hospitals and recreational structures are relocated near to the first group of houses and all amenities are then concentrated near this group of houses, while the other group remains far from all amenities.[5] The lack of variation is due to the order followed in the aggregation process for calculating the index. Assuming K amenities and N housing units, the procedure for calculating the hedonic quality of life index aggregates first each amenity across housing units, to obtain the average for each amenity; second, the average amenity quantity are aggregated summing up them through a weighted sum, where we know from Chapter 2, that the weightings correspond to the implicit prices of amenities. If the degree of association among the distribution of amenities in the statistical population is considered important, the reverse sequence should be adopted to calculate a quality of life index: first the K variables, measuring amenities, should be aggregated into a single indicator for each population unit; second, the N indicators, obtained by the first step, should be aggregated over the N population units to obtain a quality of life index. This procedure, which we call henceforward a reverse procedure, has frequently been used to measure multidimensional inequality, welfare and poverty and is supported by neat axiomatic results (see Atkinson, 2003; Aaberge and Peluso, 2012; Croci-Angelini and Michelangeli, 2012; Tsui, 1995, among many others). As regards the measurement of urban quality of life, as far as we know, there is only one recent work by authors (Brambilla *et al.*, 2013) who adopt the reverse procedure to calculate an urban quality of life index, called an equity-adjusted quality of life index. The name is used because it enables adjustment to the hedonic quality of life index *à la* Roback (1982) by explicitly taking into account the unequal distribution of amenities within a city. The main assumption is that an unequal availability of amenities within a city has a negative impact on the evaluation of its overall quality of life. The more unbalanced the distribution of amenities across neighborhoods, the lower the value of the equity-adjusted quality of life index. This index can be used to disentangle the effect of each amenity on quality of life from their joint effect. A further advantage is that in the first step of the procedure, i.e. K amenities aggregated across N statistical units, it is possible to account for the complement/substitute nature of amenities. Amenities are substitutes if a decrease in one amenity can be compensated by an "equivalent" increase in another amenity, leaving quality of life unchanged. Whereas, they are complements if in order to raise the quality of life the increase in one amenity must be accompanied by an increase in another amenity. A weakness of the reverse procedure is that all amenities must be either substitutes or complements in determining quality of life, but this assumption is not necessarily satisfied in empirical configurations. In the real world, some amenities may be linked by a substitution relationship and others might be complementary. Hence, theoretical extensions able to overcome this difficulty mathematically could extend the potential field of application of the methodology based on the reverse procedure remarkably.

4.5 Equity as equality of opportunities

It is widely accepted that equality and equity coincide only under special conditions. For instance, a situation where two individuals have the same productivity, work the same number of hours and earn the same wage, can easily be seen as equitable. But if we consider the case of two individuals who are identical but one makes much more effort than the other, a fair pay system may differ from egalitarian treatment, since it seems more reasonable ethically to reward the more productive worker with more money, rather than pay the same wage to both. In more realistic cases, where individuals differ in personal aptitudes, skills or different life situations, the criteria to adopt to ensure equitable treatment is still being debated since the discussion got under way in the early 1960s, featuring Milton Friedman, Amartya Sen, John Rawls and many other scholars. Albeit from different points of view, all these theories try to establish how to ensure equitable outcomes between individuals. Recently, Roemer (1998), van de Gaer (1993) and Fleurbaey (2008) have developed a theory, where equity is interpreted in terms of equality of opportunity, rather than equality of outcome. According to this theory, individual outcomes derive from three main factors: individual effort, circumstances beyond individual responsibility (family background, age, country of birth, etc.) and public policies. Equality of opportunity arises when all the differences of outcomes generated by effort are maintained (reward principle), while those due to circumstances are neutralized by appropriate policies (compensation principle).[6] Equality of opportunity is a relevant variable in urban planning. An unequal distribution of opportunities contributes to increased social stratification and residential segregation; it exacerbates xenophobia, crime and frustration, triggering social unrest. Living in deprived neighborhoods also undermines the accumulation of social capital by generating harmful peer pressure and social stigma, and reducing aspirations for a good quality of life. Future opportunities are compromised, especially for children, who are more vulnerable and are not responsible for the negative circumstances to which they are subjected. The effects of bad circumstances at the local level on the distribution of personal opportunities raises non-trivial equity concerns and suggests compensatory policies to equalize opportunities. Even in this respect, a fair provision of public goods to all citizens is absolutely essential to guarantee equal opportunities to everyone. In the next section, we contrast these general ideas with the specific equity concerns raised in recent decades by planning literature.

102 *Marco Giovanni Brambilla et al.*

4.6 Territorial justice

The relevance of the provision of urban commons has been discussed by, among others, Gidwani and Baviskar (2011), who identified two types of urban commons (or public goods) that are worth foregrounding, namely: ecological commons (air, water bodies, wetlands, etc.) and civic commons (streets, public spaces, education facilities and public transport).

Urban planning decisions may affect citizen well-being via different channels. The provision of goods and local taxation directly affects individual extended income and wealth. By extended income, we mean the sum of disposable cash income plus the value of public in-kind transfers. Aaberge *et al.* (2013) study the distributional impact of public in-kind transfers in 23 European countries, ranking these countries on the basis of extended income inequality, and financial poverty. They show that these rankings change when the value of in-kind transfers is included in the definition of income.

To assess public policies in terms of equity, three main criteria can be identified, based respectively on equality, need and preferences (Harvey, 1973; Lucy, 1981; Hay, 1995; Talen, 1998; Soja, 2010). At a purely abstract level, equity criteria can be defined in terms of resources or achievements. According to the first criterion, an equal level of services or achievements may be the objective of the planner. Equity as equal access to urban commons means that every resident should have access to the same amount of public resources, regardless of his economic endowment and willingness to pay. Equalizing public services does not guarantee equal outcomes, since individual needs and preferences contribute to the process of transformation from commodities to functionings (Sen, 1985). However, this criterion is partly consistent with the idea of leveling the playing field developed in equality of opportunity literature: the differences in outcomes are driven by the initial endowment of resources and talents and by individual decisions. In the equality of opportunity vocabulary, this approach implies a neat preference for the reward principle against the compensation principle. The second criterion subordinates the distribution of services to the different needs of citizens. The "territorial justice" concept, introduced by Davies (1976) "requires that service provision is proportional to service needs at the inter-area level" (Boine and Powell, 1991). It is clear that by shifting the focus from equal resources to equal achievements, the second criterion becomes a special case of the first, after appropriate correction for equivalence scales in the measurement of income inequality. This approach is consistent with the compensation principle of the equality of opportunity theory, provided that needs depend on exogenous circumstances outside individual control. Practically, it is not easy to check for responsibility in this setting. If children's needs can be deemed beyond their responsibility, the link between needs and objective circumstances becomes much more tricky when location choices are relevant to creating needs. This is a non-trivial point that requires further investigation.

With regard to public service provision, these services could be sized by consumer preference: people using public transport or walking in a park are displaying consumer demand and can express the wish for a change in the quantity or quality of the services. Their preferences can be investigated in surveys and the provision of such services may reflect their willingness to pay. The distributional outcomes based on one of the previous criteria may sharply differ from the others. Mladenka and Hill (1977) provide the example of libraries: the demand criterion recommends more libraries in wealthier neighborhoods, while a needs-based or a purely egalitarian criterion would recommend an entirely different location pattern. If these concepts are clearly defined and easily understandable, some problems might arise when applied to planning processes. As for equality, parks, libraries and police stations cannot be equidistant from everyone; needs must be correctly identified and treated. Territorial justice requires that people with different needs are unequally treated and this requires consensus at the political level. Finally, the criteria based on demand and preferences can be biased by income or education levels; surveys to elicit the preferences of residents are not sufficiently representative of the city population and people may not wish to reveal a willingness to pay for goods that are usually free of charge, because they are indirectly financed by one system or another of local taxation.

Recent literature has explored how standard inequality measures can be used to implement different equity principles in public facility location problems where space matters. Marsh and Schilling (1994) put forward an analytic scheme based on three basic concepts: locating a public facility in a given place produces measurable effects (depending on the location and size of the facility) on several groups, which are well identified on the basis of one or more traits. A general equity criterion requires that each group receives its fair share of the effects generated by the facility.

Some effects may depend on the distance, such as access to a public library, but others may not, due to external factors such as traffic congestion. The degree of fairness of the effect received by each group depends on the definition of the group and on the specific equity criterion implemented by the planner. In general, a simple scaling operation is sufficient to reconcile the first equity criterion—equality—with needs, or preference criteria. For instance, the right number of ambulances in each area may be proportionate to its population, but may also depend on average age or on specific needs, illness or demand from some inhabitants. The size of the area may also be taken into account. Following this broad perspective, territorial equity becomes an allocation problem, where the proportional rule is used to allocate the effects of the specific type of facility or burden considered among several groups. Defining groups, effects and scaling is crucial and may be shaped by cultural values, precedent and contextual aspects that reflect inhabitants' needs, demands or preferences. If spatial equity requires equal proximity to public facilities, different access measures may be considered. Talen and Anselin (1998) integrated the simple count of facilities in a real unit with an accessibility measure based on average travel distance, and another accessibility measure based on the "gravity model," where accessibility increases with the number and size of available facilities of a given type and decreases with a decay factor depending on the distance from the facility. These accessibility measures

104 *Marco Giovanni Brambilla et al.*

partly completed by global and local spatial autocorrelation analysis, and implemented through a local version of the Moran index, are able to detect local spatial association and to check whether the global pattern of associations is uniform throughout the data set.

In the following section, we turn our attention towards positive models, where the location problem is simplified but the link between individual preferences and public facility provision is clearly characterized.

4.7 Positive models

Urban amenities such as city parks, libraries, museums and cultural centers are provided publicly to improve inhabitants' quality of life. The provision of amenities may be resolved by referendum and financed through lump-sum or proportional taxes, allocated over all the city inhabitants. Or the benefits of urban amenities may not be spread equally over the population: residents living nearer to the public good are obviously advantaged. Two different approaches have been pursued to investigate this problem. Following Tiebout (1956), several authors have analyzed how household location depends on preferences for a public good (Nechyba, 2004; Walsh, 2007; Banzhaf and Walsh, 2008, among many others). This literature has investigated the sorting of households into communities on the basis of their preferences for a public good, when a majority aggregative rule determines the level of a public good.

On the other hand, a huge amount of literature on public choice and political economy has studied the determinants of the size and the location of public goods and services provided through majority voting, for a given distribution of people in the territory. The policy choice can be horizontal for the location of a public good, or vertical (like the budget allocated to education, housing, etc.), or both.[7] De Donder *et al.* (2012a) clarify under which distribution of individual characteristics (such as income and preferences for the location of the public good) a majority voting (or Condorcet) equilibrium exists, when voting simultaneously over the location and size of the public good. Even assuming the simplest location choice, that is placing the public good over a segment, the conditions that guarantee a simultaneous voting equilibrium are rather stringent and unrealistic. These complex results reflect the difficulties in assessing the outcomes of majority rule in pure location problems. Some authors who address this issue (Banks and Austen-Smith, 1999; Ordeshook, 1986) have studied the case with quadratic preferences—where a different center represents the preferred location of each individual—and have demonstrated the possibility of different types of sequential equilibria, such that some do not correspond to any voter's most-preferred policy (see De Donder *et al.*, 2012b for an illustration). Considering sequential equilibria (where people first vote on funding, then on the location of the public good) Alesina *et al.* (1999) and Perroni and Scharf (2001) assumed both income and preference heterogeneity. De Donder *et al.* (2012a) showed that in this case, a median voter-type equilibrium exists if the public service is financed through lump-sum taxation, while if the public good is financed by proportional income taxation, the equilibrium levels of taxation depend on the shape and the correlation of income and preference distributions. The positive approach is to focus increasingly on specific urban problems such as pollution, congestion and traffic (see Russo, 2013; Alesina and Passarelli, 2014) and represent a promising field of investigation and application of concepts of political economy to urban economics. We now complete the survey by presenting some attempts to embed individual preferences in normative judgments.

4.8 Preferences, quality of life, and values

Individuals are attracted by cities with the best combination of amenities according to their preferences. Choosing which city to live in forces individuals to trade off money and the best bundle of amenities. The link between preferences and utility provided by urban amenities has been modeled by the hedonic approach developed by Rosen (1979) and Roback (1982) and extensively described in Chapter 2. Within this framework, Brambilla *et al.* (2013) show how preferences for equity can be introduced into the quality of life assessment of a city through a correction term for the standard hedonic quality of life index. They obtain a new index called equity-adjusted quality of life index, already mentioned in Section 4.4. The correction term is obtained as the sum of unidimensional inequality indices, accounting for the dispersion of each amenity within the city, plus a residual term summarizing any correlation among the distribution of amenities. This formulation allows us to disentangle the contribution of the dispersion of each amenity to the overall quality of life index from the joint effect of the amenities. The correction term depends on as many parameters as the number of amenities under examination. Each parameter registers the aversion to the unequal availability of the corresponding amenity within the city. The model is therefore sufficiently flexible to allow for a specific degree of aversion to the unequal availability of each amenity.

The equity-adjusted quality of life index is used to assess quality of life in Milan over the period 2004–2008. Data on amenities include information on environmental characteristics, public transport, education, shopping facilities, recreational activities, and socio-economic characteristics. The results show that the uneven availability of amenities within the city reduces the standard hedonic quality of life index by 28 percent. Recreational activities, public transport and environmental characteristics turn out to be the more unequal amenities distributed across city neighborhoods, while the socio-economic composition is the amenity for which the inequality aversion is higher than the unequal distribution of the other amenities.

4.9 Conclusions

This chapter presents the main consequences—at the urban level—of the increasing inequality accompanying per-capita GDP growth in many developing and developed countries. It discusses two aspects of the methodology currently used to analyze the spatial pattern of increasing inequality in countries and regions. We point out the limits of standard breakdown techniques normally used to account for the spatial dimension of inequality; and we highlight the need to adopt a

106 *Marco Giovanni Brambilla et al.*

multidimensional setting in order to provide suitable measures of individual well-being and urban quality of life. Since there is still little literature that seeks to assess the spatial variations of inequality in a multidimensional setting, the extension to the multidimensional setting of inequality breakdown techniques to check the MAUP is a promising line for further investigation. We also suggest combining some recent ideas in the economic theory of justice with the equity criteria developed in urban planning literature, in order to establish a link between equality of opportunity and territorial justice. These comparisons deserve further investigation, especially when individual opportunities are defined in terms of the availability of (or accessibility to) public facilities. Finally, the role of individual preferences and demand in defining urban equity criteria and quality of life measurement are examined. Some advances in the urban economics literature have been made recently that account for citizens' preferences for public facilities in the construction of quality of life indices sensitive to equity. Individual preferences can be revealed through a hedonic price analysis of the housing and labor markets, and appropriate multidimensional inequality indices can be used to make the quality of life index sensitive to the uneven availability of public facilities in different areas present at the urban level. Several relevant topics are sidelined in our analysis, in particular the impact on quality of life of urban segregation and the various endogenous processes related to segregation and social stratification within the city, such as those studied by Shelling (1969).

Notes

1 UN-Habitat is the United Nations Human Settlements Programme, established in 1978 within the United Nations system and dedicated to urbanization.
2 The Gini coefficient is a measure of inequality varying from 0 (every individual received an equal share of income, then there is perfect equality) to 1 (one individual receives all the income, then there is perfect inequality).
3 See Chapter 3, Section 3.1 for a short introduction to the social indicators approach.
4 To simplify the analysis, the labor market is not considered but the reasoning holds even if it is included.
5 The invariance of the Roback index holds under the assumption that citizens do not change home If people changed house, the housing market would attain a new equilibrium, changing the implicit prices associated with the amenities and then the Roback index value for the city.
6 See Roemer and Trannoy (2014) for a recent survey about the measurement of equality of opportunity, where the role of luck is also taken into account.
7 See De Donder *et al.* (2012b) for a recent presentation of this literature.

Bibliography

Aaberge, R., Langorgen, A. and Lindgren, P. (2013) *The Distributional Impact of Public Services in European Countries*, Eurostat Methodologies and Working papers, European Commission, Luxembourg.
Aaberge, R. and Peluso, E. (2012) "A Counting Approach for Measuring Multidimensional Deprivation," *IZA Discussion Papers no. 6589*, Institute for the Study of Labor (IZA).
Alesina, A. and Passarelli, F. (2014) "Regulation versus Taxation," *Journal of Public Economics*, 110, pp. 147–156.

Alesina, A. and Rodrik, D. (1994) "Distributive Politics and Ecconomic Growth," *The Quarterly Journal of Economics*, 109(2), pp. 465–490.

Alesina, A., Baqir, R. and Easterly, W. (1999) "Public Goods and Ethnic Divisions," *The Quarterly Journal of Economics*, 114, pp. 1243–1284.

Alesina, A., Di Tella, R., and MacCulloch, R. (2004) "Inequality and happiness: are Europeans and Americans different?," *Journal of Public Economics*, 88, pp. 2009–2042.

Anas, A. (2008) "Ethnic Segregation and Ghettos," in Arnott, R. and McMillen, D.P. (eds.), *A Companion to Urban Economics*, USA: Blackwell Publishing.

Atkinson, A.B. (2003) "Multidimensional Deprivation: Contrasting Social Welfare and Counting Approaches," *Journal of Economic Inequality*, 1, pp. 51–65.

Banks, J. and Austen-Smith, D. (1999) *Positive Political Theory: Collective Preference*, Vol. 1, Michigan, MI: Ann-Arbor.

Banzhaf, H.S. and Walsh, R.P. (2008) "Do People Vote with Their Feet? An Empirical Test of Tiebout," *American Economic Review*, 98(3), pp. 843–863.

Becker, G.S. (1968) "Crime and Punishment: An Economic Approach," *Journal of Political Economy*, 76, pp. 169–217.

Begovic, B. (2006) "Economic Inequality and Corruption," Center for Liberal-Democratic Studies (CLDS), Belgrade, Serbia.

Benabou, R. (1993) "Workings of a City: Location, Education and Production," *The Quarterly Journal of Economics*, 108(3), pp. 619–652.

Birdsall, N. (1996) "Why Low Inequality Spurs Growth: Savings and Investment by the Poor," Washington, DC: Inter-American Development Bank, p. 18.

Block, M. and Heineke, J. (1975) "A Labour Theoretical Analysis of Criminal Choice," *American Economic Review*, 65, pp. 314–325.

Blomquist, G.C., Berger, M.C. and Hoehn, J.P. (1988) "New Estimates of Quality of Life in Urban Areas," *American Economic Review*, 78(1), pp. 89–107.

Boine, G. and Powell, M. (1991) "Territorial Justice: A Review of Theory and Evidence," *Political Geography Quarterly*, 10(3), pp. 263–281.

Brambilla, M., Michelangeli, A., and Peluso, E. (2013) "Equity in the City: On Measuring Urban (Ine)quality of Life," *Urban Studies*, 50(16), pp. 3205–3224.

Croci Angelini, E. and Michelangeli, A. (2012) "Axiomatic Measurement of Multidimensional Well-Being Inequality: Some Distributional Questions," *Journal of Behavioral and Experimental Economics*, 41, pp. 548–557.

Datt, G. and Ravaillon, M. (1992) "Growth and Redistribution Components of Changes in Poverty Measures: A Decomposition with Applications to Brazil and India in the 1980s," *Journal of Development Economics*, 38, pp. 275–295.

Davies, B.P. (1968) *Social Needs and Resources in Local Services*, London: Michael Joseph.

Davies, B.P. (1976) "Territorial Injustice," *New Society*, 710, pp. 352–353.

De Donder, P., Le Breton, M. and Peluso, E. (2012a) "On the (Sequential) Majority Choice of Public Good Size and Location," *Social Choice and Welfare*, 39(2–3), pp. 457–489.

De Donder, P., Le Breton, M. and Peluso, E. (2012b) "Majority Voting in Multidimensional Policy Spaces: Kramer–Shepsle versus Stackelberg," *Journal of Public Economic Theory*, 14(6), pp. 879–909.

Ehrlich, I. (1973) "Participation in Illegitimate Activities: A Theoretical and Empirical Investigation," *Journal of Political Economy*, 81, pp. 521–565.

Fisher, P.F. and Langford, M. (1995) "Modelling the Errors in Areal Interpolation between Zonal Systems by Monte Carlo Simulation," *Environment and Planning A*, 27(2), pp. 211–224.

Fleurbaey, M. (2008) *Fairness, Responsibility and Welfare*, Oxford: Oxford University Press.

108 *Marco Giovanni Brambilla et al.*

Gehlke, C.E. and Biehl, K. (1934) "Certain Effects of Grouping upon the Size of the Correlation Coefficient in Census Tract Material," *Journal of the American Statistical Association*, 29, pp. 169–170.

Gidwani, V. and Baviskar, A. (2011) "Urban Commons," *Review of Urban Affairs*, 50, pp. 42–43.

Glaeser, E.L. (2011) *Triumph of the City*, London: Macmillan.

Glaeser, E.L., Resseger, M. and Tobio, K. (2009) "Inequality in Cities," *Journal of Regional Science*, 49, pp. 617–646.

Glaeser, E.L., Gottlieb, J.D. and Ziv, O. (2014) "Unhappy Cities," *Journal of Regional Science*, 49, pp. 617–646.

Harris, J.R. and Todaro, M.P. (1970) "Migration, Unemployment and Development: A Two-Sector Analysis," *American Economic Review*, 60(1), pp. 126–142.

Harvey, D. (1973) *Social Justice and the City*. London: Edward Arnold.

Hay, A.M. (1995) "Concepts of Equity, Fairness and Justice in Geographical Studies," *Transactions of the Institute of British Geographer*, 20, pp. 500–508.

Kelly, M. (2000) "Inequality and Crime," *Review of Economics and Statistics*, 82(4), pp. 530–539.

Kornhauser, R.R. (1978) *Social Sources of Delinquency: An Appraisal of Analytic Models*, Chicago, IL: University of Chicago Press.

Lucy, W. (1981) "Equity and Planning For Local Services," *Journal of the American Planning Association* 47(4), pp. 447–457.

Marsh, M. T. and Schilling, D.A. (1994) "Equity Measurement in Facility Location Analysis: A Review and Framework,"*European Journal of Operational Research*, 74, pp. 1–17.

Merton, R. (1938) "Social Structure and Anomie," *American Sociological Review*, 3, pp. 586–593.

Mladenka, K. and Hill, K.Q. (1977) "The Distribution of Benefits in an Urban Environment: Parks and Libraries in Houston," *Urban Affairs Quarterly*, 13, pp. 73–94.

Nechyba, T. (2004) "School Choice and School Quality in the US," *CESifo DICE Report*, Ifo Institute for Economic Research, 2(4), pp. 33–38.

Nielsen, F. and Alderson, A.S. (1997) "The Kuznets Curve and the Great U-Turn: Income Inequality in U.S. Counties, 1970 to 1990," *American Sociological Review*, 62(1), pp. 12–33.

Openshaw, S. and Taylor, P.J. (1979) "A Million or so Correlation Coefficients: Three Experiments on the Modifiable Areal Unit Problem," in Wrigley, N. (ed.), *Statistical Applications in Spatial Sciences*, London: Pion, pp. 127–144.

Openshaw, S. and Rao, P.J. (1995) "Algorithms for Reengineering 1991 Census geography," *Environment and Planning A*, 27(3), pp. 425–446.

Ordeshook, P. (1986) *Game Theory and Political Theory*, Cambridge: Cambridge University Press.

Perroni, C. and Scharf, K. (2001) "Tiebout with Politics: Capital Tax Competition and Constitutional Choices," *Review of Economic Studies*, 68, pp. 133–154.

Persson, T. and Tabellini, G. (1994) "Is Inequality Harmful for Growth?," *American Economic Review*, 84(3), pp. 600–621.

Peyton Young, H. (1994) *Equity in Theory and Practice*, Princeton, NJ: Princeton University Press.

Reynolds, D.W. (1997) "The Lost Architecture of Ancient Rome, Insights from the Several Plan and the Regional Catalogues," *Expedition*, 39(2), pp. 15–24.

Roback, J. (1982) "Wages, Rents and Quality of Life," *Journal of Political Economy*, 90(6), pp. 1257–1278.

Roemer, J. (1998) *Equality of Opportunity*, Cambridge, MA: Harvard University Press.

Roemer, J. and Trannoy, A. (2014) "Equality of Opportunity," in *Handbook of Income Inequality*, vol. 2, Atkinson, A. and Bourguignon, F. (eds.), Amsterdam: Elsevier.

Rosen, S. (1979) "Wage-based Indexes of Urban Quality of Life," in Mieszkowsi, P. and Stratzheim, M. (eds.), *Current Issues in Urban Economics*, Baltimore, MD: John Hopkins Press.

Russo, A. (2013) "Voting on Road Congestion Policy," *Regional Science and Urban Economics*, 43(5), pp. 707–724.

Sen, A.K. (1985) *Commodities and Capabilities*, Amsterdam: Elsevier.

Shaw, C. and Mckay, H. (1942) *Juvenile Delinquency and Urban Areas*, Chicago, IL: University of Chicago Press.

Shelling, T. (1969) "Models of Segregation," *American Economic Review*, 59(2), pp. 488–493.

Shorrocks, A. and Wan, G. (2005) "Spatial Decomposition of Inequality," *Journal of Economic Geography*, 5(1), pp. 59–81.

Soja, E.W. (2010) *Seeking Spatial Justice*, Minneapolis, MN: University of Minnesota Press.

Talen, E. (1998) "Visualizing Fairness: Equity Maps for Planners," *Journal of the American Planning Association* 64(1), pp. 22–38.

Talen, E. and Anselin, L. (1998) "Assessing Spatial Equity: An Evaluation of Measures of Accessibility to Public Playgrounds," *Environment and Planning A*, 30, pp. 595–613.

Tiebout, C.M. (1956) "A Pure Theory of Local Expenditures," *The Journal of Political Economy*, 64(5), pp. 416–424.

Tobler, W.R. (1989) "Frame Independent Spatial Analysis," in Goodchild, M. and Gopa, S. (eds.), *The Accuracy of Spatial Databases*, London: Taylor & Francis, pp. 115–122.

Tsui, K.Y. (1995) "Multidimensional Generalizations of the Relative and Absolute Inequality Indices: The Atkinson-Kolm-Sen Approach," *Journal of Economic Theory*, 67, pp. 251–265.

UN-Habitat (2013) *Urban Equity in Development Cities for Life*, London: Earthscan.

United Nations Human Settlements Programme (UN-Habitat) (2008) *State of the World's Cities 2008/2009*, Harmonious Cities, London: Earthscan.

Urban Age Programme (2009) *Cities and Social Equity, Detailed Report*, London: London School of Economics and Political Science.

Uslaner, E.M. (2011) "Corruption and Inequality," *CESifo DICE Report 2/2011*, pp. 20–24.

van de Gaer, D. (1993) *Equality of opportunity and investment in human capital*, PhD thesis, Leuven University.

Walsh, R. (2007) "Endogenous Open Space Amenities in a Locational Equilibrium," *Journal of Urban Economics*, 61(2), pp. 319–344.

Wong, D.W.S. (2001) "Location-Specific Cumulative Distribution Function (LSCDF): An Alternative to Spatial Correlation Analysis," *Geographical Analysis*, 33(1), pp. 76–93.

Wong, D.W.S. (2004) "The Modifiable Areal Unit Problem (MAUP)," in Janelle, D.G., Warf, B. and Hansen, K. (eds.), *WorldMinds: Geographical Perspectives on 100 Problems*, Kluwer Academic Publishers, pp. 571–573.

You, J. and Khagram, S. (2005) "A Comparative Study of Inequality and Corruption," *American Sociological Review*, 70, pp. 136–157.

5 Urban sustainability and individual/household well-being

Constantinos Antoniou and Nathalie Picard

5.1 Introduction

Sustainability is a concept that has been used extensively in many domains over the past decades and it is generally accepted that it covers three spheres: society, environment, and economics. This multidimensionality makes quantifying sustainability a challenging task and therefore different ways to operationalize it have been developed. Urban sustainability, as a special case of sustainability, deals with the specific nature of cities and becomes increasingly more important as urbanization constantly increases and the problems associated with cities become more severe. In this chapter, we focus on urban sustainability, individual well-being and quality of life. Clearly, these are all desirable outcomes of urban design and whether they can be achieved in parallel, or whether there are some conflicts, is an interesting question.

Figure 5.1 presents Google ngrams, which count how many times the requested term appears in books published in the particular year, for the following three relevant terms: (1) indicators, (2) quality of life, and (3) sustainability. Arguably, it can be interpreted as a sort of indication of popularity/relevance of terms over time. All three terms show similar trends, i.e. a slow initial increase, followed by a steep adoption. Indicators (a term that is broad and applied to many fields) start seeing some significant mention at the end of the nineteenth century, while quality of life only really becomes noticeable in the 1970s. Finally, sustainability starts being mentioned in the 1980s, but catches up to quality of life by the early 2000s.

In this chapter we propose an innovative definition of urban sustainability as the sum of several components, one of which is the quality of life. Our definition of sustainability includes a quantifiable measure of quality of life as a function of residential location and local amenities, which is an interesting contribution. We consider models describing preferences and behaviour of both individuals and households that seek to maximize their immediate well-being. We present specific examples of approaches to model in detail aspects of urban life that have a strong impact on an individual's well-being, such as the commute to work and residential and work-place choice. Particular emphasis is given to the interdependencies of these decisions and behaviours between household members.

Urban sustainability and well-being 111

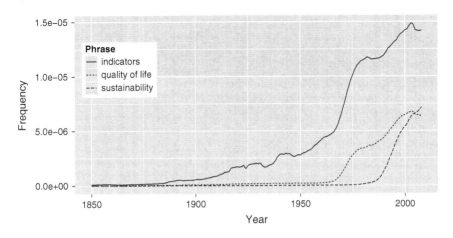

Figure 5.1 Popularity (expressed through Google ngrams) of three relevant terms: (1) indicators, (2) quality of life, and (3) sustainability.

Source: Author's own construct.

The structure of the chapter is as follows. Urban sustainability and its link with quality of life are first introduced, including indicators to express, quantify and measure urban sustainability. Taking advantage of advances in computational performance and data collection techniques, modelling and simulation today is moving from static to dynamic and from macroscopic/aggregate to microscopic/disaggregate. Considering these trends, we then explore disaggregate models and in particular the distinction between individual and household well-being, and how it affects their decisions. The heterogeneity in the willingness to pay for local amenities is discussed next, followed by a presentation of models for couples' joint mode choice and joint residential location choice. The question of whether observed location behaviour allows for the measuring of individual or household welfare is explored next, followed by a concluding section that discusses outlooks and extensions of this topic.

5.2 Urban sustainability and quality of life

A large number of definitions have been formulated for sustainability, in general, and urban sustainability, in particular. While these are useful, an overall accepted definition has not been reached, and in most cases, it is not clear how these definitions might evolve depending on the size and other characteristics of the conurbation.

Among the various definitions of urban sustainability, some are more relevant for the topic and focus of this book. For example, Maclaren (1996) defines urban sustainability as "a desirable state or set of conditions" that persist over time and may include: intergenerational and intragenerational equity, protection of the natural environment, minimal use of non-renewable resources, economic activity and

112   Constantinos Antoniou and Nathalie Picard

prosperity, and individual well-being. The relative weight of each of these components may change depending on the particular characteristics and the priorities of each urban environment. Arguably, less developed cities might put a higher priority on covering the basic needs of their citizens while more advanced cities might put a higher emphasis on issues such as equity, considering that the more elementary needs of the citizens are already covered.

The evolution of modern societies (and also the enrichment of the literature on sustainability) suggests that sustainability is no longer restricted to environmental concerns, but also incorporates economic and social dimensions (Dempsey *et al.*, 2011). While environmental processes may have significant similarities across cities and regions, economic and – especially – social issues need to be carefully considered in context. Therefore, in order to better capture the subtle differences across different urban areas, it becomes important to describe and specify in detail the components that make up urban sustainability.

The concept of urban quality of life is in itself complex and, arguably, could be broader than urban sustainability. Quality of life is often mostly linked to health, but this can lead to a limited, myopic definition. For example, according to Mitchell (2000) urban quality of life is determined by health, physical environment, natural resources, goods and services, community development, personal development, and security. We will see in subsequent sections that most of these dimensions of the quality of life are actually valued by households in their residential location choice. Economic aspects, which are not considered in this definition, are usually considered as one of the major pillars of quality of life (Van Kamp *et al.*, 2003). Indeed, dwelling prices are among the main determinants of residential location, and the weight attached to dwelling prices in residential location choice depends on household income. Urban development and evolution inherently use up resources from the ecosystem, thus potentially leading to a deterioration of the quality of the urban environment. To assess whether the "progress" is positive or negative, one needs to find a way to balance and compare the positive results of development, on the one hand, with the adverse impacts of using up limited natural resources, on the other hand. It becomes apparent that sustainability is affected by positive as well as negative effects of urban development. One approach for modelling urban sustainability is the metabolism model (Newman, 1999), where the urban ecosystem is viewed as a human body. According to this approach, the goal of sustainability in a city coincides with the reduction of the city's use of natural resources and the production of waste.

The United Nations Development Programme (Malik, 2013) has integrated various development indicators into a "human development index" (HDI): life expectancy, educational attainment, and command over the resources needed for decent living. Nowadays, most Western cities perform well in this index, while urban areas in the developing world are seeing rapid improvement. Observed trends in these indicators for countries in the developing areas confirm that there have been significant social and economic advances over the last three to four decades. It is clear that human well-being is a combination of many factors, and cannot simply be captured via economic indicators, such as GDP and its growth rate. In recent years, interest in using subjective data to measure well-being has steadily been increasing and it is now considered that subjective well-being is one of the three conceptual approaches to measuring quality of life (Stiglitz *et al.*, 2009). Of course, one significant difficulty with dealing with subjective measures of happiness is that there is often no objective, measurable counterpart. Some subjective measures of human well-being that can be related to actual performance are satisfaction with the quality of health care and education. These are good indicators, as it is possible to provide high standards of health care and education even when overall economic indicators are not performing well (one example is that the highest value of satisfaction with education quality is 94 per cent in Cambodia, while the global average is 64 per cent).

Another (objective) way to measure individual well-being is the hedonic approach.[1] The main assumption is that individual or household well-being is related to the utility derived both from the housing-specific and local characteristics of dwellings. Housing-specific characteristics correspond to the characteristics of the dwelling itself: total floor area, number of rooms, comfort level, etc. The local characteristics of the dwelling correspond to the local amenities (travel time and accessibility to jobs and services, quality of schools, green spaces, etc.) and neighbourhood characteristics (population density, fraction of poor and rich households, unemployment rate, fraction of singles and large families, fraction of foreigners, etc.). One could argue that such hedonic approaches lie in-between the economic indicators and the subjective well-being. In the later sections of this chapter, we develop the argument that human well-being is a combination of many factors, which are valued differently by individuals, like subjective well-being, and we propose a way to measure it more objectively, using observed behaviour.

Sustainability has both a short-term (within a generation) and a long-term (between generations) component. Proost *et al.* (2014) illustrate how these two aspects have been dealt with by economists. In this case, the goal is to provide quality of life and consumption options to future generations, through the preservation of sufficient productive capital for future generations. This capital can then be combined with other resources, such as labour, to guarantee sufficient quality of life. It should be made clear that productive capital in this case is a very broad term, including conventional "man-made capital", such as knowledge and infrastructure, as well as "natural capital", such as natural resources and the quality of the environment. Balancing these two components will be crucial for long-term sustainability and measuring them using the appropriate indicators poses an interesting challenge (Arrow *et al.*, 2004).

Population density and the types and mix of land uses play a big role in urban sustainability, as well as in households' well-being, although possibly in opposite directions. For example, while households may seek out locations with a high percentage of similar households (e.g. rich households are attracted by rich households and poor households are attracted by poor households) this may not be sustainable, as it leads to segregated cities. Urban planners argue in favour of a more compact, high-density and mixed-use urban form, as a more energy-efficient form of urban development, which allows citizens to minimize time and energy wasted on transport and spend more time on activities that serve actual needs and advance their quality of life. The increased density of urban form, however, may have conflicting impacts on social sustainability. For example, consider the definition of Bramley and Power (2009), who identify two key dimensions of social sustainability: social equity and sustainability of community. Social equity may cover access to jobs and affordable housing, as well as more access to local services, such as health care and shopping (for example, de Palma *et al.*, 2007b, address specifically this point, i.e. equity in access to local amenities). Social equity is arguably favoured by high-density urban development, as citizens have a larger number of local services available within their reach. Community sustainability at the neighbourhood level can benefit from the following conditions: interaction with other social networks, citizen participation in community activities, residential stability, security and sense of place. If citizens interact more with other people and participate in activities close to their residence, then they will have stronger ties to the community. And people are more eager to interact with other people when these other people are similar to themselves, resulting in social homogamy. A section on the heterogeneity of individuals' preferences that leads to this phenomenon is provided later in this chapter.

Furthermore, it is argued that high-density urban development might lead to more mixed/less segregated areas (compared to the typical "suburban sprawl" situation). On the other hand, people typically indicate that they prefer low-density suburban residential areas, which may be a reflection of a long-lasting projected image (from the popular media) of higher quality of life in these areas.

Urban sustainability is linked not only to purely economic and environmental factors, but also to the quality of life of citizens. One can easily consider a city that is designed in a way that maximizes its economic performance and minimizes its environmental impact, but at the same time leaves its residents unhappy and with low quality of life. Such a city would not be "sustainable", even if some measures show it as such. The several definitions of sustainability that have been proposed over the past decades, which are often overlapping and even contradicting, make it difficult for policy-makers to plan accordingly (Proost *et al.*, 2014). One of the factors that complicate the issue is the scope of sustainability, i.e. whether it includes only ecological capital, or also economic capital and social capital (Hediger, 2000). When only ecological capital is considered, strong sustainability is implied; on the other hand, when total capital is considered, we are talking about weak sustainability. Weak sustainability allows for substitution and trade-offs between ecological capital and other types of capital, with the aim of maximizing the overall level of social welfare.

One way to assess the link of urban sustainability and quality of life is to study the relocation decisions of residents within a city, assuming of course that the movement is driven by the need to maximize the overall satisfaction of the person (or family) making the move (Seo, 2002). Of course, not all moves are voluntary or discretionary, and this makes it much harder to assess the topic. A clear distinction can be made between the reasons for residence, and the satisfaction for each factor, between the inner city and the central city. Seo (2002) discusses the responses in

Urban sustainability and well-being 115

reference to the findings of a national opinion poll (Findlay *et al.*, 1988), which identifies the following six characteristics as the priorities in the places people wanted to live in: (1) minimal crime, (2) good health services, (3) low pollution, (4) low cost of living, (5) good shopping facilities, and (6) cultural diversity.

Urban ecosystems and open/green areas can have a strong impact on the well-being of citizens (Bolund and Hunhammar, 1999), as they provide recreational benefits including aesthetic and cultural attractions in the city. For example, it has been found that residents under stress (Ulrich *et al.*, 1991) and patients in a hospital (Ulrich, 1984) had much better experiences when exposed to natural environments (e.g. their room window was facing a green park). Of course, when one considers an urban component, one needs to also consider the possible externalities of ecosystems in cities, such as some tree species that may contribute to urban smog and ozone problems (Slanina, 1997), increased mosquito hatching and bad odours near ponds, and increased crime during the night in parks.

It becomes apparent from this discussion that dealing with sustainability relies on a multitude of heterogeneous and hard to measure factors. Monitoring urban sustainability requires some of the key aspects, such as the quantification of sustainable levels of energy, water use, food consumption, and the use of non-renewable resources, transportation, housing, and waste (Walsh *et al.*, 2006). Of course, there are many more aspects that need to be addressed before urban sustainability requirements are fully covered. The next section provides an overview of indicators for urban sustainability, in an effort towards this direction.

5.3 Urban sustainability indicators

Many researchers have attempted to develop a set of indicators that are complete and easy to compute and apply. However, it is clear that this ideal set of indicators has not yet been identified. Tanguay *et al.* (2010) present a meta-analysis of the use of urban sustainable development indicators (SDI) in developed Western countries and find that there are serious limitations in this "state-of-the-art". In particular, there is a lack of consensus on the conceptual framework and approach, but also on the selection and optimal number of indicators to use. This suggests that the problem is not simply one of fine-tuning and optimizing an already available set of indicators, but that there are open questions that remain.

Maclaren (1996) outlines the following steps in an overall process of reporting on urban sustainability: (1) define the goals; (2) scope the problem to determine how many indicators are suitable; (3) choose an appropriate indicator framework (e.g. domain-based, goal-based, sectorial, issue-based, causal or combination); (4) define indicator selection criteria; (5) identify a set of potential indicators; (6) evaluate the indicators and select a final set; (7) collect data and analyse the indicator results; (8) prepare and present the urban sustainability report; (9) assess the indicator performance. Such a linear process can be further improved through the incorporation of feedback mechanisms (Alberti, 1996). In such a framework for measuring urban sustainability, three main elements can be envisaged: (1) key variables to describe urban and environmental systems and their interrelationships;

116   *Constantinos Antoniou and Nathalie Picard*

(2) measurable objectives and criteria that enable assessing these interrelationships; and (3) feedback mechanisms to refine the selection of key variables and objectives, so that they serve the task at hand more effectively. A useful set of indicators should be able to support decisions on whether urban quality and performance is improving or deteriorating in relation to certain criteria or targets and how these trends can be linked to trends in urban development and organization (Alberti, 1996).

Besides determining the individual indicators that can be used, it is important to underline that indicators should not be considered in isolation, but combined (Sahely *et al.*, 2005). Furthermore, it is essential to highlight the distinction between indicators and criteria, i.e. yardstick values against which indicator values can be measured. It is also important to note that the most valuable use of indicators is to monitor and identify relative changes of urban sustainability over time, and not to compare them against some absolute, reference numbers. Clearly, different urban environments have different needs, resources, and capacities for further improvement; it is easy for a city starting from a very low level to quickly improve, while it may be very hard for a city that has already covered all the "low-hanging fruit", to further increase its urban sustainability. In all cases, however, it is important to know whether a city or a region is moving toward or away from environmentally sustainable paths. One way to monitor this is using a natural capital approach (Olewiler, 2006), which includes guidelines for the development and selection of natural capital indicators that can help predict the current environmental sustainability trends of a city.

Munda (2006) discusses and compares various concepts for urban sustainability policy-making, including concepts from ecology and economics, and proposes social multi-criteria evaluation (SMCE) as a general, multidimensional framework for urban sustainability policies. Selected indicators include percentage of houses owned, residential density, use of private car, mean travel time to work, income disparity, households below the poverty line, and crime rate.

Dempsey *et al.* (2011) explore the relationship between urban form and social sustainability and identify two main dimensions of social sustainability: equitable access to local services (such as post office, supermarket, primary school, library, public open spaces, and primary health care) and sustainability of the community itself. Fehr *et al.* (2004) propose a comprehensive list of indicators for urban sustainability in a developing country (Brazil), covering demographic evolution, public transportation, solid waste handling, liquid effluent handling, air monitoring, fresh water supply, public education, public health care, cultural issues, energy supply, park availability and maintenance, and land use and resource preservation. Identifying these indicators is only the first step in a long process of implementing them, which is hampered by many difficulties, such as the challenge of quantification of these indicators. Furthermore, the challenge of maintaining long-term compliance and a management model for the application of the indicators is discussed as a key parameter of long-term success.

Shen *et al.* (2011) review and compare different urban sustainability indicator practices and propose a comparative categorization named the International Urban

Sustainability Indicators List. The aim is to support decisions about which a set of indicators may be more suitable for each case, considering four dimensions: environmental, economic, social, and governance. Transportation enters directly into the environmental and social dimensions. Singh *et al.* (2009) provide an overview of sustainability indicators applied in policy evaluation and discuss issues related to sustainability indices formulation strategy, scaling, normalization, weighting, and aggregation. Wilson *et al.* (2007) compare six sustainable development indicators, both in tabular format and spatially in a map. An application in Canada illustrates the differences of the various measures, which are discussed in an effort to elucidate their differences.

The level of aggregation of the analysis is also an important issue. Brereton *et al.* (2008) use disaggregated data at the individual and local level and use an indirect utility function of well-being that comprises spatial factors (such as commuting time and proximity to the coast) and socio-economic and demographic characteristics.

Keirstead and Leach (2008) examine urban sustainability indicators, considering London as a case-study, and find that there is a gap between theory and practice. The authors attribute this issue partly to the vague definition of urban sustainability. When trying to operationalize urban sustainability through indicators, it is essential to be as clear and concrete as possible regarding the nature of urban sustainability itself. Therefore, specific research questions are often pursued in this direction, such as the discussion of weak versus strong sustainability, i.e. the extent to which man-made capital can be substituted for lost environmental capital, or the relative weight of the different components of urban sustainability, such as social, economic, and environmental. Cities are unique structures with special characteristics, and therefore these individual features should be explicitly considered when attempting to quantify the puzzle of urban sustainability components.

The PROPOLIS project (Lautso *et al.*, 2004; Spiekerman and Wegener, 2004) was a research project partly funded through the European Union Fifth Framework Programme. The project aimed to research, develop, and test integrated land-use and transport policies, tools, and comprehensive assessment methodologies in order to define sustainable long-term urban strategies and demonstrate their effects in European cities. One of the objectives of the PROPOLIS project was to identify policies that could simultaneously improve all dimensions of urban sustainability, compared to a reference solution, instead of sacrificing one dimension to improve another. The findings, based on the output of the project, were optimistic, as they suggested that a set of approaches, combining pricing, investment and land-use policies, reached this goal in most of the cities that were used as cases in the project. Therefore, it is argued that these policies could be transferable to other cities as well. Three sets of indicators were developed for the quantification and assessment of these policies: environmental indicators, social indicators and economic indicators. Interestingly, they include the total net benefit from transport as an economic indicator. As a result, there is at least the option to compare environmental benefits and the costs of realizing them.

Bradley Guy and Kibert (1998) discuss the systems approach of sustainable development, which also includes economic and social factors, making the process of selecting sustainability indicators an inherently human value-driven process. Jabareen (2006) presents seven design concepts of sustainable urban form: (1) compactness; (2) sustainable transport; (3) population density; (4) mixed land uses; (5) diversity; (6) passive solar design; (7) greening. These concepts are being used by Jabareen (2006) in an assessment matrix in order to assess the sustainability of different urban forms.

Proost *et al.* (2014) stress that sustainability also encompasses social aspects and that equity and a minimum access to basic amenities for the poor should be considered. The equity dimension of a policy can be considered by giving higher weight to the cost components of the poorest groups or individuals. The relative weights of the income classes may be chosen based on the degree of the inequality aversion (Atkinson, 1970) of the policy-maker. Other social indicators, such as the quality and intensity of social interactions, may be more difficult to quantify and evaluate, also due to strong externalities between individuals and network effects that are difficult to foresee (Schelling, 1978).

5.4 Microsimulation models for the analysis of urban sustainability

The preceding discussion has illustrated the conceptual and methodological challenges associated with the understanding and measurement of urban sustainability and its links with individual well-being and quality of life. In this section, we explore how state-of-the-art modelling approaches can support the analysis of urban sustainability.

The exponential advances in computational capabilities accompanied by the emerging data collection techniques have resulted in an overall shift in modelling and simulation, from static to dynamic and from aggregate to disaggregate. Land-use and transport interaction software comprise one of the fields in which this shift has been particularly evident, with software, such as UrbanSim (Waddell, 2002; Waddell *et al.*, 2007), becoming increasingly more attractive and widely used.

Integrated Land-Use and Transport – or Land-Use and Transport Interaction – (LUTI) models are sets of interacting sub-models that are used to forecast urban development after the implementation of a policy. LUTI models form the mathematical, quantitative approach for predicting the direct and indirect effects of urban planning policies on the environment, society and economy that the theoretical, qualitative approach is unable to predict itself.

LUTI models combine agent (households and jobs) location choice, transition, real estate price (rent and purchase) and development, and transport (activity and agent-based) models, in an integrated framework. The sub-models are first separately estimated using base-year data, and then applied in simulations of different time intervals (e.g. every year). For every simulated period, the data set generated from the previous simulation is used. Due to the complicated nature of the interacting agents in agent-based LUTI models, disaggregate social and structural data are required. Since the analysis in the agent-based models takes place at the individual level detailed, microscopic models are used. Therefore, such frameworks are called microscopic simulation or microsimulation frameworks, in contrast to macroscopic or more aggregate models, which are much faster to develop and run, and therefore may be suitable for other applications.

These models allow the simulation of entire urban areas or conurbations in very fine detail, which in turn allows the evaluation of a wide range of indicators. The consideration of these indicators allows for a well-rounded, multi-dimensional assessment of urban sustainability and, in turn, social welfare and well-being. In this chapter, we use such disaggregate models that operate on millions of citizens, couples/households, and dwellings, to demonstrate the differences between individual and household decisions on their individual and combined well-being.

Proost *et al.* (2014) present a unifying and integrated evaluation framework for microsimulation models. To evaluate policies simulated by the microsimulation model, one can feed the outputs of the model to a social welfare function, which will be used to produce concise estimates of social welfare. In essence, this function would be used to evaluate a number of indicators over all individuals in the city, for each scenario, and thus provide an aggregate value of the expected social welfare under the considered scenario. One advantage of this approach is that one can use the underlying LUTI model to simulate various policy scenarios and perform predictions of their impacts on a microscopic level, and then compute point estimates (or ranges of estimates) of the expected social welfare. The weighting of the different components may differ based on the criteria of the policy decision maker and the objectives that are set. A sensitivity analysis of the resulting solution should also be performed, to ensure that the selected policy is robust and might not change subject to minor fluctuations in the input parameters.

Proost *et al.* (2014) provide a general framework for a social welfare specification that can be further operationalized depending on the data and issues at hand. This specification includes the value of the local stock (of both natural and physical capital) left for the next generations at the end of the time horizon, the cost of implementation of the policy, and the discounted sum of the revenues collected (these include the tax revenues as well as the tolls and the revenues from public transport).

5.5 Individual vs. household well-being and individual vs. household decisions

The analysis of well-being at the household level is not necessarily consistent with the analysis of the same variables at the individual level. Peluso and Trannoy (2007) analyse the conditions under which the individual's and household's points of views are consistent with each other. The analysis of income distribution at the household level and at the individual level often reveals significant differences. As a consequence, we argue that the family should be considered when computing sustainability indicators as well as well-being indicators.

Switching from the individual to household or family point of view is relevant and often necessary in three major cases. The first case is when the choices themselves are important for the family (marriage, divorce, number of children,

120 *Constantinos Antoniou and Nathalie Picard*

children's education, etc.). The second case is when individual choices generate externalities to the other members of the household (competition among family members for using a joint car, chore sharing, spatial mobility, retirement plans, etc.). The third case is when decisions are naturally or necessarily taken jointly (joint residential location or joint leisure activities, for example).

The first case naturally comes to the researcher's mind, and it has given rise to a large body of literature, but there are few examples of it in the urban context. The second one, with many examples in the urban context, is crucial for welfare analysis, which is central to this chapter, and the third one is essential for understanding household decisions and their interactions with public policies.

Taking into account individual and family aspects is of particular relevance in the family context, since the preferences and constraints of different family members usually vary in this context. When several individuals with different preferences and constraints have to take a joint decision, or a series of individual decisions involving consequences for other family members, the bargaining process can be rather complex. However, when a bargaining process takes place within the family, specific considerations such as altruism or repeated interaction usually ease the process, leading to a Pareto-optimal decision. A decision is Pareto-optimal if it leads to a situation where it would not be possible to increase the well-being of one family member without decreasing the well-being of at least one other family member.

Chiappori (1988) has developed collective models based on the Pareto-optimality assumption. He has shown that, under some basic and rather realistic assumptions, when the outcome of a joint decision is Pareto-optimal, it can be solved by maximizing a weighted average of the utilities of the different family members. The weight of a given family member's utility is called his/her Pareto weight; it depends on the within-family bargaining power of the family member considered.

The very simple example developed below will illustrate the need to disentangle bargaining power from preferences in joint decisions in order to perform welfare analysis in the context of family decisions.

Consider that individual well-being only depends on commuting time, and is proportional to commuting time (with a negative coefficient, since the more time you spend commuting the less happy you are; the opposite of this coefficient is called the Value of Time, or VOT). Let us denote by μ the woman's Pareto weight and by tt_g the commuting time of gender g, with $g = m$ for the husband and $g = f$ for the wife. Then, the household welfare function can be written as:

$$W = constant - \mu \cdot VOT_f \cdot tt_f - +(1 - \mu) \cdot VOT_m \cdot tt_m \qquad (5.1)$$

Consider a reference household, R, with constant $= 15$, $\mu = 0.5$ and $VOT_f = VOT_m = 10 \text{€}$ per hour, and $tt_f = tt_m = 1$ hour. Consider now household A with the same constant, Pareto weights and travel times, but with $VOT_f = 12$ and $VOT_m = 8$. Then the household welfare level is the same in these two households, but the woman is worse-off in household A than in the reference household, because she is more sensitive to commuting time, and the man is better-off in household A than in the reference household, because he is less sensitive to commuting time. Consider now household B with the same constant, values of time, and travel times as the reference household, but with $\mu = 0.6$. Then the welfare level of household B is the same as that of the reference household and in household A. In addition, the individual well-being level of the woman (respectively man) is the same in household B as in the reference household, but the woman (respectively man) is better-off (respectively worse-off) in household B than in household A. Now, the household welfare function is equal to $15 - 5 \cdot tt_f - 5 \cdot tt_m$ in the reference household, whereas it is equal to $15 - 6 \cdot tt_f - 4 \cdot tt_m$ in households A and B. Since the household welfare functions are equal in household A and B, these two households will behave the same way, and they will look identical if Pareto weight is not disentangled from preferences. However, the well-being of individual members in these two households is totally different, since the woman (respectively man) is more (respectively less) affected by commuting time in household A than in household B. By contrast, the preferences of individual members are the same in household B and in the reference household, but their behaviour will be different since the Pareto weights are different.

To conclude this example, individual well-being only depends on individual preferences, whereas household welfare function and behaviour depends both on individual preferences and Pareto weights.

Collective models are very general in the sense that they do not rely on a restrictive specific bargaining process, and they do not impose any restrictive specification for each member utility function. Collective models have proved on many occasions to perform better than the usual unitary models employed to explain observed behaviour (Vermeulen, 2002).

The main restriction in the early literature on collective models is that it rules out altruism. By contrast, Chiappori (1992) has shown that most of the results of collective models easily extend to the case of caring preferences. When a family member has caring preferences, his/her global utility function depends on his/her own well-being (or sub-utility) and on the well-being of the other family members. The global utility of any family member is increasing in the sub-utility of any family member. Altruism is reflected in the individual global utility, but there is no altruism in the individual sub-utilities: the individual sub-utility of a given family member only depends on the variables chosen by this family member. With caring preferences, maximizing global utilities is equivalent to maximizing sub-utilities. It means that any joint Pareto-optimal decision is such that it would not be possible to increase the global utility of any family member without decreasing the global utility of at least another family member, and that it would not be possible to increase the individual sub-utility of any family member without decreasing the sub-utility of at least another family member. With caring preferences, a Pareto-optimal solution maximizes the weighted average of individual global utilities, and the weight of a given member's global utility reflects his/her bargaining power. The same Pareto-optimal solution also maximizes the weighted average of individual sub-utilities, but in this case, the weights merge the effect

122   Constantinos Antoniou and Nathalie Picard

of bargaining power and the effect of altruism. This distinction is particularly important for welfare analysis.

We now turn to specific examples on the measurement of individual well-being in the urban context, with empirical applications in the Paris region, using data from the 1999 General Census.

5.5.1   Heterogeneous preferences and willingness to pay for local amenities

In the context of residential location, individual or household well-being can be measured by the utility derived from the dwelling. Following Rosen (1974), if real estate markets were perfect, the value of dwelling characteristics would be perfectly reflected in prices, which would "clear the market". Market clearing implies that prices adjust so as to make any household indifferent between any locations. When a location becomes more attractive, this increases the utility of living in this location, but at the same time, this increases the price to be paid to live there, which in turn decreases the utility to live there. Equilibrium in perfect real estate markets implies that these two effects exactly compensate. Heterogeneity of preferences makes market clearing conditions more complex, and imperfections in real estate markets prevent prices from clearing the market. We thus depart here from this literature because there is clear evidence that prices do not clear the markets in the Paris region, as discussed in de Palma et al. (2007a). Instead, we focus on the effect of amenities and dwelling prices (per square meter) and on individual or household well-being, measured by a utility function.

Inoa et al. (2014) show that preferences for local amenities are highly heterogeneous across individuals and households. They focus on singles and one-worker couples. Chiappori et al. (2012), by contrast, focus on dual-earner couples. We discuss below the heterogeneity of preferences across these different household categories, showing that what matters for individual or household well-being depends on individual and household characteristics.

Preferences differ across individuals and households, not only as a function of their characteristics, but also in relation to their (chosen) tenure status and dwelling type, as discussed in Dantan and Picard (2014).

For example, households with children value a lot of green spaces, or good quality schools, whereas young singles are more interested in leisure infrastructures. Such heterogeneity can be taken into account by estimating a discrete choice model for residential location in which local amenities are crossed with individual/household characteristics, as in de Palma et al. (2005, 2007a). Under perfect markets assumption, individuals or households choose the location that provides the largest utility and individual-specific well-being can be measured by the indirect utility using a multinomial logit model. The coefficients of the local amenities and other explanatory variables (globally referred to as attributes) are then proportional to the marginal utility of the associated attribute, or to the willingness to pay for the attributes.

Household preferences depend on income, measured by:

$$\log(\text{income}) = \log(\text{income of the household considered/average income}$$
$$\text{in the region}).$$

This variable is equal to 0 when household income is equal to average income in the region, positive for richer households and negative for poorer households.

For all real estate sub-markets, the price coefficient has the expected negative sign, meaning that the utility of a household with average income decreases when dwelling prices increase. The price elasticity becomes less and less negative when income increases, which is consistent with the fact that a dwelling is rather a luxury good, and richer households are often less sensitive to dwelling prices than poorer households. The price elasticity even becomes positive for the richest households, which mainly reflects the effect of unobserved local amenities. Indeed, richer households pay more attention than poorer households to local amenities, and this increases the equilibrium real estate prices. When such a characteristic is not observable, its effect is included in the price coefficient.

We find a strong preference of households for cities which are well endowed with public goods and transport, and for living close to households that are similar in terms of composition, age, and wealth. We also find that the preferences for local amenities, such as public parks, forests, or sporting facilities, significantly depend on the number of children in the household, which contributes significantly to the social homogamy in terms of number of children. This adds to the fact that, ceteris paribus, households with children are attracted by other households with children: families with children tend to locate close to each other, both because they enjoy similar amenities and because they enjoy living close to similar households.

5.5.2 Commuting time and couples' joint mode of transport choice

One of the main determinants of individual well-being in large cities subject to severe congestion, such as the Paris region, is commuting time. This is because most of the jobs are located in the centre of the region, whereas many households, especially those with children, are located in the suburbs. In addition, many households are not able to afford several cars; this makes it very difficult for the two spouses to commute by car in dual-earner households, and induces competition between spouses to use the car when there is only one car in the household.

Spouses' mode of transport choices are interdependent for several reasons. First, spouses may enjoy commuting together, because time spent together seems shorter. Second, commuting together allows sharing of the commuting cost. However, commuting together is possible or interesting only when spouses commute in similar directions. Third, there is a kind of "competition for the car" in households with only one car and two spouses commuting to different destinations. Picard *et al.* (2013) analyse in detail mode of transport choice between couples and evaluate the importance of competition for using the car for commuting trips; they also evaluate the welfare of each spouse in this joint model.

124 *Constantinos Antoniou and Nathalie Picard*

In this bargaining model, the household maximizes the weighted average utility of the woman and the man. The weight of the woman's utility corresponds to her Pareto weight, and depends on spouses' characteristics (age, nationality, education, etc.), whereas the weight of the man's utility is normalized to 1 minus the woman's weight.

We focus in this section on the part of individual welfare, which depends on commuting time, namely the (monetary and psychological) commuting cost. Each spouse's commuting cost has an individual-specific and mode-specific fixed part corresponding to the monetary and subjective cost of taking the car or public transport to go to work, and an individual and mode-specific variable part corresponding to the monetary cost and psychological displeasure of spending time commuting. The variable cost is proportional to commuting time, which depends on the mode and on a potential "detour". For example, there is a detour for the man if he drops the woman to her work before he drives to his own work. He may decide to do so because he enjoys the company of his wife, or in order to share operating costs.

We consider dual-earner couples and compare the welfare of each spouse in different, alternative scenarios:

1   Both spouses use public transport (reference case, with the utility of both spouses normalized to 0). This alternative is available whatever the number of cars in the household; the following ones require at least one car.
2   The woman commutes by car and the man by public transport.
3   The man commutes by car and the woman by public transport.
4   Each spouse uses his/her own car. This alternative is available only in households with at least 2 cars.
5   The man drops the woman on his way to his own job. This implies a detour for the man, which is a longer trip than his trip in the drive alone case.
6   The woman drops the man on her way to her own job. This implies a detour for the woman, which is a longer trip than her trip in the drive alone case.

Each of these six alternatives involves specific commuting times for each spouse, which can be computed, and thus specific fixed and variable costs.

In the census data we use, we can observe the mode choice of each spouse, so we can identify alternatives 1 to 3. When both spouses commute by car, we know that the couple selected one alternative among alternatives 4 to 6 if there are two cars in the household, or one alternative among alternatives 5 and 6 if there is only one car in the household, but we cannot observe directly which of these 2 or 3 alternatives was chosen. However, these three alternatives lead to different welfare levels for each spouse, and we can compute the likelihood of each of these alternatives for each couple.

Of course, the number of cars in the household is not exogenous, but is chosen by the household. Buying one or two cars offers the possibility to use it or them for commuting trips, but also for other occasions. Thus, buying one or two cars increases household welfare by enlarging the choice set in the mode choice

Urban sustainability and well-being 125

decision. This is anticipated in the decision of buying one or two cars. However, buying and maintaining cars is costly and thus reduces utility by reducing the budget available for other expenses.

Dantan and Picard (2013) have developed a model to measure individual's and couples' welfare resulting from the joint decisions to buy no car, or one or two cars, and of each spouse's mode choice. Using this model and observing the joint mode choice of each couple, they can estimate the Pareto weights and the fixed and variable cost of each alternative. Using these estimates, they can compute the welfare of each individual and each household. It is then possible to evaluate the welfare effects of any policy aiming at reducing commuting time, by improving either the public transport network or the private transport network.

The results in Dantan and Picard (2013), and subsequent ongoing research, show that the woman's bargaining power increases with her age and decreases with the man's age. The woman's bargaining power is larger is she is native than if she is a foreigner, and it is larger if she lives with a foreigner than if she lives with a native man.

The fixed cost of commuting by public transport is larger than the fixed cost of commuting by car alone, both for the husband and the wife. This means that, for very short trips, both men and women prefer driving to using public transport. This preference for the car compared to public transport is a mix of subjective preferences and of the fixed cost of using either mode of transport.

However, the marginal commuting cost is larger by car than by public transport. This is consistent with the fact that most commuters using public transport use a monthly card allowing them to travel freely, implying no marginal monetary cost for public transport (only a subjective marginal cost corresponding to the disutility of spending time on public transport). By contrast, the marginal cost of operating a car (including fuel expense) is not negligible at all.

The combination of the fixed cost and variable cost by mode is such that the man would prefer using public transport than driving alone for any trip more than 1 hour and 10 minutes for both modes, and he would prefer driving alone than using public transport for any trip less than 1 hour and 10 minutes for both modes. The estimated switching time is only 20 minutes for women. This is consistent with the fact that most women commute by public transport and most men commute by car.

The estimated fixed cost of driving together is larger than the weighted[2] average fixed cost of spouses driving alone. This may reflect the cost of scheduling constraints: commuting together implies leaving at the same time, which may be inconvenient when the husband's and wife's ideal schedules differ. The variable cost of commuting together in the same car is larger than the weighted variable cost of spouses commuting alone by car when the woman drives, but it is lower when the man drives. Consider the case of equal Pareto weights (0.5 for each spouse), and spouses working at the same place, so that there is no detour if they commute together by car. Then, it will never be optimal that the woman drives and the man is the passenger, since both fixed and variables costs are larger in this case than when either the man drives and the woman is a passenger, or both spouses

126 *Constantinos Antoniou and Nathalie Picard*

use their own car. However, it is optimal that the man drives and the woman is the passenger for short trips, i.e. for trips shorter than 47 minutes (when both spouses work at the same place).

Overall, our results show that improving the public transport network would benefit women more than men. More precisely, it would benefit most of the women, whereas it would benefit only men working very far away (more than one hour) from the place where they live. By contrast, improving the private network (roads) would benefit more men than women. More precisely, it would benefit most of the men, whereas it would benefit only women working quite close to the place where they live (less than 20 minutes, but not walking distance).

5.5.3 Couples' joint residential location

Since commuting time is one of the major determinants of individual well-being in large cities subject to severe congestion, individuals and households do their best to reduce this time. The previous section analysed how commuting time can be reduced by choosing the appropriate mode of transport (subject to potential competition for the car, when there is only one in the household), conditional on residential location and on spouses' workplaces. We now analyse how households may choose their residential location (conditional on each spouse's workplace) in order to reduce the commuting time of either spouse, thus increasing his/her welfare.

Picard *et al.* (2013) show that women's commuting time is lower than men's in the Paris region. The average difference is 5.7 minutes out of 45 minutes by public transportation, and 2.2 minutes out of 15 minutes by private car. This difference may a priori come from two different phenomena: (1) the marginal distributions of dwellings (irrespectively of male and female workplaces) are such that dwellings are on average closer to female jobs than to male jobs; (2) the endogenous distribution of dwellings conditional on female and male workplaces is such that, for a specific household, the dwelling is closer to the woman's workplace than to the man's workplace. However, Picard *et al.* (2013) show that the first explanation does not hold, since the marginal distributions of dwellings (irrespectively of male and female workplaces) are such that dwellings are on average slightly closer to male jobs than to female jobs. This suggests that household residential location is endogenously chosen so that it minimizes the wife's commuting time more than the husband's commuting time, that is, in order to maximize the wife's welfare more than the husband's welfare. This result is also consistent with Abraham and Hunt (1997), who notice that the probability of moving is more strongly related to commuting distance for women than for men, which results in shorter commuting distances for women after a relocation.

The observed shorter commuting times for wives than for husbands suggest a larger degree of bargaining power for women than men in the residential location choice, but this could also be compensated for by other decisions. For example, the woman usually spends more time caring for children and taking them to school or other activities.

Urban sustainability and well-being 127

Picard *et al.* (2013) estimate a multinomial logit model of residential location conditional on husband and wife workplaces, as a function of local dwelling price (per square metre, in log, which has the expected negative sign) and spouses' actual travel time, by mode and gender. Their results show that household location is slightly more sensitive to women's than men's travel time by private car, but it is twice more sensitive to women's than men's travel time by public transport. Interacting travel times with the number of cars in the household helps in understanding such differences. Travel time by private car (both for husband and wife) has no influence on household location for households owning no car, which is fully consistent. Households do not care how much time a husband or wife would spend commuting by car, when they have no access to any car. The difference between the coefficients of travel time by private car for the wife in households with no or one car is not statistically significant. For the husband, it is the difference between one and two cars, which is not significant. This means that the husband's commuting time by private car becomes relevant in residential location choice as soon as there is at least one car in the household. By contrast, the wife's commuting time by car becomes really relevant only when there are at least two cars in the household. This gives a strong indication that the husband has priority use of the car to commute, when there is competition between spouses for the use of the unique car. This competition was analysed in greater detail in the previous section.

The influence of travel time by public transportation on residential location is decreasing with the number of cars in the household, both for the wife and for the husband. This influence nearly disappears for men, when there are two cars in the household, suggesting that the husband usually commutes by car and does not care about transit travel times when there are two cars in the household. These results are consistent with the fact that, on the one hand, public transportation is a substitute for the private car, when household members can easily reach a station, which is usually the case in the centre and inner ring in Paris, whereas it is a complement when individuals have to drive to the station in order to use public transportation. The fact that the husband's transit commuting time plays virtually no role in residential location of two-car households, whereas the wife's transit commuting time still matters suggests that, when there are two cars in the household, husbands will, regardless, entirely commute by car, whereas wives may go to the station by car.

Based on the above results concerning the use of the car, Chiappori *et al.* (2012) estimate a structural collective model for household location conditional on spouses' workplaces, in which travel times are computed assuming the man has priority access to the car in households with only one car. The commuting time considered is then by public transport for both spouses if there is no car; the minimum between private car and public transport for both spouses if there are two cars. In households with only one car, the travel time considered is by public transport for the woman and the minimum between private car and public transport for the man.

Consistently with collective models, Chiappori *et al.* (2012) analyse a structural model explicitly taking into account both spouses' individual preferences and respective bargaining powers (or Pareto weights) rather than mixing them in a household utility function, which may or may not be consistent with rationality. They develop a method to disentangle the Pareto weights and the spouses' values of time and to measure separately the influence of explanatory variables on the Pareto weights and on the value of time, that is, on individual well-being. To the best of our knowledge, this is the only contribution to the literature that takes into account the role of the within-family decision process and spouses' bargaining powers in a residential location choice. The other contributions, such as Abraham and Hunt (1997) or Beharry-Borg *et al.* (2009), do consider the influence of individual characteristics on residential location choices, but the associated coefficients mix the influence of individual preferences and bargaining powers.

Spouses may or may not have diverging preferences concerning local amenities, and these preferences probably differ from the preferences of singles. The same individual will tend to enjoy bars and discos, when she/he is single, and open spaces, when she/he is married with children. Given this change in preferences of the same individual when she/he marries, it is not possible to disentangle respective bargaining powers and spouses' preferences for local amenities. Instead, they consider a joint preference of the household for local amenities, and they compute the joint welfare that the household gets from local amenities rather than trying to recover the well-being that each spouse – separately – gets from the same local amenities.

By contrast, it is obvious that the husband's preference for his own commuting time[3] is different from the wife's preference for the husband's commuting time. The influence of the husband's commuting time on household residential location mixes (1) the role of the husband's VOT, which a priori depends only on the husband's individual characteristics and (2) the role of respective spouses' Pareto weights, which a priori depends both on the husband and wife individual characteristics. Similarly, the influence of the wife's commuting time on household residential location mixes the role of the wife's VOT and of the respective spouses' Pareto weights. As a result, neglecting spouses' respective Pareto weights leads to biased estimates of the values of time of the household members, and, therefore, biased estimates of each spouse's well-being. Each spouse's Pareto weights is normalized to one-half in the reference case (i.e. the two spouses are native and 20 years old), and the husband and wife Pareto weights always sum to 1, so that Pareto weights can be interpreted as percentages. Any increase in the woman's Pareto weight corresponds to a decrease of the same percentage for the husband's Pareto weight. The econometric results show that the woman's age and man's nationality play a crucial role in determining Pareto weights, as do educational differences.

The Pareto weight of the husband is reduced by about 4.5 per cent when he is foreign, whereas the wife's Pareto weight does not significantly depend on her nationality. The wife's Pareto weight is larger when she is older and/or more educated than her husband, and the husband's Pareto weight is larger when he is more educated than his wife (compared to a couple in which spouses have the same age and educational level).

Urban sustainability and well-being   129

The econometric results of this model also show a large bias in the measurement of spouses' well-being when the bargaining power is not taken into account in a residential location model. For example, there is a 20 per cent underestimation of the welfare loss due to commuting time for a 40-year-old native man, which becomes an 18 per cent overestimation for a 40-year-old native man. For the wife, the welfare loss due to commuting time is always overestimated when the Pareto weight is omitted, and the bias is 15 per cent for a 40-year-old native woman and 10 per cent for a 20-year-old native woman. There is an additional bias upwards in the measurement of the welfare loss due to commuting time for foreign men when the Pareto weight is omitted.

5.5.4   _How to measure the welfare generated by the access to a well-suited job?_

One important source of individual welfare in modern urban economies is the opportunity to find a job well-suited to the individual's preferences and skills, and to be able to commute to this job daily, in a reasonable commuting time. When she/he chooses a job conditional on his/her residential location, an individual trades off between the characteristics of this job (is it well suited to the individual's preferences and skills?) and the time required to commute to this job. When she/he chooses his/her residential location, the individual anticipates future job location choices. In the transport literature relying on discrete choice literature (see Anderson _et al._, 1992, for details), this anticipation is translated in an accessibility variable measuring the expected maximum utility of potential workplaces. Accessibility also corresponds to the weighted average of the utility of each potential workplace, the weight corresponding to the probability that this workplace is chosen.

If all individuals had the same skills and preferences for jobs, and the same VOT, the accessibility to jobs would be universal, i.e. identical for all individuals and only dependent on residential location. However, skills and preferences for different job types, as well as VOT, are highly heterogeneous. As a result, the accessibility of jobs should be individual-specific, as argued by Inoa _et al._ (2014). Accessibility of jobs depends on gender, fertility, age and, more importantly, on education, as illustrated in Figure 5.2. For the lowest educational level (elementary and middle school), accessibility is high inside Paris, as well as inside and around the denser cities in the suburbs. This is consistent with the fact that less-educated people mainly look for low-qualification jobs close to their residence, and such jobs are concentrated in the denser cities. By contrast, highly educated people look for qualified jobs, and such jobs are concentrated in specific places, such as Paris CBD or La Défense, which are well connected to the public and private transport networks.

As a result, accessibility for highly educated people is high in all locations that are well connected to Paris CBD or to La Défense through either the public or the private transport network. This explains the differences between the two maps in Figure 5.2.

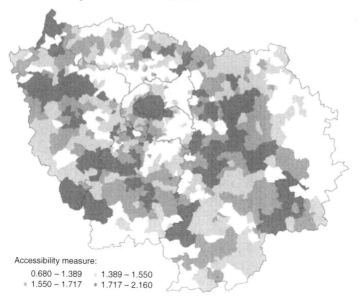

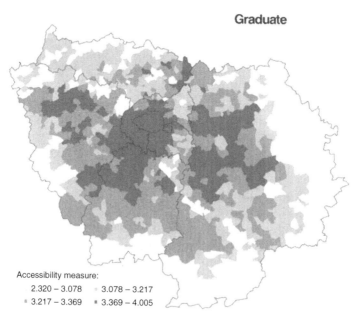

Figure 5.2 Accessibility measures, by education level.
Source: Author's own construct.

Finally, estimation results for residential location choices show that well-being is better explained by such an individual-specific accessibility measure than by the universal accessibility measure usually used in transport literature.

5.5.5 Does observed location behaviour allow measuring individual or household welfare?

The analysis of well-being relies on the measurement of the utility of individuals or households. Under perfect market conditions, utility governs residential location choices and can be estimated from observed choices. By contrast, under imperfect markets, individual and household behaviour do not perfectly reflect utility. In this case, the analysis of well-being requires to disentangle the roles of preferences and constraints.

Two major types of constraints can be considered in location choice models. Capacity constraints analysed in de Palma *et al.* (2007a) prevent some households from locating in their preferred place, whereas liquidity constraints analysed by Dantan and Picard (2014) prevent some households from buying their dwelling. Both constraints are related to imperfections in the dwelling market and would not hold if prices could clear the market.

5.5.5.1 Capacity constraints

One important issue that has not yet received sufficient attention in the literature, and that is the central focus of this subsection, is the role of availability constraints in households' choices. In estimating location choice models by observing agents' choices among a set of alternatives, it is implicitly assumed that the alternatives are all available, as they would be in a perfect real estate market. However, in the housing market, limited availability is not at all uncommon. For example, a particular neighbourhood may be highly desired, while few vacancies may be available to those searching in the area. A standard assumption in economics is that prices adjust and clear the market, and therefore putting prices on the right-hand side of the model is sufficient to address this concern. However, casual observation supported by data suggests that this assumption may be too strong in many housing markets, especially in the Paris region. Various forms of friction make the housing market less than perfectly efficient. High transaction costs, regulation constraints, attachments to social networks, non-trivial search costs, and low turnover in some locations, among other factors, suggest that prices may not fully clear the market. These factors give rise to supply constraints in some locations.

If the assumption that prices clear the market is not valid, then it follows that coefficients estimated for discrete choice models (and hence the formulation of welfare functions) in markets that experience some level of availability constraints will be biased, confounding the effect of the constraints with the agents' preferences. An important policy implication of this concern is that if these constraint effects are not corrected for in estimation of a choice model, predicted shifts in demand in response to an exogenous change (such as the change in accessibility due to major transportation investments) would also be biased, leading

132 *Constantinos Antoniou and Nathalie Picard*

to potentially misleading conclusions regarding the relative costs and benefits of alternative policy choices. A second important policy implication is that welfare levels computed from the estimation of such models are also biased.

De Palma *et al.* (2007a) have developed an allocation process, when supply is smaller than demand in some alternatives. They assume that the final allocation mechanism should obey some simple explicit rules (or axioms). From these assumptions, they compute the ex post allocation. That is, they only describe the ex ante choice (i.e. the choice which ignores the capacity constraints) and the ex post allocation (i.e. the individual choice once the competition for scarce housing resources has taken place). Therefore, in the proposed approach, they do not specify the complex dynamics that characterize the adjustment process from ex ante to ex post allocation. They develop the model specifications and estimation algorithms for markets with constrained availability of at least some alternatives. Their method is applied to the Paris region using the 1999 General Census data.

Their results show that about half the alternatives ("communes") have greater demand than supply. When the system is constrained, the (ex post) probability that a household is allocated to an alternative differs from the ex ante probability that this household prefers this alternative. As a result, the ex post demand, corresponding to the sum of (ex post) allocation probabilities over all households differs from the ex ante demand, corresponding to the sum over all households of ex ante preference probabilities.

When an alternative is constrained ex ante, i.e. the ex ante demand is greater than supply, it can be shown that this alternative j is also usually constrained ex post. The excess demand in alternatives constrained ex ante induces an overflow, increasing the ex post demand in all alternatives that were not constrained ex ante. As a result, when an alternative is unconstrained ex ante, i.e. the ex ante demand is lower than supply, this alternative may be constrained ex post if the ex post demand exceeds supply, or it may remain unconstrained ex post otherwise.

De Palma *et al.* (2007a) solve the model using two basic assumptions: free allocation and no priority rule. Free allocation means that if an individual prefers an alternative which is unconstrained ex post, he can be sure to be allocated to it. Free allocation implies that the IIA property (independence from irrelevant alternatives), specific to the MNL (multinomial logit) model, still holds in a constrained system, for the unconstrained alternatives. That is, for two alternatives unconstrained ex post, the ratio of (ex post) allocation probabilities is equal to the ratio of (ex ante) choice probabilities. Free allocation also implies that the individual ratio of the ex post allocation probability to the ex ante preference probability is the same across all unconstrained alternatives. This household-specific allocation ratio is necessarily greater than 1. An allocation ratio of 1.1, for example, means that for any unconstrained alternative, the probability that an individual is allocated to this alternative is 10 per cent higher than the probability that he prefers this alternative. This also means that, if this individual is allocated to this alternative unconstrained ex post, the probability that it is not his/her preferred alternative is $(1.1 - 1)/1.1 = 9.09$ per cent.

No priority rule is a fairness criterion stating that, in an alternative constrained ex post, the individual ratio of the ex post allocation probability to the ex ante preference probability is the same for all households, and equal to the ratio of supply to ex ante demand for this alternative. This alternative-specific ratio is necessarily lower than 1 in alternatives constrained ex ante. A ratio of 0.8 means that the probability that an individual is allocated to this constrained alternative is 20 per cent lower than the probability that he/she prefers this alternative.

De Palma *et al.* (2007a) developed an iterative algorithm based on these two basic assumptions, allowing them to disentangle (possibly heterogeneous) preferences from capacity constraints using data on observed choices. According to their estimates, 43 per cent of the communes are constrained ex ante and 72 per cent of the communes are constrained ex post, due to overflow. However, the constraints are not very severe in most of these alternatives, and the average allocation ratio is 1.13 ex ante and 1.30 ex post, which means that 30 per cent of households are not located in their preferred commune, i.e. the welfare cannot be directly computed from observed choices for 30 per cent of the households, but should rather be corrected for the bias resulting from capacity constraints.

5.5.5.2 *Credit constraints*

We now analyse the relevance of different public policies for improving well-being through increased access to ownership and social desegregation. Demand-oriented policies, such as fiscal deduction of loan interest, "a house for 15 euros a day", or interest-free loans, aim at alleviating the liquidity constraints on the poorest households, thus improving their access to ownership. Supply-oriented policies, such as social housing or building of houses for 100,000 euros, aim at increasing the supply of dwellings. Both policies often neglect the interaction between tenure status and residential location, and may result in worsening residential segregation by inducing the poorest households to buy a dwelling in a cheaper location with a large concentration of poor households, instead of renting a dwelling in a more expensive and less segregated location (welcoming a balanced mix of rich and poor households). Modelling housing preferences for both dwelling type and local amenities is then essential to evaluating housing public policies.

Indeed, if segregation is found to be due to different valuations of local characteristics between poor and rich households, then supply-side policy should attempt to adapt local characteristics so as to attract households of different social categories. However if segregation is found to be due to stronger credit constraints on poor households, a desegregative policy should consist of relaxing those constraints by redistributing incomes or proposing advantageous loan terms to poorer households.

Social segregation, which is a source of social un-sustainability, can be explained partly by the fact that preferences (for local amenities and for dwelling prices) differ between poor and rich households and partly by credit constraints affecting mainly the poorest households. When household preferences depend on the local composition of the population, welfare analysis and policy evaluation are subject to strong externalities between households.

If social segregation mainly comes from preferences, for example, if rich (respectively poor) households enjoy living in places with a large fraction of rich (respectively poor) households, then the fact that a new rich (respectively poor) household comes to a place increases the welfare of all rich (respectively poor) households in this place. In this case, policies aiming at improving the social mix may reduce the welfare of a large fraction of households, since they will reduce the social homogamy which is positively valued in household welfare.

By contrast, if social segregation mainly comes from credit constraints, then poor households will care about the fraction of rich and poor households around only if this has a significant effect on dwelling prices. In this case, a policy aiming at alleviating credit constraints would increase the welfare of the poorest households without affecting the other households if the effects on equilibrium prices were negligible. Dantan and Picard (2014) show that policies aiming at alleviating credit constraints on the poorest households may have large counter-productive effects because they would induce a massive relocation of households from Paris to the suburbs, thus dramatically changing dwelling prices.

They consider a three-level nested model explaining tenure status, dwelling type and location, and extend it to credit constraints according to Figure 5.3. The model is estimated using data on the 1999 French survey, which contains information on the

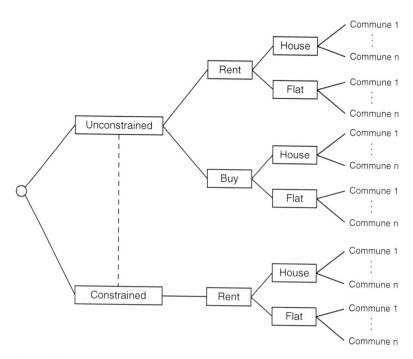

Figure 5.3 Extended nested model explaining credit constraints, tenure status, dwelling type and location.

Source: Author's own construct.

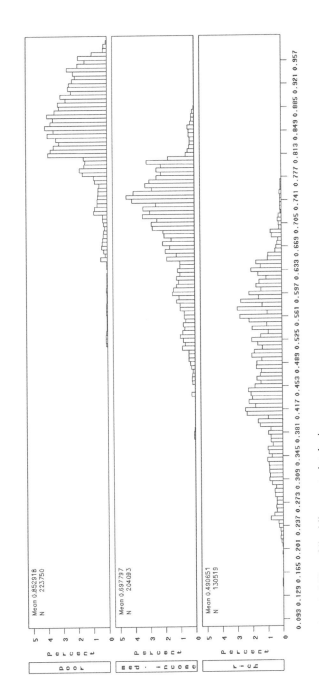

Figure 5.4 Probability of liquidity constraint, by income group.

Source: Author's own construct.

tenure status, dwelling type and residential location of about five million households in Ile-de-France. No information on credit constraints is directly available in this data, but it can be inferred statistically from the structure of the model.

Consistently with intuition, estimates show that, ceteris paribus, the probability of liquidity constraint is a decreasing function of household income and an increasing function of household size; it is lower when the household head is older or married and larger when she/he is young or a foreigner.

The influence of income on the probability of liquidity constraint is very large, as shown in Figure 5.4. This probability varies between 65 per cent and 96 per cent for most of the poor households (see the top sub-figure of Figure 5.4), between 45 per cent and 88 per cent for middle income households (middle), and between 20 per cent and 70 per cent for the rich households (bottom). These very large differences suggest a large bias in welfare measurement when welfare is directly measured from residential location choices, assuming that all households are located in their preferred location and neglecting credit constraints.

Liquidity constraints also vary geographically (Figure 5.5). More than 70 per cent of the households that moved to Paris City or to the close suburbs in 1998 were credit constrained, and forced to rent, because they could not buy a dwelling in such expensive places, except in the western part of the region, where the fraction of credit-constrained households is only 60–70 per cent

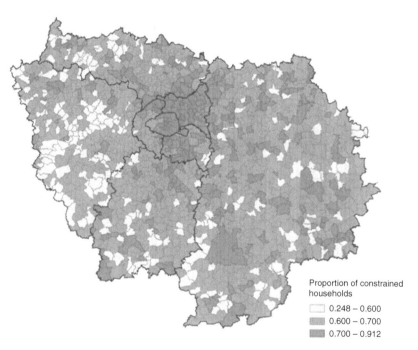

Figure 5.5 Proportion of constrained households per commune.

Source: Author's own construct.

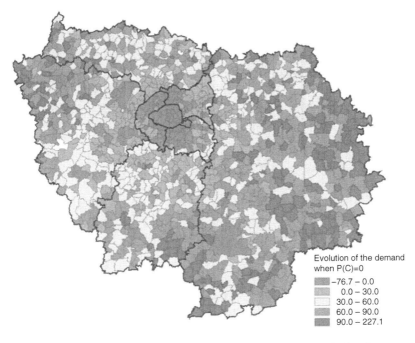

Figure 5.6 Per cent change in demand when credit constraints are alleviated.
Source: Author's own construct.

(middle-income and moderately rich households can afford to buy a dwelling in Hauts-de-Seine, but not inside Paris). The fraction of credit-constrained households is between 25 per cent and 60 per cent in many communes in the further away western suburbs (and some of the communes in more distant suburbs of Paris), because middle-income and a small number of poor households can afford to buy a dwelling there.

Dantan and Picard (2014) ran some partial simulations, ignoring equilibrium effects in order to assess the effect of liquidity constraints on household location. The purpose of these partial simulations was not to predict what would happen if liquidity constraints were alleviated for all households, because such a policy would dramatically change equilibrium prices and would induce huge capacity constraints, since it would move the demand to places with a low supply of dwellings of the desired dwelling and/or tenure type. Their objective was rather to compute the difference between actual choices and preferences, i.e. what a given household would do if liquidity constraints were alleviated for this specific household only, which is the relevant way to evaluate well-being. The results displayed in Figure 5.6 show a large decrease in the population inside Paris and a more moderate decrease or a marginal increase in the nearest suburbs. This means that credit constraints induce many households to rent inside Paris or in the local

138 Constantinos Antoniou and Nathalie Picard

suburbs, whereas they would prefer (and could afford if they were allowed to borrow) to buy a dwelling in the distant suburbs, especially in the very distant eastern and north-western suburbs, where selling prices are currently low. This therefore also means that liquidity constraints limit urban sprawl.

5.6 Conclusions

According to the World Health Organization, the majority of the human population already lives in cities and this number is expected to rise to seven out of ten people by 2050. Life in cities has advantages (e.g. possibly shorter commuting times and greater accessibility to amenities and work), but also imposes challenges (e.g. scarcity of resources). Sustainability, in general, and in cities in particular, becomes particularly important and the focus of research by economists, environmentalists, and engineers, among other disciplines.

Urban sustainability and individual/household well-being thus become critical for the viability of cities (and especially mega-cities). In this chapter we have considered a definition of sustainability as the sum of several components – one of which is the quality of life – including recent developments on how they can be quantified and modelled. Considering the ongoing shift from aggregate to disaggregate models, individual/household-based models have been presented, demonstrating the depth and insights that can be obtained when rich data sets and detailed modelling techniques are combined.

These models require very large and detailed data bases that are very costly to obtain and, often, of not very good quality. Advanced modelling techniques are being developed to operationalize their analysis. Consequently, the applications considered here may be difficult to reproduce in other cities. On the other hand, powerful LUTI models, such as UrbanSim (Waddell, 2002; Waddell et al., 2007) are being developed, which attempt to incorporate many of these models into a single model system. Of course, this leads to further complications, as discussed, for example, in Picard et al. (2010). The individual models that are incorporated in these LUTI models (such as residential location choice or mode choice) are often simple and do not reflect the state of the art in these fields. For example, in this chapter, we present elaborate couples' joint residential location and joint mode choice models that may not be easily incorporated into the current versions of these models. As stated by Chiappori (1992), such joint models can be used for welfare analysis, and should be used instead of individual models. A few elaborate models, such as the one involving capacity constraints, were successfully introduced in UrbanSim, allowing a more precise evaluation of household well-being to be made than could be achieved with simpler models (which merge the roles of preferences and constraints).

The disaggregate nature of these models allows the detailed quantification of social welfare at the individual/household level, which in turn allows the analysis of spatio-temporal trends and issues such as equity. Examples of analyses using spatial econometric real estate models are presented by Efthymiou and Antoniou (2013, 2014), for example; they consider the impact of transport infrastructure on real estate prices. As urban sustainability and individual/household well-being continue to attract the attention of researchers and policy-makers alike, it is expected that novel ideas will emerge that will improve our ability to describe them in a way that corresponds with observed conditions, thus providing additional insight.

Notes

1 A comprehensive presentation of the hedonic approach is provided in Chapter 2.
2 Weighted by Pareto weights, which are equal to 0.5 for each spouse in the reference couple.
3 Let's call it Value of Time, although it is more complex when utility is not linear in travel time because then VOT is given by the local derivative of utility with respect to commuting time, and it varies with commuting time.

Bibliography

Abraham, J. E. and Hunt, J. D. (1997) "Specification and estimation of nested logit model of home, workplaces, and commuter mode choices by multiple-worker households", *Transportation Research Record*, 1606, pp. 17–24.

Alberti, M. (1996) "Measuring urban sustainability", *Environmental Impact Assessment Review*, 16(4), pp. 381–424.

Anderson, S., de Palma, A. and Thisse, J. (1992) *Discrete choice theory of product differentiation*, MIT Press, Cambridge, MA.

Arrow, K., Dasgupta, P., Goulder, L., Daily, G., Elhrlich, P., Heal, G., Levin, S., Mailer, K. G., Schneider, S., Starrett, D. and Walker, B. (2004) "Are we consuming too much?", *Journal of Economic Perspectives*, 18(3), pp. 147–172.

Atkinson, B. A. (1970) "On the measurement of inequality", *Journal of Economic Theory*, 2, pp. 244–263.

Beharry-Borg, N., Hensher, D. and Scarpa, R. (2009) "An analytical framework for joint vs separate decisions by couples in choice experiments: The case of coastal water quality in Tobago", *Environmental and Resource Economics*, 43(1), pp. 95–117.

Bolund, P. and Hunhammar, S. (1999) "Ecosystem services in urban areas", *Ecological Economics*, 29(2), pp. 293–301.

Bradley Guy, G. and Kibert, C. J. (1998) "Developing indicators of sustainability: US experience", *Building Research & Information*, 26(1), pp. 39–45.

Bramley, G. and Power, S. (2009) "Urban form and social sustainability: the role of density and housing type", *Environment and Planning. B, Planning & Design*, 36(1), pp. 30–48.

Brereton, F., Clinch, J. P. and Ferreira, S. (2008) "Happiness, geography and the environment", *Ecological Economics*, 65(2), pp. 386–396.

Chiappori, P.-A. (1988) "Rational household labor supply", *Econometrica*, 56(1) pp. 63–90.

Chiappori, P.-A. (1992) "Collective labor supply and welfare", *Journal of Political Economy*, 100(3), pp. 437–467.

Chiappori, P.-A., de Palma, A. and Picard, N. (2012) "Couple residential location and spouses workplaces", THEMA working paper no. 3.3, Cergy-Pontoise University.

Chiesura, A. (2004) "The role of urban parks for the sustainable city", *Landscape and Urban Planning*, 68(1), pp. 129–138.

Dantan, S. and Picard, N. (2013) "Do housing borrowing constraints cause residential segregation in the Paris region?", mimeo, THEMA, Cergy-Pontoise University.

Dantan, S. and Picard, N. (2014) "The role of preferences and constraints in residential segregation: methodology and empirical evidence", paper presented at the *13th International Workshop Spatial Econometrics and Statistics*, 15–16 April 2013, Toulon, France.

Dempsey, N., Bramley, G., Power, S. and Brown, C. (2011) "The social dimension of sustainable development: defining urban social sustainability", *Sustainable Development*, 19(5), pp. 289–300.

de Palma, A., Motamedi, K., Picard, N. and Waddell, P. (2005) "A model of residential location choice with endogenous housing prices and traffic for the Paris region", *European Transport*, 31, pp. 67–82.

de Palma, A., Picard, N. and Waddell, P. (2007a) "Discrete choice models with capacity constraints: an empirical analysis of the housing market of the greater Paris region", *Journal of Urban Economics*, 62(2), pp. 204–230.

de Palma, A., Motamedi, K., Picard, N. and Waddell, P. (2007b) "Accessibility and environmental quality: inequality in the Paris housing market", *European Transport*, 36, pp. 47–74.

Efthymiou, D. and Antoniou, C. (2013) "How do transport infrastructure and policies affect house prices and rents? Evidence from Athens, Greece", *Transportation Research Part A: Policy and Practice*, 52, pp. 1–22.

Efthymiou, D. and Antoniou, C. (2014) "Measuring the effects of transportation infrastructure location on real estate prices and rents. Investigating the current impact of a planned metro line", *EURO Journal on Transportation and Logistics*.

Fehr, M., Sousa, K. A., Pereira, A. F. N. and Pelizer, L. C. (2004) "Proposal of indicators to assess urban sustainability in Brazil", *Environment, Development and Sustainability*, 6(3), pp. 355–366.

Findlay, A., Morris, A. and Rogerson, R. (1988) "Where to live in Britain in 1988: quality of life in British cities", *Cities*, 5(3), pp. 268–276.

Hediger, W. (2000) "Sustainable development and social welfare", *Ecological Economics*, 32, pp. 481–492.

Inoa, I., Picard, N. and de Palma, A. (2014) "Effect of an accessibility measure in a model for choice of residential location, workplace, and type of employment", *Mathematical Population Studies*.

Jabareen, Y. R. (2006) "Sustainable urban forms their typologies, models, and concepts", *Journal of Planning Education and Research*, 26(1), pp. 38–52.

Keirstead, J. and Leach, M. (2008) "Bridging the gaps between theory and practice: a service niche approach to urban sustainability indicators", *Sustainable Development*, 16(5), pp. 329–340.

Lautso, K., Spiekerman, K., Wegener, M., Sheppard, I., Steadman, P., Martino, A., Domingo, R. and Gayda, S. (2004) *Propolis. Planning and research of policies for land use and transport for increasing urban sustainability.* Final report, Technical report, LT Consultants, Helsinki.

Lloyd, K. M. and Auld, C. J. (2002) "The role of leisure in determining quality of life: issues of content and measurement", *Social Indicators Research*, 57(1), pp. 43–71.

Malik, K. (2013) *Human Development Report 2013. The rise of the South: Human progress in a diverse world*, United Nations Development Programme (UNDP).

Maclaren, V. W. (1996) "Urban sustainability reporting", *Journal of the American Planning Association*, 62(2), pp. 184–202.

Mitchell, G. (2000) "Indicators as tools to guide progress on the sustainable development pathway", in Lawrence, R. J. (ed.), *Sustaining Human Settlement: A Challenge for the New Millennium.* North Shields: Urban International Press, pp. 55–104.

Munda, G. (2006) "Social multi-criteria evaluation for urban sustainability policies", *Land Use Policy*, 23(1), pp. 86–94.

Newman, P. W. (1999) "Sustainability and cities: extending the metabolism model", *Landscape and Urban Planning*, 44(4), pp. 219–226.

Olewiler, N. (2006) "Environmental sustainability for urban areas: the role of natural capital indicators", *Cities*, 23(3), pp. 184–195.

Peluso, E. and Trannoy, A. (2007) "Does less inequality among households mean less inequality among individuals?", *Journal of Economic Theory*, 133(1), pp. 568–578.

Picard, N., Antoniou, C. and De Palma, A. (2010) "Econometric models. Sustain City", THEMA Working Paper no. 2.4, Cergy-Pontoise University.

Picard, N., de Palma, A. and Dantan, S. (2013) "Intra-household discrete choice models of mode choice and residential location", *International Journal of Transport Economics*, XL(3), pp. 419–445.

Proost, S., Van der Loo, S., Antoniou, C. and Efthymiou, D. (2014) "Indicators of sustainable development for microsimulation models", in *Integrated transport and land use modeling for sustainable cities*, Bierlaire, M., de Palma, A., Hurtubia, R. and Waddell, P. (eds.), Ch. 2.11, EPFL Press.

Rosen, S. (1974) "Hedonic prices and implicit markets: product differentiation in pure competition", *Journal of Political Economy*, 82, pp. 34–55.

Sahely, H. R., Kennedy, C. A. and Adams, B. J. (2005) "Developing sustainability criteria for urban infrastructure systems", *Canadian Journal of Civil Engineering*, 32(1), pp. 72–85.

Schelling, T. (1978) *Micromotives and Macrobehaviour, Technical Report*, New York: W. W. Norton.

Seo, J. K. (2002) "Re-urbanisation in regenerated areas of Manchester and Glasgow: new residents and the problems of sustainability", *Cities*, 19(2), pp. 113–121.

Shen, L. Y., Jorge Ochoa, J., Shah, M. N. and Zhang, X. (2011) "The application of urban sustainability indicators – A comparison between various practices", *Habitat International*, 35(1), pp. 17–29.

Singh, R. K., Murty, H. R., Gupta, S. K. and Dikshit, A. K. (2009) "An overview of sustainability assessment methodologies", *Ecological Indicators*, 9(2), pp. 189–212.

Slanina, S. (1997) *Biosphere-atmosphere Exchange of Pollutants and Trace Substances*, Berlin: Springer.

Spiekerman, K. and Wegener, M. (2004) "Evaluating urban sustainability using land-use transport interaction models", *European Journal of Transport and Infrastructure Research*, 4(3), pp. 251–272.

Stiglitz, J. E., Sen, A., and Fitoussi, J.-P. (2009) *Report by the Commission on the Measurement of Economic Performance and Social Progress*, Paris.

Tanguay, G. A., Rajaonson, J., Lefebvre, J. F. and Lanoie, P. (2010) "Measuring the sustainability of cities: an analysis of the use of local indicators", *Ecological Indicators*, 10(2), pp. 407–418.

Ulrich, R. (1984) "View through a window may influence recovery from surgery", *Science*, 224, pp. 420–421.

Ulrich, R. S., Simons, R. F., Losito, B. D., Fiorito, E., Miles, M. A., Zelson, M. (1991) "Stress recovery during exposure to natural and urban environments", *Journal of Environmental Psychology*, 11, pp. 201–230.

Van Kamp, I., Leidelmeijer, K., Marsman, G. and De Hollander, A. (2003) "Urban environmental quality and human well-being: towards a conceptual framework and demarcation of concepts; a literature study", *Landscape and Urban Planning*, 65(1), pp. 5–18.

Vermeulen, F. (2002) "Collective household models: principles and main results", *Journal of Economic Surveys*, 16(4), pp. 533–564.

Waddell, P. (2002) "UrbanSim: modelling urban development for land use, transportation and environmental planning", *Journal of the American Planning Association*, 68(3), pp. 297–314.

Waddell, P., Ulfarsson, G. F., Franklin, J. P. and Lobb, J. (2007) "Incorporating land use in metropolitan transportation planning", *Transportation Research Part A: Policy and Practice*, 41(5), pp. 382–410.

Walsh, E., Babakina, O., Pennock, A., Shi, H., Chi, Y., Wang, T. and Graedel, T. E. (2006) "Quantitative guidelines for urban sustainability", *Technology in Society*, 28(1), pp. 45–61.

Wilson, J., Tyedmers, P. and Pelot, R. (2007) "Contrasting and comparing sustainable development indicator metrics", *Ecological Indicators*, 7(2), pp. 299–314.

6 Agglomeration economies and urban location benefits

The debate around the existence of an optimal city size

Roberto Camagni and Roberta Capello

6.1 Introduction

In the real world, the number of people living in cities is growing in all countries and continents. The urbanisation process is a phenomenon which, in the last decade, has been increasingly intense in the developing countries. The share of urban population in the more developed continents, such as Europe and North America, is extremely high, and at the world scale, reached 50 per cent in 2009 (United Nations, 2010). This percentage, according to official forecasts, is expected to rise yet further in future decades.[1] As a consequence of increasing population, cities physically expand through processes which have been defined as "ville éclatée", "ville éparpillée", "ubiquitous city" and, more recently, "metropolisation". The population of large cities is continuing to grow, though sometimes more slowly than previously (Camagni, 1998); this continuous trend puts at the forefront of the theoretical reflections Alonso's challenging questions: "how big is big enough?" and "how big is too big?" (Alonso, 1964). These questions have been addressed in the literature by looking for the maximum (average) location benefits that inhabitants receive from living in a particular city, once the (average) location costs are discounted, reaching an optimal city size (Alonso, 1971). After that size, there is no reason for a city to grow, since the advantages for inhabitants (which in economic terms measure the quality of life in cities) decrease.

The constantly increasing size of cities encountered in the real world is in contrast with the "optimal city size" theory. The declining rate of urban population growth recorded in the last decade in most developing countries appears to be common to all cities, independently of physical size, and represents a general slowing down, rather than a specific crisis in the larger cities. For example in Italy, during the 1970s, there were negative population growth rates in the urban system of the Po Valley in northern Italy not only in the major cities, but also a number of secondary centres of 75,000 to 150,000 inhabitants (8 out of 19) and even some smaller towns of 20,000 to 75,000 inhabitants (27 out of 113 (Camagni *et al.*, 1986)). According to the theory, however, medium-sized towns are expected to increase their size, since the advantages associated with the physical dimension are still higher than location costs.

144 *Roberto Camagni and Roberta Capello*

Does an optimal city size exist? This chapter aims to review the theoretical debate in search of a reply to this question. In particular, starting from the criticisms to the optimal city size theory contained in the literature (Section 6.2), the chapter presents the theoretical advances made by the scientific literature (Section 6.3). The main result achieved recently is that other measurable factors affecting urban costs and benefits contribute together with pure size to the equilibrium size of the city (Camagni *et al.*, 2013). The chapter aims to provide evidence on the role of local characteristics that influence net urban location benefits, irrespective of the size of cities, by presenting two empirical analyses developed by the research group of the two authors (Section 6.4). Some concluding remarks are contained in Section 6.5.

6.2 Criticisms of the optimal city size

Since the 1960s, urban economists and geographers have put at the forefront of their reflections the problem of urban growth and of optimal urban size, trying to reply to the intriguing questions of Alonso: "how big is too big?" and "how big is big enough?" (Alonso, 1964), and the issue is still on the agenda of both scientists and policy makers (Nijkamp and Kournit, 2011; Partridge *et al.*, 2009; Partridge, 2010). In particular, the main question was to identify whether increasing returns to urban size exist. The reply was for the first time given by the optimal city size theory, which claims that urban location (average) advantages increase when the city size increases (Alonso, 1971), due to externalities that stem from: (1) consumptions and investments in public services; (2) large markets of outputs; and (3) large and diversified markets of inputs (Camagni, 1998). These externalities are well known as "agglomeration economies" (Glaeser *et al.*, 1992; Rosenthal and Strange, 2001; Parr, 2002). On the other side, average urban costs decrease, while the city size increases: expenses for the implementation of fixed capital infrastructure decrease while the number of people using them increases (Richardson, 1972).

However, a general consensus exists within the literature on urban size, on the fact that agglomeration economies exist up to a certain threshold, after which urban benefits start to decrease; after that threshold, in fact, opposite mechanisms start to act and change positive into negative elements, "agglomeration economies" into "agglomeration diseconomies", while average urban costs start to increase, diminishing the net agglomeration advantage. Congestion, high urban rents, environmental costs are all elements that explain the decrease in agglomeration advantages, and the city, as each economic resource intensively exploited, shows decreasing returns.

Following this logic, average urban location costs and benefits both have a U-shaped form: the former decrease and then increase, the latter increase and then decrease. The size of the city for which the difference between total location costs and advantages is maximum, is identified as the "optimal city size".[2]

During the 1970s, additional refinements to this theory have been developed, at different theoretical levels:

1 by differentiating between optimal city size for people already living in the city and potential inhabitants; the first is obtained by the size that guarantees the maximum distance between average location costs and benefits, the latter by the size that equals marginal costs and benefits (Richardson, 1972);

2 by defining more precisely what is meant by location cost, identified merely in the urban rent that inhabitants have to pay for an urban location (Alonso, 1971);

3 by adding environmental aspects into urban costs (Anderson and Crocker, 1971): already in 1956, Duncan mentions crimes and urban pollutions as the main elements to determine urban size. Richardson (1972) underlines the distinction between public and private location costs, the former having in their definition all environmental costs. Cities might grow more than their optimal city size, since the location choice of individuals is based on private costs and benefits that achieve the optimum for higher city sizes than social costs and benefits.

The simplicity and the validation of the theoretical expectations from the reality have produced a level of success around these studies. However, some criticisms started to emerge when looking more carefully into the optimal city size theory. No economic rules, models, or theories exist that interpret increasing and decreasing returns to scale of a resource like the city. The theory exists, since it is empirically demonstrated; if this were not the case, it would be difficult, or even impossible, to guarantee the existence of agglomeration economies. In this field, econometric studies support the theory: as Mills (1993) said: "this is one of the few fields in which economics is more advanced than theory".

The seemingly mistaken interpretation of the real world by the "optimal city size theory" has already been pointed out by various authors. Richardson (1972) was the first to present a "sceptic's view", by underlining that an apparent paradox existed between the theoretical acceptance of an "optimal city size" and the contradictory development patterns of urban systems in the real world. According to Richardson, this paradox could be explained by the existence of other determinants influencing urban agglomeration economies, not merely physical size. Since Richardson's paper, other interpretations have been given to this apparent paradox, through the "urban life cycle" theory,[3] and through the integration of dynamic elements, such as innovation, continuous information, and knowledge acquisition, into the static framework of "optimal city size theory".

Although demonstrated by a large number of empirical estimations, many criticisms have been made of the neoclassical approach to optimal city size theory. These include the observations that (as formulated by Capello, 2002):

- Cities are different from one another. They are characterised by different functions and perform different specialisations (Henderson, 1985, 1996). The use of the same urban production function for all cities in econometric analyses estimating optimal city size is extremely restrictive. In the words

146 *Roberto Camagni and Roberta Capello*

of Richardson: "we may expect the efficient range of city sizes to vary, possibly dramatically, according to the functions and the structure of the cities in question" (1972: 30).

- If cities are different from one another, the optimal city size may be different, depending on the specific characteristics. Richardson elegantly compares the "optimal city size" theory with the theory of the behaviour of firms. We would never expect the optimal position for each and every firm to occur at the same level of output, so why should we expect the optimal point in each city to be located at the same population level?
- Cities exist in an inter-urban environment. The optimal city size theory, on the contrary, does not consider the spatial context in which cities operate.
- Cities generate a large variety of externalities as a result of the qualitative characteristics of the urban production environment. Already in 1961, Chinitz expressed some doubts about the fact that urban factor productivity depends mainly on the physical size of cities. He emphasised, on the contrary, the importance of a diversified and competitive urban production system as a source of urban productivity. Such a system is able to provide a far larger variety of externalities for small firms than an oligopolistic and specialised urban structure. Chinitz supported his thesis with an empirical analysis of New York, a large and diversified urban area, and Pittsburgh, a highly specialised city.[4]

The necessity to overcome the limits of the theory on the optimal city size has increased in recent years, when the urbanisation process has drastically been affected by rapid growth.

6.3 Agglomeration economies and territorial capital

Given the limits highlighted in the optimal city size theory, for a long time scientific efforts were redirected outside the problem of searching for an "optimal" size and mainly dedicated to the identification of urban specificities that affect urban costs and benefits. Recently, this effort implied departing from the consideration of the pure physical structure and the pure indivisibilities that accompany the supply of services and the markets for inputs and output, and linking instead benefits and costs of city size to intangible elements of a different nature, impinging both on static and dynamic efficiency of cities through continuing information, innovation, and knowledge acquisition (Camagni *et al.*, 2013). In other words, the theoretical step forward in the explanation of the capacity of cities to take advantage from agglomeration economies lies in the presence of strategic territorial capital assets (Camagni, 2009).

In fact, two groups of territorial capital assets can be identified in this sense. The first group is more conventional, highlighting elements like urban atmosphere, human capital, and agglomeration economies on the benefits side, and social conflicts/malaise, and costs of the city in general (urban land rent), on the costs side. These elements are closely correlated with city size, and influence its location benefits and costs. A second, more recent and unconventional type of literature encompasses the role of urban functions (embedded in dynamic urban models), the role of the city within inter-urban cooperation agreements (the so-called city-network paradigm) on the benefit side, and the loss of efficiency and sustainability brought in by dispersed urban forms, on the costs side.

Both conventional and more innovative determinants of agglomeration costs and benefits are considered, merging economic, social, environmental, and physical factors (urban form). In particular, conventional determinants of agglomeration economies are highlighted in the following.

6.3.1 Indivisibilities and productivity

In the early approaches concerned with the economics of urban size, the reflection mainly concerned scale economies in the supply of private and public fixed capital, and the provision of the consequent services, and on general productivity of the economic fabric. In some studies the optimal city size was even erroneously searched as the size guaranteeing the minimum location costs, with no attention to location advantages.

Along this line, in the first part of the 1970s, theorisation was accompanied by empirical studies mainly concentrated on the analysis of per capita expenses for public services. Ladd (1992); Alonso (1971), and Mera (1973) estimated, on a sample of American and Japanese cities, that per-capita public expenses are greater for cities with more than one million inhabitants. Beyond that size, per-capita expenses increase, witnessing a U-shaped curve for average urban costs.[5] Hirsch (1968) showed that this rule was valid only for specific services, like firemen, while the average cost curve had either a constant shape with respect to urban size for some services, like education, or a decreasing functional shape for others, like water, gas, and electricity.

On the benefit side, a large body of literature emphasised the role of agglomeration economies as sources of productivity increases. Alonso (1971) showed that the average labour productivity is greater in American cities that have more than five million inhabitants, and demonstrates, like many others later, that the minimum of the location cost curve is achieved for an urban size smaller than the size guaranteeing the maximum of location advantages. Through the estimate of an aggregate urban Cobb-Douglas production function on a sample of 58 American cities, Segal (1976) demonstrated that the parameter of the urban size variable was significant: metropolitan areas with more than three million inhabitants showed a factor productivity which is 8 per cent higher than the other cities. In a cross-sectional study on 230 American cities, Marelli (1981) achieved similar results: larger cities had a greater factor productivity than smaller cities, but this held up to a certain urban size, after which factor productivity again showed decreasing returns. Other empirical studies found out that the productivity was 30 per cent greater in the Île de France and 12 per cent greater in Marseille, Lyon, and Nice than in the rest of the French cities (Rousseaux and Proud'homme, 1992; Rousseaux, 1995).

148 *Roberto Camagni and Roberta Capello*

6.3.2 *Environmental costs and social conflicts*

On the cost side, a large body of literature tried to disentangle from the general urban location costs those costs specifically related to the natural environment (Anderson and Crocker, 1971; Clark and Kahn, 1989), to criminality and air pollution (Duncan, 1956), and to environmental costs associated with urban size (Richardson, 1972). Hedonic price models became a diffused methodology to measure environmental costs and social conflicts – implicitly embedded in urban rent – and highly dependent on urban size (Ridker and Henning, 1967; Freeman, 1971; Getz and Huang, 1978; Izraeli, 1987). The endogenous interaction with population and rent is tackled with a spatial econometric simultaneous regression model in Jeanty *et al.* (2010). They use Michigan census tract-level data and eventually find that local neighbourhoods tend to register increases in housing values when gaining population, while on the contrary being more likely to lose population following an increase in housing values, controlling for spatial simultaneity, spatial interaction, and unobserved spatial autocorrelation in the data.

6.3.3 *Agglomeration as a facilitator of social interaction*

As mentioned before, the benefits associated with agglomeration engender productivity increases. This aspect has been recently explained with the role played by density in creating an "urban atmosphere". Density, in fact, enriches the probability of exchange of ideas, knowledge, and social interaction; all such elements are at the basis of greater productivity in agglomerated areas. A relatively recent wave of quantitative assessments found that pure density may explain up to half the total variance of output per worker (Ciccone and Hall, 1996). Proximity is a reducer of spatial impedance, and therefore is expected to raise the levels of efficiency of economic actors. Besides, firms may benefit from the relocation of other firms, being technologically compatible, in their proximity. Empirical evidence on this issue is provided in Martin *et al.* (2011). Also, this notion within the general spatial equilibrium approach à la Roback (1982) is behind Partridge *et al.* (2009), which deals with the spatial distribution of factor prices as influenced by various measures of remoteness. Incomplete access to the productivity gains accruing to firms and individuals in agglomerated areas is testified with a set of GMM (Generalised Method of Moments) estimates on US counties. The authors find, in analogy with the classical Central Place Theory, that median earnings and housing costs decline respectively from 5 per cent to 9 per cent, and from 12 per cent to 17 per cent in remote areas as an average penalty across cities of different rank.

Agglomeration effects on wages are also divided between level and growth effects in Glaeser and Mare (2001). The authors find that coordination and learning may be at the roots of the wage increases accruing to workers relocating in dense urban areas. In this literature, level effects are those, stemming mainly from reduced transport costs, accruing to individuals (in terms of higher productivity, and hence, wages) relocating to urban areas. Growth effects are instead related to the faster wage growth characterising individuals in urban areas. Both these effects

Agglomeration economies 149

attract knowledge workers to urban areas, which fosters cities' innovativeness, which in turn backfires and causes a higher attractiveness of large urban areas to knowledge workers (Faggian and McCann, 2009).

In addition to pure agglomeration effects, Glaeser and Mare (2001) show that sorting of skilled individuals in large urban areas may be a partial, but convincing, explanation of wage premia and higher productivity of urban workers and entrepreneurs. Interestingly, their empirical findings are valid only for very large urban areas, while medium and small cities seem to bring fewer advantages to people willing to relocate there.

6.3.4 Urban diversity as a source of creativity

Moreover, a large body of literature addresses the large variety of externalities that result from the qualitative characteristics of the urban production environment. In 1961, Chinitz expressed some doubts about the fact that urban factor productivity depends mainly on the physical size of cities. He emphasised, on the contrary, the importance of a diversified and competitive urban production system as a source of urban efficiency and growth. Such a system is able to provide a far larger variety of externalities for small firms than an oligopolistic and specialised urban structure in which the internalisation of service functions inside large firms reduces urbanisation economies. Chinitz supported his thesis with an empirical analysis comparing New York, a large and diversified urban area, with Pittsburgh, a city highly specialised in monopolistic sectors; his findings supported the idea that in more diversified urban areas, urban productivity depends on urbanisation advantages, while in more specialised cities it depends on economies of scale.[6] A similar view was expressed by Jacobs, who emphasised that it is not the mere physical proximity that generates economies of scale, but the diversity of activities located in large cities giving rise to higher creativity for people working and living in large cities (Jacobs, 1969).

A large debate was formulated in the literature about whether industrial specialisation or diversification had a higher effect on urban productivity (Sveikauskas et al., 1988). In order to test for sectoral specificity, some studies estimated the size effects at the sectoral level. Through a CES (Constant Elasticity of Substitution) production function, Shefer witnesses the existence of wide economies of scale in 10 sectors located in American cities (Shefer, 1973); Carlino divides the index used by Shefer in three parts, in order to capture economies of scale and economies of localisation and urbanisation in 19 manufacturing sectors, and finds significant results for both localisation and urbanisation economies in 12 industries out of 19 (Carlino, 1980). Sveikauskas estimates industrial labour productivity in 14 sectors, and finds that productivity increases by 6.4 per cent as city size doubles (Sveikauskas, 1975). Moomaw comes to similar conclusions, with sectoral productivity increase associated with a doubling in city size equal to 6 per cent (Moomaw, 1983).

Recently, a microfounded general equilibrium model has been set up in Duranton and Puga (2005), which shows how cities can first host innovative firms,

150   Roberto Camagni and Roberta Capello

which produce prototypes (*nursery cities*). Then, firms find it optimal to relocate in lower rank cities in order to look for lower production costs and switch to mass production. This provides evidence to the Jacobs conjecture about the higher innovativeness of industrially diversified cities.

6.3.5   Human capital and local synergies as sources of learning

An important part of the literature deals with the role played by large cities as nurseries of new ideas and seedbeds for learning processes, embedded in human capital and 'tacit knowledge' (Polanyi, 1966; Bathelt *et al.*, 2004). When interpreted in dynamic terms, the urban environment supports cooperation, synergy and relational proximity, which influence the innovativeness of firms. Shared values, common codes of behaviour, a sense of belonging and mutual trust are features which the urban archetype shares with the *innovative milieu* archetype (Camagni, 1999), accounting for the ability to reduce uncertainty and generate processes of knowledge socialisation and collective learning, and supporting the identification of an urban milieu, defined as a network of informal or selected linkages developed around a specialisation sector or filière, developing inside the urban context or the urban production system (Camagni, 1999).

6.3.6   Amenities as sources of urban attractiveness

More generally, "urban amenities", in the form of accessibility to high quality public services (schools and hospitals, etc.), to a variety of recreational services (theatres and cinemas, etc.), to high education services (universities), to cultural capital (museum and historical monuments, etc.) (Clark and Kahn, 1989), have been highlighted as intangible advantages present in the large city (Clark and Cosgrave, 1991; Cropper, 1981; Henderson, 1982). Their economic assessment is usually based on hedonic price models. Along this line, many studies devoted their efforts to measure the quality of life in urban areas (Berger *et al.*, 1987; Blomquist *et al.*, 1988; Burnell and Galster, 1992; Roback, 1982, 1988; Rosen, 1979; Carlino and Saiz, 2008) as source of attractiveness for firms and individuals. Recent empirical literature also identifies "consumption" amenities (e.g. nice weather: Rappaport, 2007; Cheshire and Magrini, 2006) as a source of urban attractiveness (see Chapter 2).

With respect to unconventional determinants of agglomeration economies, the main ones highlighted in the literature may be summarised as follows.

6.3.7   Urban functions and urban ranks

The difference among cities in terms of urban functions was brought to the fore by Richardson in the 1970s, and formalised in a supply-oriented dynamic model (SOUDY) (Camagni *et al.*, 1986). The model assumes that an "efficient" city size interval exists separately for each hierarchical rank, associated with rank-specific economic functions. In other words, for each economic function characterised by a specific demand threshold and a minimum production size, a minimum and a

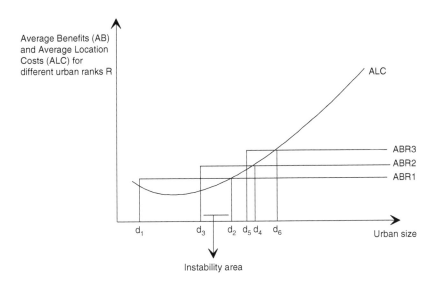

Figure 6.1 Efficient city-size for different urban functions.
Source: Camagni *et al.* (1986).

maximum city size exists beyond which urban location diseconomies overcome production benefits typical of that function.

As Figure 6.1 shows, under these conditions for each economic function and each associated urban rank, it is possible to define a minimum and a maximum city size in which the city operates under efficiency conditions (i.e. with net positive gains) (d1–d2 for the function – and centre – of rank 1; d3–d5 for the function – and centre – of rank 2, and so on). The higher the production benefits (profits) of the single functions (increasing with rank), the higher the efficient urban size interval associated to such function.

As each centre grows, approaching the maximum size compatible with its rank ('constrained dynamics'), it enters an instability area (e.g. in d3–d2 in Figure 6.1) where it becomes a potentially suitable location for higher order functions, thanks to the achievement of a critical demand size for them. In dynamic terms, each city's long-term growth possibilities depend on its ability to move to higher urban ranks, developing or attracting new and higher-order functions ('structural dynamics'). This "jump" is not mechanically attained: it represents a true urban innovation and is treated as a stochastic process in the dynamic model.

The interest of this model resides in the fact that it overcomes some of the limits of the "optimal" city size theory, by suggesting:

- the need to replace optimal size by an "interval" within which the city size is "efficient",[7] i.e. where average production benefits exceed average location costs;

152   *Roberto Camagni and Roberta Capello*

- the need to allow different "efficient" urban sizes according to the functions actually performed by the cities;
- the possibility of decoupling urban ranks from urban size. Differently from Christaller's approach, two cities of the same size (for example, size d_2 in Figure 6.1) can belong to two subsequent ranks (1 and 2 in the example), depending on their capacity to attract/develop higher functions.[8]

Indeed, a recent contribution (Duranton and Puga, 2005) provides evidence on the increasing pattern of functional, rather than sectoral, specialisation in US cities, with an impressive concentration of managerial functions in large urban areas and a symmetric pattern of concentration in production plants in smaller cities.

6.3.8   *City networks*

Born in the field of industrial economics (Chesnais, 1988), the concept of network behaviour has been transferred into urban economics, providing a successful theoretical framework to overcome the limiting interpretative power of the traditional central place model.[9] In fact, real city-systems in advanced countries have deeply departed from the abstract Christaller pattern of a nested hierarchy of centres and markets, showing (Camagni, 1993):

- processes of city specialisation and presence of higher order functions in centres of lower order;
- horizontal linkages between similar cities, not allowed in the traditional model (e.g. the financial network among top cities in the worldwide hierarchy or linkages among similar centres performing headquarter and advanced services functions (Camagni and Capello, 2004)).

This empirical evidence supported the idea that new and increasing relationships among centres follow a network logic, where specialisation patterns are the main reasons to establish economic relationships. While the organisational logic underlying Christaller's central place model is territorial, emphasising a gravity-type control over market areas, in the network model a different logic prevails, based on long distance competition and cooperation, regardless of the distance barrier (Camagni, 1993). While in the more traditional analysis, transport costs and economies of scale were the principal forces shaping the spatial organisation of functions and cities, in the new logic other elements come to the fore – economies of vertical and horizontal integration, and network externalities similar to those emerging from "club goods". These elements provide the possibility for cities to reach higher critical mass and scale economies through network integration – in the economic, logistic, and organisational fields – with other cities.

Two main typologies of city networks are considered: linkages among centres of similar size performing different functions, aiming at the achievement of economies of vertical integration, division of labour and market size ("complementarity networks"), and linkages among centres performing similar functions aiming at the achievement of economies of horizontal integration and network externalities ("synergy networks") (Camagni, 1993).

The city-network model allows single cities to upgrade their economic functions without necessarily increasing their individual size. Therefore cities of intermediate size are being increasingly looked upon as the places that could well host the growth of the years to come: limited city sizes, in fact, facilitate environmental equilibrium, efficiency of the mobility system and the possibility for citizens to withhold a sense of identity, provided that a superior economic efficiency and scale economies are reached through cooperation networks with other cities – located in the same regions or distant but well connected.

Urban productivity was empirically found to be much more closely related to urban connectivity – another concept similar to urban network relations – than to urban scale (McCann and Acs, 2011), thus supporting the global city argument.

The joint application of the SOUDY model and the city-network paradigm has relevant implications for urban efficiency and growth: size is not the only determinant of factor productivity and agglomeration economies. The presence of higher urban functions and integration inside city-networks are also extremely important elements in the explanation of the competitive advantage of cities, allowing them to boost productivity even in presence of limited urban sizes.

6.3.9 Urban form and sprawl

A different recent research programme concerns the inspection of urban form and its relevance for the efficiency of cities. In this case, urban form is "optimal" when it allows cities to grow in physical terms, with the lowest social and environmental costs and the maximum social and economic benefits. A dispersed urban form, in fact, increases environmental costs associated with higher mobility on private cars, easily generates social segregation, and limits inter-personal interaction. Unfortunately such sprawling models are spreading in many advanced and developing countries (Breheny, 1992; Owens, 1992), following the American pattern. A land consumption index calculated by the French *Agences d'Urbanisme* shows that between 1950 and 1975, in 22 French urban areas, population has doubled while the territory occupied has increased only by 20–30 per cent; however, between 1975 and 1990 population has increased by 25 per cent, while the territory occupied by urban activities has doubled (Camagni, 1999). Other studies have calculated the collective cost of urban sprawl; in the Lombardy region, in the Milan metropolitan area, for example, an analysis of 186 municipalities shows the "wasteful" character of sprawling development patterns in terms of land consumption, public costs for infrastructure and services, and collective, environmental costs linked to urban mobility (Camagni et al., 2002).

International institutions like the European Commission and OECD have long since pointed out the economic and social costs of sprawl, while more recently the European Environment Agency (EEA, 2006) has indicated urban sprawl as the a crucial but up to now unmet and "ignored" challenge. In theoretical terms, it looks

154 *Roberto Camagni and Roberta Capello*

justified to hypothesise urban form as a necessary qualification and complement to urban size in the determination of urban efficiency.

6.4 Empirical evidence from European cities

An important message emerges from the previous theoretical debate. Not only does city size affect agglomeration economies: the presence of specific territorial capital assets influences location benefits. Cities are supposed to share the same complex cost and production functions with heterogeneous, substitutable factors linked not just to economic functions but to other context conditions. There-fore each of them maintains its specificity and consequently its "equilibrium" size, but comparability (and the possibility of running cross-sectional analyses) is saved, as is the possibility of devising policy strategies for urban growth or containment.

The statement was empirically tested in two recent empirical analyses run by the research group the authors are leading. The first one, conducted by Capello and Camagni (2000), was an econometric estimate of a sample of 58 Italian cities of different size, and of two average urban costs and benefits functions, made dependent on size (measured in terms of absolute population), high level functions and the degree of a-spatial linkages, and represented respectively in the following translog functions:

$$\ln ALB = \ln \eta + \alpha_1 \ln D + \alpha_2 \ln FUN + \alpha_3 \ln NET + \beta_1 \frac{1}{2} (\ln D)^2$$
$$+ \beta_2 \frac{1}{2} (\ln FUN)^2 + \beta_3 \frac{1}{2} (\ln NET)^2 + \delta_1 \ln D \ln FUN$$
$$+ \delta_2 \ln D \ln NET + \delta_3 \ln FUN \ln NET \tag{6.1}$$

and:

$$\ln ALC = \ln \eta + \alpha_1 \ln D + \alpha_2 \ln FUN + \alpha_3 \ln NET + \beta_1 \frac{1}{2} (\ln D)^2$$
$$+ \beta_2 \frac{1}{2} (\ln FUN)^2 + \beta_3 \frac{1}{2} (\ln NET)^2 + \delta_1 \ln D \ln FUN$$
$$+ \delta_2 \ln D \ln NET + \delta_3 \ln FUN \ln NET \tag{6.2}$$

for the average location costs, where:

- *ALB* represents the average location benefits (an unweighted sum of different social, economic and environmental advantage indicators, namely the share of people holding a university degree; the number of schools, of bank branches, and the supply of urban services with respect to urban population, the per-capita square metres of green areas in cities, the per capita use of energy, petrol and water).

- *ALC* represents the average urban location costs, (an unweighted sum of different social, economic, and environmental cost indicators, namely: per-capita NO_x emission; per-capita quantity of urban waste; number of vehicles per km^2; the share of unemployment in the total urban population; the number of crimes per urban population),
- *D* represents the absolute population of the city.
- *FUN* represents the type of urban functions developed in the city, measured as the share of private tertiary value-added produced by the city.
- *NET* represents the network integration level achieved in the city, measured as the stock of per-capita telephone subscribers.

The originality of the empirical analysis was based on the consideration that in an urban area three environments exist, the *physical (natural and built)* environment, the *economic* environment and the *social* environment, each of them explaining in part or in combination the existence and persistence of a city. All three environments generate advantages and disadvantages, i.e. user benefits and costs for a city. All three have to be considered together, because they interact with one another and represent, or express, goals, means and constraints to human action in the city. For each interaction between social, economic and environmental spheres, indicators were built in order to measure the location benefits (labelled city effect) and location costs (labelled urban overload), and therefore the externalities stemming from the interactions (see Table 6.1).

Table 6.1 Indicators of city effect and urban overload indicators

	Interaction between economic and physical environment	*Interaction between economic and social environment*	*Interaction between social and physical environment*
City effect indicator (Average Location Benefits ABL)	Per-capita energy use Per-capita petrol use Per-capita water use	Number of graduates/ population Number of schools/ population Number of banks/ population Supply of public services/population Urban rent per m^2	M^2 of green areas in city per capita
Urban overload indicator (Average Location Costs ALC)	Per-capita NOx emissions Per-capita kg of urban waste Number of vehicles per m^2.	Unemployment/ population	Number of murders/ population

Source: Capello and Camagni (2000).

156 *Roberto Camagni and Roberta Capello*

The *city effect*, or *location benefit*, takes into account the following positive aspects of the interaction between the three environments, namely:

- positive externalities stemming from the interaction between the economic and the physical environment. The indicators chosen here are the per-capita use of energy, petrol, and water;
- positive externalities stemming from the interaction between the economic and the social environment. In this area, the indicators chosen are: the share of people holding a university degree; the number of schools, of bank branches, and the supply of urban services with respect to urban population;[10] and the price of new houses per m². In microeconomic terms, this last factor is generally regarded as a cost, like in the Alonso type of location cost curve. In our macro-urban approach, urban rent is assumed as a proxy for urban economics and well-being of inhabitants, as it reflects the income and economic wealth of the city;
- positive externalities stemming from the interaction between the physical and the social environment. The indicator chosen is the per-capita square metres of green areas in cities.

Each indicator was divided by its maximum value, in order to standardise the different values and thus sum the different indices.[11] The general "city effect" (benefit) indicator is in fact calculated as the unweighted sum of the different indices obtained; the indices refer to cross-effects between the different environments, and therefore the choice of a weighted sum would imply an arbitrary choice of weights. The first group of indices, relating to the interaction between the economic and the natural environment enter the sum with their "complement to one" value, reflecting their negative correlation with city size.

In the same way, the *urban overload* (cost) indicator takes into account the negative aspects of the interaction between the three environments, namely (see Table 6.1):

- negative externalities stemming from the interaction between the economic and the physical environment. Here, all social costs for the natural environments have to be taken into account: per-capita NO_x emission; per-capita quantity of urban waste; number of vehicles per km²;
- negative externalities stemming from the interaction between the economic and the social environment. In this area, the indicator chosen is the percentage of unemployment in the total urban population;
- negative externalities stemming from the interaction between the physical and the social environment. The indicator chosen is the number of crimes per urban population.

Also, in this case, the overall indicator is the unweighted sum of the different indicators, each divided by its maximum value before being aggregated.

Other two indicators are necessary for the analysis, since they act as independent variables. The first concerns the types of high-order economic functions developed in the city. For this, the share of private tertiary value-added produced by the city is used. The second relates to the level of network integration of the city with the rest of the world: the lack of statistical information on the flows of interaction between our sample cities (duration of phone calls or number of phone calls) for these groups of cities has obliged us to choose a variable representing the stock of per-capita telephone subscribers. However, the share of flows of international phone calls (both duration and number of phone calls) and the per-capita telephone subscribers available for a different group of cities (municipalities) in the metropolitan areas of Milan have shown a correlation equal to 0.80.

The translog function (Equations 6.1 and 6.2) allowed us to estimate the elasticity of benefits (or costs) directly with respect to any of the right-hand-side variables, that is the percentage cost (benefits) change due to 1 per cent change of a specific determinant, other things being equal. If D is the absolute size of the city, in order to test whether the size reduces benefits, it is enough to calculate from Equation 6.1 the following expression, and to test the sign of e_D:

$$e_D = \alpha_1 + \beta_1 \ln D + \delta_1 \ln FUN + \delta_2 \ln NET \qquad (6.3)$$

where e_D is the size elasticity of the urban advantages. Based upon Equation 6.3, the interaction of the elasticity of benefits with the other two determinants can be studied. The same logic applies for the cost function, so the size-elasticity of urban costs with the other two determinants can be studied with the same methodology applied to the benefit curve (Capello and Camagni, 2000).

Equation 6.3 has been estimated on the sample of 58 Italian cities used to estimate Equations 6.1 and 6.2. The results are summarised in Figure 6.2. The first results regard the variable traditionally interpreted in the literature as the most important source of urban average benefits and costs: urban size.

Figure 6.2 (graphs a and b) shows the estimated benefits and urban costs functions for different levels of urban size. In economic terms, the calculated parameters reflect the elasticity of the urban benefits and costs with respect to size, i.e. how the city benefits and urban costs change with an increase in size of 1 per cent, for different urban sizes. The results obtained are in line with the abstract interpretation of the optimal urban size theory. In fact, the curves are "well-behaved", showing benefits which increase with urban size up to a certain point (approximately 361,000 inhabitants) and then decrease.

Urban location costs show a decreasing trend up to a certain urban size (approximately 55,500 inhabitants) and an increasing trend afterwards, once again in line with the traditional expectations. Medium-sized cities appear to have a greater endogenous capacity to keep social, economic, and environmental costs under control.[12] Interestingly enough, we can see from Figure 6.2a that the urban costs reach a minimum value at a lower urban size than the maximum urban benefits. This result confirms the outcome of other econometric studies, which show a

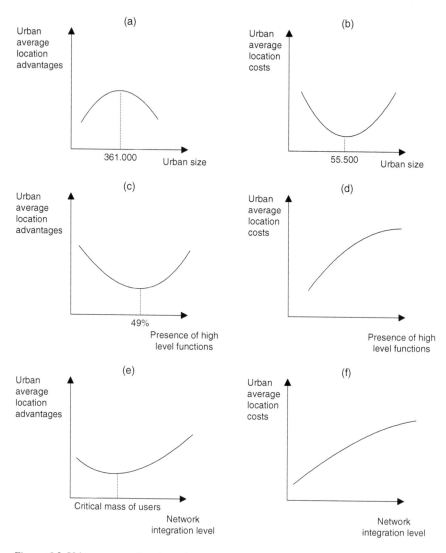

Figure 6.2 Urban average location advantages and costs for different urban sizes, higher urban functions, and degree of networking.

Source: Capello and Camagni (2000).

lower "optimal size" of the city when cost-efficiency factors are utilised than when advantages are taken into consideration directly.

The picture changes when the analysis is made on the basis of the different types of economic functions which can characterise a city. The results are quite interesting. The results on the urban benefits are in line with the conclusions suggested by the SOUDY model. The estimated curve confirms the theoretical hypotheses of the SOUDY model (Figure 6.2c and d): higher order functions guarantee a greater average benefit, due to the positive returns generated, up to a certain share of service activities (49 per cent of its total activities).

The urban costs increase at a decreasing rate when there is a strong presence of high level functions. This means that the increase in value-added functions tends to entail congestion and location costs, but that this negative aspect does not occur in a disruptive and uncontrollable way, as in the case of increasing urban size (Figure 6.2d). The urban average costs increase at a decreasing rate, which indicates that higher order functions produce economic development and also local congestion costs, but with a decreasing marginal productivity, and thus in a more controlled way.

The results of the size elasticity of the urban benefits and costs for different levels of network integration produce an interesting picture (Figure 6.2e and f). As far as the benefits are concerned, they decrease up to a certain level of network integration, when they start to increase. These results are stimulating, since they suggest that:

- for low levels of network integration, advantages of autarchy and independence take place, although these results seem to be statistically weak;
- when the network integration process starts, cities are vulnerable and are weak partners, risking in general being exploited by the network, rather than exploiting the advantages of a network. This result is in line with the general idea that being part of a network does not necessarily mean obtaining advantages from it (Camagni, 1993). As expected, this is true up to a certain level of network integration;
- after a certain threshold level, the city is able to exploit the advantages associated with the interconnected economy and network externality advantages are in full operation. Through the network, the city is able to exploit more dispersed information collection, the acquisition of more know-how and more qualified input factors, as well as a wider market for final goods.

For the urban costs, the picture which emerges is similar to that for different levels of high-order functions (Figure 6.2f). When the level of network integration increases, urban costs increase, too. This is what would be expected: higher levels of network integration stimulate more economic activities and generate higher urban benefits, but with the negative counterpart of increasing costs. What is rather interesting is that urban costs exhibit decreasing growth rates. Again, this result is different from the exploding situation, which occurs when the city size is taken into consideration.

A more recent empirical analysis has been run on a sample of 59 European cities, with data at FUA level, by Camagni *et al.* (2013), looking at the same empirical issue from a different angle. Starting from a theoretical model, the aim of the work is to empirically analyse the determinants of "equilibrium" urban size.

Urban costs and benefits are in fact made both dependent on size, and on traditional aspects like urban rent, un-efficient urban structure (sprawl) (Glaeser

160 *Roberto Camagni and Roberta Capello*

and Kahn, 2003) and social malaise – the former – and amenities and sectoral diversity – the latter – in a traditional Cobb-Douglas form:

$$C = size^\alpha \, rent^\beta \, sprawl^\gamma \, malaise^\delta \tag{6.4}$$

and

$$B = amenities^\zeta \, humancapital^\eta \, diversity^\vartheta \, size^\kappa \tag{6.5}$$

The equilibrium city size, representing the size at which cities do not have any advantage in increasing their size, is obtained by equating marginal costs and benefits with respect to size. The following equation is obtained, expressed in logarithmic terms (Camagni *et al.*, 2013):

$$\ln(size) = \frac{\ln(\kappa/\alpha)}{(\alpha - \kappa)} + \frac{\zeta}{(\alpha - \kappa)} \ln(amenities) + \frac{\vartheta}{(\alpha - \kappa)} \ln(diversity)$$

$$+ \frac{\chi}{(\alpha - \kappa)} \ln(density) + \frac{\mu}{(\alpha - \kappa)} \ln(functions)$$

$$+ \frac{\nu}{(\alpha - \kappa)} \ln(networks) + \frac{\beta}{(\alpha - \kappa)} \ln(rent)$$

$$- \frac{\delta}{(\alpha - \kappa)} \ln(malaise) - \frac{\gamma}{(\alpha - \kappa)} \ln(sprawl) \tag{6.6}$$

Equation 6.6 has been estimated on a sample of 59 European cities with data at FUA level.[13] The different variables have been proxied with (Camagni *et al.*, 2013):

- urban amenities, by the inflows of tourists in the Metropolitan Area representing a measure of urban attractiveness;
- diversity, by the Jacobsian source of externality stemming from a diversified labour market, calculated as the share of non top five industries (at NACE 2 digits) in total employment (Glaeser *et al.*, 1992);
- agglomeration economies, by population density;
- city-networks, by the number of Framework Programme 5 projects to which institutions of Metropolitan Areas jointly participate over the total workforce of the area;
- high level urban functions, by the share of the labour force in ISCO professions 1 and 2 (respectively legislators, senior officials, managers, and professionals);
- rent, by the prices m^2 of average quality apartments in downtown metropolitan areas;
- social distress, by the number of crimes recorded for the FUA;
- sprawl, by the share of non-urbanised land inside FUA. This indicator captures the degree of fragmentation of a FUA territory, typical of a dispersed urban form.

In order to avoid multicollinearity that might exist between networks, functions, and urban size, instrumental variables have been applied. Empirical results show the expected significance and sign of parameters in Equation 6.5. What is of particular interest is that both variables representing unconventional elements, in particular functions and networks, show a positive and significant sign; ceteris paribus, cities with higher-order functions or higher networking achieve a higher equilibrium size. Ceteris paribus, the equilibrium city size increases when higher-order functions or the degree of networking of the city increase.

6.5 Conclusions and policy implications

The present work has revised the theoretical paradigms that, since the 1970s, have been put in place to overcome the limits of the "optimal city size theory". The influence of urban size on urban costs and advantages, as explained by the "optimal city size" theory, exists and is important, but cannot be efficiently assessed without overcoming some of the limitations imposed by the theory. What the recent theoretical paradigms suggest is that it is not a problem of *optimal* city size, but of *efficient* size, which largely depends on what the city produces, how it produces, and the way in which it cooperates within the urban system. Urban size inevitably influences location costs and benefits, however the same also holds for territorial capital assets on which the city can invest in order to achieve higher location benefits, and therefore a higher level of quality of life.

The chapter presents two recent empirical works that validate empirically the assumptions on the role of unconventional elements on urban benefits. In particular, the type of economic function and the degree to which the city is integrated in an urban system appear to be strategic elements for the definition of location benefits and costs, analysed in relation to all aspects constituting the city, i.e the social, environmental, and economic aspects.

Urban growth appears to be a never-ending story; the constant positive trend of urban size of world cities has important normative consequences. Cities need a constant monitoring of urban dynamics, of its determinants, also through serious research analyses. Moreover, our cities need efficient urban policies, which aim to upgrade the economic functions within the city, as well as the development of linkages outside the city, such as alliances, cooperation agreements, advanced international transport, and telecommunications infrastructures. All of these elements and strategic policies are undoubtedly important for guaranteeing the survival of a modern city.

In particular, set against the recent issue of whether in a crisis period like the present one policy makers should concentrate their limited resources in larger cities in order to exploit agglomeration economies, or spread their investment in a larger set of cities, the answer comes logically after these reflections. Investment should be devoted to cities in order to enable any of them, despite their size, to turn their risk of decreasing returns into agglomeration economies, by investing in the renovation their functions and their ways of cooperation.

Notes

1 For a comprehensive description of urbanisation process, see Chapter 1.
2 Alonso (1971) stressed the mistaken tendency of many authors to look for "optimal city size" only by minimising the location cost function. As he argued, this would be sensible only if output per capita were constant (ibid.: 70).
3 On this theory see, among others, van den Berg *et al.* (1983) and Camagni *et al.* (1985).
4 Carlino (1980) provides a criticism of Chinitz' analysis, and demonstrates on a sample of 65 American towns that economies of scale, both internal and external to the firm, play a role in the definition of urban productivity.
5 A doubt remains, though, with these results: in larger cities higher per-capita expenses may be due to a higher willingness to pay for public services than to dis-economies of scale. Moreover, the difference in per-capita income between large and small cities exceeds the difference in average costs; therefore, if an optimal dimension exists, this is characterised more by productivity than by average costs.
6 Carlino (1980) provides a criticism of Chinitz' analysis, and demonstrates on a sample of 65 American towns that economies of scale, both internal and external to the firm, play a role in the definition of urban productivity. See on this debate also Kawashima (1975).
7 Richardson (1972) suggests replacing the concept of optimal city size with an efficient interval of urban size in which urban marginal benefits are greater than marginal location costs.
8 The two cities will differ, though, in dynamic terms: the one belonging to the lower rank (ABR_1) will not grow further, having reached the maximum size of its interval, while the one having developed the higher functions (linked to rank 2) will grow, due to the presence of new and wide net urban benefits (profits).
9 Camagni (1993) theorised the concept, applying it to urban systems. The same concept was already utilised in other fields, such as the behaviour of the firm and macroeconomic organisational behaviour. For a review of the concept, see Capello and Rietveld (1998).
10 In this case, the information used is in fact the number of people using public services, i.e. the demand, which is used as a proxy for the supply, as the latter data is unavailable.
11 Many methods exist for standardising the variables. The one chosen has been applied by Biehl (1986), where an aggregate physical infrastructure index was obtained as the sum of different indices of different physical infrastructures.
12 The trend of our location cost curve differs from the traditional location cost curve of Alonso. Also our more macro type of cost function, where the social cost to the environment and the social disamenities associated with urban size are contained, has an increasing shape, but only from a certain urban size. Before that level, other mechanisms, which are not considered in Alonso's microeconomic type of location cost curve, take place and allow small cities to increase their size without paying in terms of the economic, environmental, and social diseases that physical growth may imply.
13 For the conceptual model, the methodology, the data, and the detailed econometric results, see Camagni *et al.* (2013).

Bibliography

Alonso, W. (1964) *Location and Land Use: Towards a General Theory of Land Rents*, Cambridge, MA: Harvard University Press.

Alonso, W. (1971) "The Economics of Urban Size", *Papers and Proceedings of the Regional Science Association*, 26, pp. 67–83.

Anderson, R. and Crocker, T. (1971) "Air Pollution and Residential Property Values", *Urban Studies*, 8(3), pp. 171–180.

Bathelt, H., Malmberg, A. and Maskell, P. (2004) "Clusters and Knowledge: Local Buzz, Global Pipelines and the Process of Knowledge Creation", *Progress in Human Geography*, 28(1), pp. 31–56.

Berg van den, L., Drewett, R., Klaassen, L., Rossi, A. and Vijverberg, C.H.T. (1983) *Urban Europe: a Study of Growth and Decline*, Oxford: Pergamon.

Berger, M., Blomquist, G. and Waldner, W. (1987) "A Revealed-Preference Ranking of Quality of Life for Metropolitan Areas", *Social Science Quarterly*, 68(4), pp. 761–778.

Biehl, D. (1986) *The Contribution of Infrastructure to Regional Development, Regional Policy Division*, Brussels: European Community.

Blomquist, G., Berger, M. and Hoehn, J. (1988) "New Estimates of the Quality of Life in Urban Areas", *American Economic Review*, 78(1), pp. 89–107.

Breheny, M. (1992) "Sustainable Development and Urban Form: An Introduction", in Breheny, M. and Owens, S. (eds), *Sustainable Development and Urban Form*, London: Pion.

Burnell, J. and Galster, G. (1992) "Quality-of-life Measurements and Urban Size: An Empirical Note", *Urban Studies*, 29(5), pp. 727–735.

Camagni, R. (1991) "Local Milieu, Uncertainty and Innovation Networks: Towards a Dynamic Theory of Economic Space", in R. Camagni (ed.) *Innovation Networks: Spatial Perspectives*, London: Belhaven-Pinter, pp. 121–144.

Camagni, R. (1992) *Economia Urbana. Principi e Modelli*, Rome: NIS.

Camagni, R. (1993) "From City Hierarchy to City Network: Reflections about an Emerging Paradigm", in Laschmanan, T. and Nijkamp, P. (eds), *Structure and Change in the Space Economy*, Berlin: Springer Verlag, pp. 66–90.

Camagni, R. (1998) "Sustainable Urban Development: Definition and Reasons for a Research Programme", *International Journal of Environment and Pollution*, 10(1), pp. 6–26.

Camagni, R. (1999) "The City as a Milieu: Applying the GREMI Approach to Urban Evolution", *Revue d'Economie Régionale et Urbaine*, 3, pp. 591–606.

Camagni, R. (2009) "Territorial Capital and Regional Development", in Capello, R. and Nijkamp, P. (eds), *Handbook of Regional Growth and Development Theories*, Cheltenham: Edward Elgar, pp. 118–132.

Camagni, R. and Capello, R. (2004) "The City Network Paradigm: Theory and Empirical Evidence", in Capello, R. and Nijkamp, P. (Eds), *Urban Dynamics and Growth: Advances in Urban Economics*, Amsterdam: Elsevier, pp. 495–532.

Camagni, R., Capello, R. and Caragliu, A. (2013) "One or Infinite Optimal City Sizes? In Search of an Equilibrium Size for Cities", *The Annals of Regional Science*, 51(2), pp. 309–341.

Camagni, R., Curti, F. and Gibelli, M.C. (1985) "Ciclo Urbano: le Città tra Sviluppo e Declino", in Bianchi, G. and Magnani, I. (eds), *Sviluppo Multiregionale: Teorie, Problemi, Metodi*, Milan: Franco Angeli, pp. 197–234.

Camagni, R., Diappi, L. and Leonardi, G. (1986) "Urban Growth and Decline in a Hierarchical System: A Supply-oriented Dynamic Approach", *Regional Science and Urban Economics*, 16(1), pp. 145–160.

Camagni, R., Gibelli, M.C. and Rigamonti, P. (2002) "Urban Mobility and Urban Form: The Social and Environmental Costs of Different Patterns of Urban Expansion", *Ecological Economics*, 40(2), pp. 199–216.

Capello, R. (2002) "Economie di scala e dimensione urbana: teoria e empiria rivisitate", *Scienze Regionali*, 2, pp. 79–100.

Capello, R. and Camagni, R. (2000) "Beyond Optimal City Size: An Evaluation of Alternative Urban Growth Patterns", *Urban Studies*, 37(9), pp. 1479–1497.

164 *Roberto Camagni and Roberta Capello*

Capello, R. and Rietveld, P. (1998) "The Concept of Network Synergy in Economic Theory: Policy Implications", in Button, K., Nijkamp, P. and Priemus, H. (eds) *Transport Networks in Europe*, Cheltenham: Edward Elgar, pp. 57–83.

Carlino, G. (1980) "Constrast in Agglomeration: New York and Pittsburgh Reconsidered", *Urban Studies*, 17(3), pp. 343–351.

Carlino, J. and Saiz, A. (2008) "Beautiful City: Leisure Amenities and Urban Growth", Federal Reserve Bank of Philadelphia Working Paper SSRN-1280157.

Cheshire, P. and Magrini, S. (2006) "Population Growth in European Cities: Weather Matters – but Only Nationally", *Regional Studies*, 40(1), pp. 23–37.

Chesnais, F. (1988) "Technical Cooperation Agreements among Firms", *STI Review*, OECD, n. 4.

Chinitz, B. (1961) "Constrast in Agglomeration: New York and Pittsburgh", *American Economic Review*, 51(2), pp. 279–289.

Ciccone, A. and Hall, R.E. (1996) "Productivity and the Density of Economic Activity", *American Economic Review*, 86(1), pp. 54–70.

Clark, D. and Cosgrave, J. (1991) "Amenities versus Labour Market Opportunities: Choosing the Optimal Distance to Move", *Journal of Regional Science*, 31(3), pp. 311–328.

Clark, D. and Kahn, J. (1988) "The Social Benefits of Urban Cultural Amenities", *Journal of Regional Science*, 28(1), pp. 363–377.

Clark, D. and Kahn, J. (1989) "The Two Stage Hedonic Wage Approach: A Methodology for the Valuation of Environmental Amenities", *Journal of Environmental Economics and Management*, 16(2), pp. 106–120.

Conway, H. and Liston, L. (1981) *The Good Life Index*, Conway Publications, Atlanta, GA.

Cropper, M. (1981) "The Value of Urban Amenities", *Journal of Regional Science*, 21(3), pp. 359–374.

Douglas, R. (1967) "Selected Indices of Industrial Characteristics for US Metropolitan Statistical Areas, 1963", Discussion Paper no. 20, Regional Science Research Institute, Philadelphia.

Duncan, O. (1956) "The Optimum Size of Cities", in Spengler, J. and Ducan, O. (eds) *Demographic Analysis*, Free Press.

Duranton, G. and Puga, D. (2005) "From Sectoral to Functional Urban Specialization", *Journal of Urban Economics*, 57(2), pp. 343–370.

European Environment Agency (2006) "Urban Sprawl in Europe: The Ignored Challenge", EEA Report no. 10, Copenhagen.

Faggian, A. and McCann, P. (2009) "Human Capital, Graduate Migration and Innovation in British Regions", *Cambridge Journal of Economics*, 33(2), pp. 317–333.

Freeman, M.A. III (1971) "Air Pollution and Property Values: A Methodological Comment", *The Review of Economics and Statistics*, 53(4), pp. 415–416.

Getz, M. and Huang, Y. (1978) "Consumer Revealed Preference for Environmental Goods", *Review of Economics and Statistics*, 60(3), pp. 449–458.

Glaeser, E. and Kahn, M.E. (2003) "Sprawl and Urban Growth", Harvard Institute of Economic Research, Discussion Paper no. 2004, Harvard University.

Glaeser, E., Kallal, H., Scheinlman, J. and Shleiffer, A. (1992) "Growth in Cities", *Journal of Political Economy*, 100(6), pp. 1126–1152.

Glaeser, E.L. and Mare, D.C. (2001) "Cities and Skills", *Journal of Labor Economics*, 19(2), 316–342.

Henderson, J. (1982) "Evaluating Consumer Amenities and Interregional Welfare Differences", *Journal of Urban Economics*, 11(1), pp. 32–59.

Henderson, J. (1985) *Economic Theory and the Cities*, Orlando: Academic Press.

Henderson, J. (1996) "Ways to Think about Urban Concentration: Neoclassical Urban Systems vs. the New Economic Geography", *International Regional Science Review*, 19(1–2), pp. 31–36.

Hirsch, W.Z. (1968) "The Supply of Urban Public Services", in Perloff, H. and Wingo, L. (eds), *Issues in Urban Economics*, Baltimore: John Hopkins Press.

Izraeli, O. (1987) "The Effect of Environmental Attributes on Earnings and Housing Values Across SMSAs", *Journal of Urban Economics*, 22(3), pp. 361–376.

Jacobs, J. (1969) *The Economy of Cities*, New York: Random House.

Jeanty, P., Partridge, M. and Irwin, E. (2010) "Estimation of a Spatial Simultaneous Equation Model of Population Migration and Housing Price Dynamics", *Regional Science and Urban Economics*, 40(5), pp. 343–352.

Kawashima, T. (1975) "Urban Agglomeration Economies in Manufacturing Industries", *Papers of the Regional Science Association*, 34(1), pp. 157–175.

Ladd, H. (1992) "Population Growth, Density and the Costs of Providing Public Services", *Urban Studies*, 29(2), pp. 237–295.

McCann, Ph. and Acs, Z.J. (2011) "Globalization: Countries, Cities and Multinationals", *Regional Studies*, 45(1), pp. 17–32.

Marelli, E. (1981) "Optimal City Size, the Productivity of Cities and Urban Production Functions", *Sistemi Urbani*, 3(1–2), pp. 149–163.

Martin, P., Mayer, T. and Mayneris, F. (2011) "Spatial Concentration and Plant-level Productivity in France", *Journal of Urban Economics*, 69(2), pp. 182–195.

Mera, K. (1973) "On the Urban Agglomeration and Economic Efficiency", *Economic Development and Cultural Change*, 21(2), pp. 309–324.

Mills, E. (1993) "What Makes Metropolitan Areas Grow?", in Summers, A., Cheshire, P. and Senn, L. (eds) *Urban Change in the United States and Western Europe*, Washington: The Urban Institute, pp. 193–216.

Moomaw, R. (1983) "Is Population Scale a Worthless Surrogate for Business Agglomeration Economies?", *Regional Science and Urban Economics*, 13(2), pp. 525–545.

Nijkamp, P. and Kournit, K. (2011) *Urban Europe. Global Challenges and Local Responses in the Urban Century*, Joint Programme Initiative (JPI), Free University of Amsterdam.

Owens, S. (1992) "Energy, Environmental Sustainability and Land Use Planning", in Breheny, M. and Owens, S. (eds), *Sustainable Development and Urban Form*, London: Pion, pp. 79–104.

Parr, J. (2002) "Missing Elements in the Analysis of Agglomeration Economies", *International Regional Science Review*, 25(2), pp. 151–168.

Partridge, M. (2010) "The Dueling Models: NEG vs Amenity Migration in Explaining U.S. Engines of Growth", *Papers in Regional Science*, 89(3), pp. 513–536.

Partridge, M., Rickman, D.S., Ali, K. and Olfert, M.R. (2009) "Do New Economic Geography Agglomeration Shadows Underlie Current Population Dynamics Across the Urban Hierarchy?", *Papers in Regional Science*, 88(2), pp. 445–467.

Polanyi, M. (1966) *The Tacit Dimension*, New York: Doubleday & Co.

Rappaport, J. (2007) "Moving to Nice Weather", *Regional Science and Urban Economics*, 37(3), pp. 375–398.

Richardson, H.W. (1972) "Optimality in City Size, Systems of Cities and Urban Policy: A Sceptic's View", *Urban Studies*, 9(1), pp. 29–47.

Ridker, R.G. and Henning, J.A. (1967) "The Determinants of Residential Property Values with Special Reference to Air Pollution", *The Review of Economics and Statistics*, 49(2), pp. 246–257.

166 *Roberto Camagni and Roberta Capello*

Roback, J. (1982) "Wages, Rents, and the Quality of Life", *Journal of Political Economy*, 90(6), pp. 1257–1278.

Roback, J. (1988) "Wages, Rents and Amenities: Differences among Workers and Regions", *Economic Inquiry*, 26(1), pp. 23–41.

Shefer, D. (1973) "Localisation Economies in SMA's: A Production Function Analysis", *Journal of Regional Science*, 13: pp. 55–64.

Rosen, S. (1979) "Wage-based Indices of Urban Quality of Life", in Mieszkowski, P. and Straszheim, M. (eds), *Current Issues in Urban Economics*, Baltimore: Johns Hopkins University Press, pp. 74–104.

Rosenthal, S. and Strange, W. (2001) "The Determinants of Agglomeration", *Journal of Urban Economics*, 50(3), pp. 191–229.

Rousseaux, M.-P. (1995) "Y a-t-il une surproductivité de l'Île de France?", in Savy, M. and Veltz, P. (eds), *Économie globale et Réinvention du Local*, Paris: DATAR/éditions de l'aube, pp. 157–167.

Rousseaux, M.-P. and Proud'homme, R. (1992) *"Les bénéfis de la concentration parisienne"*, Paris (FR): L'Oeil-Iaurif, Paris.

Segal, D. (1976) "Are There Returns to Scale in City Size?", *Review of Economics and Statistics*, 58(3), pp. 339–350.

Sveikauskas, L. (1975) "The Productivity of City Size", *Quarterly Journal of Economics*, 89(3), pp. 393–413.

Sveikauskas, L., Gowdy, J. and Funk, M. (1988) "Urban Productivity: City Size or Industry Size", *Journal of Regional Science*, 28(2), pp. 185–202.

United Nations (2010) *World Urbanization Prospects: The 2009 Revision—Highlights.* New York: Department of Economic and Social Affairs, ESA/P/WP/215, March.

Index

agglomeration economies 4–5, 17–19, 144–7
amenities 45, 150
Atkinson, A. 100, 118

capital: man-made capital 113, 117; natural capital 113, 116
commuting costs 16, 56
cost-of-living 49–50, 59, 61

Easterlin paradox 68
equality of opportunity 101

Generalized Entropy indices 96
Gibrat's law 27–8
Gini index 96

human development index (HDI) 112

Land Use and Transport Interaction (LUTI) models 118–19, 138

marginal willingness to pay 46, 48
metabolism model 112
microsimulation 118–19
modifiable areal unit problem (MAUP) 98, 106
monocentric: city 20–1; model 15–17, 20

networks: city network paradigm 147, 153; complementarity networks 153; network integration 157, 159; synergy networks 153
New Economic Geography 17, 28

Pareto: distribution 4, 7, 28; optimal decision 120–121; weight 120–1, 124–5, 128–9
Pigou-Dalton principle 95
polycentric city 20–1
population density 18, 58–5, 113–14
PROPOLIS 117

replication invariance 95
Roback, J. 45, 47, 49, 51
Rosen, S. 45–6, 48–9

scale invariance 95
scaling laws 19
Sen, A. 101–2
spatial model 45, 49–50
stratification 101, 106
sustainability: environmental sustainability 35, 116; global sustainability 35; social sustainability 114; strong sustainability 114, 117; urban sustainability 114–15, 117–18; UrbanSim 118; weak sustainability 114

territorial capital 146, 154, 161
territorial justice 102–3, 106
Tiebout, C.M. 48, 58, 104
treadmill 68–9

urban commons 102
urban sprawl 5–6, 11, 20

Value of Time (VOT) 120, 128

Zipf's law 4, 7, 18, 26–8

eBooks
from Taylor & Francis

Helping you to choose the right eBooks for your Library

Add to your library's digital collection today with Taylor & Francis eBooks. We have over 50,000 eBooks in the Humanities, Social Sciences, Behavioural Sciences, Built Environment and Law, from leading imprints, including Routledge, Focal Press and Psychology Press.

Choose from a range of subject packages or create your own!

Benefits for you
- Free MARC records
- COUNTER-compliant usage statistics
- Flexible purchase and pricing options
- 70% approx of our eBooks are now DRM-free.

Benefits for your user
- Off-site, anytime access via Athens or referring URL
- Print or copy pages or chapters
- Full content search
- Bookmark, highlight and annotate text
- Access to thousands of pages of quality research at the click of a button.

Free Trials Available

We offer free trials to qualifying academic, corporate and government customers.

eCollections

Choose from 20 different subject eCollections, including:

- Asian Studies
- Economics
- Health Studies
- Law
- Middle East Studies

eFocus

We have 16 cutting-edge interdisciplinary collections, including:

- Development Studies
- The Environment
- Islam
- Korea
- Urban Studies

For more information, pricing enquiries or to order a free trial, please contact your local sales team:

UK/Rest of World: online.sales@tandf.co.uk
USA/Canada/Latin America: e-reference@taylorandfrancis.com
East/Southeast Asia: martin.jack@tandf.com.sg
India: journalsales@tandfindia.com

www.tandfebooks.com